AFTERMATH OF A NUCLEAR ATTACK

A Case Study on Post-strike Operations

AFTERMATH OF A NUCLEAR ATTACK

A Case Study on Post-strike Operations

Anil Chauhan

PENTAGON PRESS

Centre for Land Warfare Studies

The Centre for Land Warfare Studies (CLAWS), New Delhi, is an autonomous think tank dealing with contemporary issue of national activity and conceptual aspects of land warfare, including conventional and sub-conventional conflicts and terrorism. CLAWS conducts research that is futuristic in outlook and policy-oriented in approach.

Centre for Land Warfare Studies
RPSO Complex, Parade Road, Delhi Cantt, New Delhi-110010
Phone: 011-25691308 • Fax: 011-25692347
email: landwarfare@gmail.com • website: www.claws.in

Aftermath of a Nuclear Attack: A Case Study on Post-strike Operations / Anil Chauhan

ISBN 978-81-8274-490-5

First Published in 2010

Published by

PENTAGON PRESS
206, Peacock Lane, Shahpur Jat,
New Delhi-110049
Phones: 011-64706243, 26491568
Telefax: 011-26490600
email: rajan@pentagonpress.in
website: www.pentagon-press.com

Printed at Avantika Printers Private Limited.

Contents

Foreword

After conducting five nuclear tests over two days in May 1998, India declared itself a state with nuclear weapons. India's nuclear doctrine, professing a 'credible minimum deterrence' is built around a policy of 'no first use'. As a corollary, India is willing to absorb a 'first strike' and has declared its intention of launching massive punitive retaliation to cause unacceptable damage. Consequently, India follows a 'counter-value' targeting strategy aimed at inflicting unacceptable punishment, as against a 'counter-force' strategy aimed at destroying the adversary's nuclear forces. India has willingly abjured the use of 'tactical' and 'theatre' nuclear weapons as these are mainly employed against battlefield targets, involve complicated command and control mechanisms, enhance the risk of unauthorised and accidental launches and are complex and costly to manufacture. India's nuclear force structure is based on a triad: SSMs (Prithvi, Agni-I and Agni-II) with nuclear warheads with the Missile Groups of the Indian Army, nuclear glide bombs under-slung on Jaguar, Mirage 2000 and SU-30 MKI fighter-bomber aircraft with the Indian Air Force, and, in due course, SLBMs on SSBNs with the Indian Navy.

May 1998 was a defining moment in India's history, as the nation decided to abandon years of self-imposed restraint on exercising the nuclear option and went ahead to conduct the Shakti series of nuclear tests. While the series of decisions by successive Prime Ministers that shaped India's nuclear arsenal remained out of public scrutiny, India stands out as the only nation that has openly and freely debated the entire range of issues connected with nuclear deterrence, prior to the decision to finally cross the nuclear Rubicon.

After the nuclear tests, India enunciated a draft nuclear doctrine and placed it in the public domain to generate an informed debate, prior to arriving at conclusions on the nature and type of nuclear force structures, delivery vectors, intelligence and early warning capabilities, and the command and control systems needed to give effect to the doctrine of credible minimum deterrence for national security. It has been a long journey and it is clear to perceptive observers that the Government of India is slowly but steadily putting into place all the building blocks that encompass the essential features of a usable deterrent.

Since the middle of the first decade of the new century, the national discourse on nuclear issues has been usurped by the debate over the advantages and disadvantages of the Indo-US nuclear cooperation agreement, and more recently, by the Nuclear Liability Bill and the China-Pakistan nuclear cooperation issue. Debates on nuclear issues like the viability of nuclear energy to meet India's long-term energy needs, contentious clauses of the 123 Agreement, a waiver from the Nuclear Suppliers Group, the options available for enrichment and reprocessing, the type of nuclear reactors desired, the availability and procurement of nuclear fuel, and participation in the International Thermonuclear Experimental Reactor (fusion reactor) project, though important for India, are peripheral to the actual development of India's nuclear weapons capability and the associated nuclear strategy that must be adopted. As a nuclear weapon state, India needs a better informed debate on the development of nuclear strategy for deterrence and for the conduct of conventional military operations under a nuclear shadow, rather than endless discussion on marginal issues. While some elements of the discussion must remain confined to insiders in political-military circles, the military hierarchy must take the lead in initiating a debate on practical issues related to nuclear deterrence so as to benefit from the knowledge and talent available in the strategic community and academia. Sustained scholarly debate is bound to generate pragmatic suggestions.

Nuclear capability of the right quality, backed by a well-reasoned doctrine, a sound strategy, and concepts and procedures that have been validated and refined through practiced drills over a period of time, are important ingredients of credible nuclear deterrence. Most research that has been undertaken in India on nuclear deterrence has focused mainly on issues that lead up to the actual decision to launch retaliatory nuclear strikes. Basically, these relate to nuclear strategy, including targeting philosophies, issues related to the command and control of nuclear weapons, measures for the passive defence of delivery vectors before and after their mating with nuclear warheads, delegation of weapon release authority and post-strike damage assessment. Very little research has been undertaken to discuss post-strike scenarios, especially the mechanism that must be in place to manage the humanitarian disaster that is bound to be caused by a nuclear strike. This aspect was probably neglected, in the understanding and hope that nuclear weapons are unlikely to be used. One cannot deny the fact that the possibility of the use of nuclear weapons, in any future conflict, remains extremely low. However, the consequences of such a horrific event, should it ever occur, will be so extraordinary that it is prudent to include such scenarios in the security calculus as a major threat and prepare accordingly. The importance of this aspect was highlighted at two places in the draft nuclear doctrine:

- India shall develop an appropriate disaster control system capable of handling the unique requirements of potential incidents involving nuclear weapons and material.

- Indian defence forces shall be in a position to execute operations in an NBC environment with minimal degradation.

The disaster management problems that will accrue after a nuclear strike cannot be ignored. Unless all aspects connected with post-strike issues have been deliberately thought through, the country will be found wanting when a nuclear crisis actually unfolds. In any future conflict, the armed forces may have to conduct military operations in an environment contaminated by radioactivity, to achieve the national aims set forth for the conflict. Both these aspects, though connected, require a different response paradigm and procedures. Developing the capability to operate in a contaminated environment will have obvious spin-offs for meeting Chemical, Biological, Radiological, and Nuclear (CBRN) threats emanating from terror attacks or nuclear incidents and accidents. The recovery of a radioactive source in a Delhi dump yard recently and the potential havoc two or three devices of such nature can cause in any city only highlights the problem at hand.

Brigadier Anil Chauhan deserves to be complimented for the excellent pioneering research he has done on the subject of post-nuclear strike disaster management and the conduct of military operations in a contaminated environment. He undertook this research during a fellowship on a sabbatical from the Army with the Centre for Land Warfare Studies (CLAWS). His work has major relevance for military and disaster management professionals and members of the strategic community dealing with the management of post-nuclear strike scenarios, which have, so far, remained completely neglected. Brigadier Anil Chauhan is a serving army officer whose experience in the NBC section at the Perspective Planning Directorate at the Army Headquarters lends added weight to his arguments and the recommendations made by him.

It is still incomprehensible that the Indian armed forces were kept out of the loop of India's nuclear weapons development process. However, as the end users of this capability, and possibly its first victims, their involvement with all aspects of nuclear deterrence will only grow in the future. It is also very encouraging that serving army officers are thinking and writing on nuclear issues which, till recently, were the domain of academicians and civilian research scholars. This book is a valuable addition to the literature on the subject and should be prescribed reading for all civilian and military professionals dealing with the nuts and bolts of nuclear deterrence.

Brig Gurmeet Kanwal (Retd)
Director
Centre for Land Warfare Studies (CLAWS)
New Delhi

Preface

Nuclear weapons evoke a sense of awe as well as revulsion because of their immense destructive potential. Proponents of nuclear weapons consider it as the 'ultimate weapon' bestowing on it an almost divine status—the '*Brahmastra*'. Opponents are equally emphatic in denouncing it as a 'blot on humanity'. In the history of warfare, no other weapon system has polarised opinion among strategic analysts, intelligentsia and indeed the common soldier on the real worth of a weapon-system which because of its enormous destructive potential has actually been rendered unusable. So we have people who may adore nuclear weapons and some who may abhor them but none can ignore them.

I am neither a proponent nor an opponent of nuclear weapons but would fall in the third category and firmly believe that nuclear weapons cannot be ignored. My interest in nuclear weapons arose for the first time when India conducted its first nuclear test on 18 May 1974. Although I kept my interest alive by keeping tabs on what was happening in the nuclear field, the exigencies of service never allowed any serious reading of the subject. This latent interest got stimulated when I was posted as Director, Threat Assessment, in the NBC Warfare section of the Perspective Planning Directorate at Army HQ. I realised there that most of the literature on nuclear warfare available in India dealt only with its offensive facets. The range of subjects included issues like nuclear targeting, force structuring, escalation dynamics, deterrence theory and its applicability in the South Asian context or the nuclear capabilities of Pakistan and China. There was very little work on the defensive aspects of nuclear warfare. I decided to put forward my views with the aim of generating awareness on this important aspect of nuclear warfare as part of my study leave project.

The initial impetus to take the plunge into the business of writing and putting forward my views was provided by Brig Anil Harnal, my immediate senior at Army HQ. Not only did he guide me in conceptualising the project, but also brainstormed some of the contingencies for nuclear weapon use in the Indian context for which I shall ever remain grateful. I would also like to thank Brig Gurmeet Kanwal, Director, CLAWS, who accepted me as a Senior Fellow and extended his wholehearted support to the project. The atmosphere at CLAWS allowed for free flow of ideas and was conducive for research. Had it not been for the atmosphere and time available at CLAWS, the project may not have seen the light of the day. I would also like to thank Professor Rajaraman of the JNU for reviewing the project report, especially the technical aspects covered in Part I of the study.

To complete a project of this magnitude in one year was a major challenge. To provide me uninterrupted time and undisturbed atmosphere at home, I would like to express my sincere gratitude to my wife Anupma. The only regret I had while working on this project was that I was unable to devote time with my daughter, Pragya, who needed me most as she was preparing for her first board exams.

Anil Chauhan

Acronyms and Abbreviations

ADS	- Advance Dressing Station
ADT	- Atomic Damage Template
AERB	- Atomic Energy Regulatory Board
ASFC	- Army Strategic Forces Command
BARC	- Bhabha Atomic Research Centre
Brig	- Brigadier
CATS	- Centralised Accident & Trauma Services
CBM	- Confidence Building Measures
CBRN	- Chemical Biological Radiological and Nuclear
CCMND	- Cabinet Committee for Management of Natural Disasters
CCS	- Cabinet Committee on Security
CDC	- Casualty Decontamination Centre
CLAWS	- Centre for Land Warfare Studies
cm	- centimetre
CMG	- Crisis Management Group
CNG	- Compressed Natural Gas
COAS	- Chief of the Army Staff
DAE	- Department of Atomic Energy
DCB	- Ditch-cum-Bund
DDMA	- District Disaster Management Authority
DF	- *Dong Feng*
DRDO	- Defence Research and Development Organisation
ECR	- Emergency Control Room
EMP	- Electro Magnetic Pulse

ERC	- Emergency Response Centre
ERW	- Enhanced Radiation Weapon
FM	- Field Manual
FNBCP	- Faculty of NBC Protection
FSC	- Forward Surgical Centre
GHQ	- General Staff Headquarters
GIS	- Geographical Information System
GZ	- Ground Zero
HOB	- Height of Burst
HQ	- Headquarters
IAEA	- International Atomic Energy Agency
ICBM	- Intercontinental Ballistic Missile
ICP	- Integrated Command Post
ICRP	- International Commission for Radiation Protection
ICV	- Infantry Combat Vehicle
IDS	- Integrated Defence Staff
IDSA	- Institute for Defence Studies and Analyses
IMD	- Indian Meteorological Department
INR	- Initial Nuclear Radiations
IPE	- Individual Protective Equipment
JL	- *Julang*
km	- Kilometre
kmph	- Kilometres per hour
kt	- Kiloton
MEA	- Ministry of External Affairs
MeV	- Million Electron Volt
MHA	- Ministry of Home Affairs
MIRV	- Multiple Independently targetable Re-entry Vehicle
MMT	- Mobile Medical Team
MoD	- Ministry of Defence
MoHFW	- Ministry of Health and Family Welfare
MOPP	- Mission Oriented Protective Posture
mSv	- millisivert

mt	- Megaton
MTC	- Minimal Treatment Centre
NATO	- North Atlantic Treaty Organisation
NBC	- Nuclear, Biological and Chemical
NCC	- National Cadet Corps
NCMC	- National Crisis Management Committee
NCT	- National Capital Territory
NDMA	- National Disaster Management Authority
NDRF	- National Disaster Response Force
NEC	- National Executive Committee
NFU	- No First Use
NGO	- Non Governmental Organisation
NIGA	- Neutron Induced Gamma Activity
NPCIL	- Nuclear Power Corporation of India Limited
NPT	- Nuclear Non-proliferation Treaty
NRRM	- Nuclear Risk Reduction Measures
NSAB	- National Security Advisory Board
NSS	- National Service Scheme
NWS	- Nuclear Weapon State
Op	- Operation
OEG	- Operational Exposure Guidance
OTA	- Office of Technology Assessment
PMF	- Para Military Forces
psi	- Pounds per square inch
rad	- Radiation absorbed dose
RALP	- Rest of Arunachal Pradesh
RED	- Radiological Emitting Device
RDD	- Radiological Dispersal Device
REC	- Radiation Exposure Criteria
RES	- Radiation Exposure Status
RNR	- Residual Nuclear Radiation
S&R	- Search and Rescue
SATA	- Surveillance and Target Acquisition

SDMA	- State Disaster Management Authority
SFC	- Strategic Forces Command
SIOP	- Single Integrated Operational Plan
SOP	- Standard Operating Procedure
TBA	- Tactical Battle Area
UAV	- Unmanned Aerial Vehicle
UN	- United Nations
US	- United States
USAF	- United States Air Force
USSR	- Union of Soviet Socialist Republics
WMD	- Weapon of Mass Destruction

Tables, Figures, Maps and Diagrams

Tables

Figures

Maps

Diagrams

1

Introduction

The Shakti series of nuclear tests by India in May 1998 had forced the clandestine nuclear weapons programme of Pakistan out of the closet. With the emergence of India and Pakistan as *de facto* if not *de jure* nuclear weapon states, the nuclearisation of the region, started by China, is now a grim reality. The region also remains conflict prone due to latent animosities, past prejudices and a host of unresolved differences, including the border issue.

Any future conflict between India on the one hand and Pakistan or China on the other, is likely to be fought within the conventional realm, albeit against a nuclear backdrop.[1] The escalation of such a conflict in the nuclear domain, leading to a limited exchange of nuclear weapons, is a possibility that cannot be discounted. Such an exchange could be a result of some miscalculation or misapprehension, exacerbated due to the prevailing tension of war leading to unauthorised or accidental use of nuclear weapons.[2] A premeditated nuclear strike to gain local or temporary military advantage or to avert a major military disaster is also a possibility. After all, the actual use or threat of use of such weapons has been the *raison d'être* for the acquisition of nuclear weapons by some of the new nuclear weapon states in the first place.

The use of nuclear weapons against India will require a multi-disciplinary response from various organs of the government. Punitive retaliatory strikes will be one of the options that will be exercised by the government. This will produce its own dynamics; however, its pressure will primarily be felt in the diplomatic and political arenas. On the other hand, the physical efforts to mitigate the effects of the strike will be most cumbersome and exacting as they will require concrete action on the ground. Such a situation may also demand the employment of the armed forces in an environment contaminated by nuclear radiations, either for humanitarian aid or to pursue conventional operations to their logical end.

The use of nuclear weapons in a counter-value or counter-force mode is a matter of conjecture and cannot be legislated in advance. In case these are used in a counter-value mode, the results will be truly catastrophic, given the density of population in towns and cities across South Asia and the coastal regions of China. Counter-force targeting, if carried out on static military installations, could include targets like air fields, naval dockyards, missile sites and military cantonments. In the Tactical Battle Area (TBA), these could be used against concentration areas, assembly areas, bridge heads or advancing mechanised columns. In case of counter-force targeting, the devastation, though lesser in scale and magnitude, will be felt by both the armed forces as well as the civilian population living in close vicinity of the border areas.

Purpose of the Study

Among weapons of mass destruction, nuclear weapons remain unique, not only because of their potential to cause large-scale destruction due to the instantaneous release of large amounts of energy in the form of blast and thermal radiation, but also due to the release of ionising radiation, which is harmful to the human body. In case detonated on or near the earth's surface, nuclear weapons can also produce a long-term radiation hazard as a result of nuclear fallout. Knowing the effects of nuclear weapons is one thing, interpreting them in simple terms from complex scientific formulae, graphs or equations to assess the damage is another, and forming a response strategy to deal with the aftermath of a nuclear strike is yet another connected issue, but it falls under an entirely different realm. The present study deals with all three issues, albeit with primary focus on the latter two aspects. In short, the study addresses three major issues. First, how and in which geographical areas could nuclear weapons be used in the South Asian context? Second, what will be the impact of such strikes in terms of human casualties and material damage? Last, what needs to be done in the aftermath of such strikes to reduce the overall damage?

The study does not claim to follow an uncharted course. Similar studies dealing with the effects of a nuclear strike on cities and to a lesser extent on the armed forces, in the regional context, have been carried out in the past. Some of these have been published in national dailies and periodicals, bringing the spectre of a nuclear holocaust closer home.[3] The purpose of most of these studies has been to inform people of the real dangers posed by nuclear weapons. However, very few have described the process of damage assessment in sufficient detail so as to form a basis for extrapolating its results on other scenarios. The following studies have not only been a source of inspiration for undertaking the present work, but have also been taken as a base model for furthering analysis on the subject:

- General K. Sundarji, *Blind Men of Hindoostan: Indo-Pak Nuclear War* (New Delhi: UBS Publishers, 1993), and 'Combat Paper No. 2' published by College of Combat (now Army War College), Mhow, Madhya Pradesh.

- Rashid Naim, "Aadhi Raat Ke Baad (After Midnight)" in Stephen P. Cohen (ed.), *Nuclear Proliferation on South Asia – The Prospects for Arms Control* (Colorado: Westview Press, 1991).
- M.V. Ramana, "Bombing Bombay? Effects of Nuclear Weapons and a Case Study of Hypothetical Explosion," International Physicians for the Prevention of Nuclear War Global Health Watch, Report No. 3, 1999.
- R. Rajaraman, Zia Mian and A.H. Nayyar, "Nuclear Civil Defence in South Asia: Is it Feasible?" *Economic and Political Weekly*, Vol. XXXIX, Nos. 46 & 47, 2004.

The purpose of the present study is twofold. First, it is to provide military and civil defence planners an idea of the scale and magnitude of the disaster that will follow a nuclear strike. Accordingly, a scenario of a tactical nuclear strike on army units has been selected to assess the damage, besides the effect of a nuclear strike on a major city and a medium-sized border town. The study also provides simplified tables that can be used in situations where the nuclear strike parameters have undergone minor modification or potential targets have been changed. Second, based on the three scenarios, the study outlines the type of operations that will have to be launched to mitigate the adverse affects of a nuclear strike. This is done with the aim of drawing out relevant lessons for the armed forces, the National Disaster Management Authority (NDMA) and various departments of the state and central governments, in the hope that this will lead to better preparedness and responses, in case we do have to deal with such a situation. For the Army, the study examines the various problems associated with operating in a radiologically contaminated environment and the decision dilemmas that the commander and staff will face while conducting post-strike operations, with a view to suggest a technically sound response strategy.

Scientific and Technical Parameters

The primary reference material for understanding the effects of a nuclear detonation and calculating the damage from individual effects has been *The Effects of Nuclear Weapons* (1977 edition) by Samuel Gladstone & Philip J. Dolan and *Effects of Nuclear War*, prepared by Office of the Technology Assessment, US Congress. Certain graphic relationships between effects and corresponding slant ranges, especially for nuclear radiation, have been referenced from *Nuclear Radiation in Warfare*, SIPRI, 1981. In addition, the following field manuals of the US Army have also been refered:

- Field Manual 3-3 on 'NBC Contamination Avoidance'.
- Field Manual 101-31-1 on 'Nuclear Weapons Employment Doctrines and Procedures'.
- Field Manual 8-9, NATO Handbook on 'Medical Aspects of NBC Defensive Operations'.

Terms of Reference

The problems associated with accessing the consequences of a limited nuclear exchange or even the assessment of damage from a single nuclear strike are manifold. First, a nuclear detonation produces both immediate and delayed destructive effects. The delayed effects can largely be attributed to nuclear fallout, the radioactivity from which can last from hours to decades.[4] Its potential to cause personnel casualties is rather difficult to predict as the entry into radioactive contaminated areas, post a nuclear strike, is a choice to be made by the defender, depending on the type and nature of operations he desires to execute in those areas. Second, the casualties from the secondary effects of a nuclear explosion like secondary fires caused due to thermal radiation or flying glass/debris caused by blast effects are difficult to ascertain, as these will depend entirely on the target posture and the availability of emergency services after the strike. Last, but not the least, is the fact that damage estimation does not take into account the social, economic or psychological trauma of a nuclear strike, which will add to the overall casualty figures.

Damage estimation techniques followed in the study are based on the immediate effects of a nuclear explosion, i.e. Blast, Thermal Radiation and Initial Nuclear Radiation. The damage potential of all these are assessed separately, as if each were present alone. The results are then aggregated as per the slant ranges till where at least two effects will be pronounced. The limitations of nuclear damage estimation techniques based on 'effects' aspects are not the only problems. For a given method of employing a nuclear weapon, the extent of damage will depend upon many external variables like visibility (especially for thermal radiation), meteorological conditions like wind speed, direction of wind (for nuclear fallout) and geographical terrain features present in the target area (for blast effects). In addition, during the actual delivery, the height of burst can be adjusted to produce an increment or decrease in the effects of blast, heat or radiation.[5] Hence the effects of a nuclear strike for a specified yield will vary with the type of burst, whether it is sub-surface, surface, low air burst, mid air or a high air burst.

The yield of nuclear weapons that can be delivered can also be varied from sub-kiloton to hundreds of megatons. Even for a specified yield, the type of nuclear weapons can range from a simple fission device[6] to a more advanced boosted fission, to a typical three-stage thermonuclear weapon. Further, each of these weapons can be manipulated to cause different effects. For example, 'salting'[7] will produce a long-term contamination hazard or the 'tampering' of the weapon can be manipulated to enhance the effects of radiations, as in case of a neutron bomb.[8] While the study will take into account most of these factors to comprehend the damage assessment and hazard prediction aspects in passing, the actual nuclear strike scenarios will be related to the likely capabilities of our adversaries and the most likely manner in which nuclear weapons will be used in the regional context.

In view of the above, the following terms of reference have been laid for the purposes of the study:

- The yields for a counter-force nuclear strike that have been considered are one kiloton neutron bomb and five kiloton and 10 kiloton fission bombs. Higher yields on a purely military target will produce no significant enhancement in effect and hence have not been included. The yields for a counter-value strike has been taken as 20 kiloton, 50 kiloton and one megaton.
- The counter-force strikes are presumed to be Surface or Low Air Burst[9] as these produce optimum conditions for the destruction of hardened targets. On the other hand, the counter-value strike on a city has been presumed to be an Air Burst[10] so as to maximise the effects.
- The damage criteria will be based on designs that are simple implosion devices. As reported in the media, Pakistan possesses such technology. Notwithstanding the inherent insanity in the use of nuclear weapons, it is assumed that there will be some sanity in the madness which will prevent the use of enhanced radiation or 'salted' nuclear weapons.
- Meteorological conditions have been assumed as would be applicable during the time of the strike.

Layout

This study is laid out in three parts as follows:

- **Part 1**: This part deals with the general effect of nuclear weapons in brief and follows it up with nuclear damage estimation and hazard prediction techniques. The findings are presented in tabulated form for easy comprehension and application.
- **Part 2**: This part analyses various areas and targets that are relatively more vulnerable to nuclear strikes, either due to their geographical locations, meteorological conditions or demography. The techniques and models developed in Part 1 are then used to assess the damage on one counter-value target, with New Delhi as a prime example, and one counter-force target.
- **Part 3**: The findings of the first two parts of the study form the basis for this part, which analyses the immediate actions that the Army and civil defence organisations will be required to undertake, both for mitigating the effects of the strike as well as to forestall the possibility of the exploitation of the adverse operational situation created by a nuclear strike. Such operations could range from large-scale casuality evacuation to vacating areas before the arrival of nuclear fallout, search-and-rescue operations and fighting in a contaminated environment. This part also

deals with certain recommendations that the Army and other institutions or establishments of the Government of India will have to consider to improve national preparedness to deal with such a crisis.

ENDNOTES

1. The Kargil Conflict of 1999 and Op Parakram in 2001, though limited in scale, were conducted under the shadow of a nuclear threat and precipitated into a nuclear crisis of sorts between India and Pakistan. Op Brasstacks in 1986 and the Kashmir insurgency in 1989 are earlier examples of nuclear sabre-rattling between the two nations.
2. The governments of India and Pakistan are engaged in talks to promote nuclear CBMs as part of the composite dialogue process, with a view to reducing accidental or unauthorised use of nuclear weapons. However, no such talks have commenced with China as it does not recognise India as a nuclear weapon state, under the terms of the NPT.
3. 'What If,' *India Today*, 10 June 2002.
4. Fission products decay as per half life, which could range from a few minutes to thousands of years.
5. A Surface Burst or Low Air Burst will produce significant nuclear fallout, thus posing a long-term contamination hazard. It may be recalled that the nuclear bombs dropped on Hiroshima and Nagasaki were both Air Burst and hence did not produce any fallout.
6. A simple fission device could be a gun barrel assembly or a more sophisticated implosion device.
7. 'Salting' is done by the use of tempering material like gold or silver, which has a longer half life for radioactive decay.
8. A Neutron Bomb or an Enhanced Radiation Weapon is usually a thermonuclear weapon that uses very little temper material. This reduces the absorption of prompt neutrons by the weapon casing.
9. In a Surface or Low Air Burst, the fireball touches the ground.
10. In an Air Burst, the weapon is exploded in the air at an altitude below 30 km but at a sufficient height, so that the fireball does not contact the surface of the earth.

PART I

EFFECTS OF A NUCLEAR STRIKE AND NUCLEAR DAMAGE ESTIMATION

2

Existing Studies and Models for Damage Estimation

If the radiance of a thousand suns were to burst at once into the sky that would be like the splendour of the Mighty One... I am become Death, the Shatterer of the Worlds.

J. Robert Oppenheimer, quoting from the Bhagavad Gita,
Alamogordo, New Mexico, 1945

A nuclear explosion involves the release of a large amount of energy[1] in a very short interval of time. It produces both immediate and delayed effects. The immediate effects are manifested in the form of blast, thermal radiation and Initial Nuclear Radiations (INR)[2] which cause significant destruction within seconds to minutes of the detonation. The delayed effects are basically due to the nuclear fallout, which inflicts damage over an extended period of time.

The purpose of the study is to arrive at certain parameters that will assist the assessment of damage from a nuclear strike, rather than going into the intricacies of a nuclear explosion phenomenon per se. Hence, the effects of a nuclear detonation will be covered only briefly, where necessary, to establish a correlation between that particular effect and its damage potential. The damage potential of individual effects, i.e. blast, thermal and nuclear radiation, is covered in detail in the following sections. This section covers damage estimation based on data available from nuclear strikes carried out at Hiroshima and Nagasaki and also includes damage estimation techniques used in available studies, carried out in the South Asian context.

Hiroshima and Nagasaki

The 'Little Boy' which destroyed Hiroshima on 6 August 1945 was a crude device, nearly three metres long and weighing about 4,000 kg. It was a gun barrel type of assembly which had an explosive yield of about 15 kilotons. In contrast, the 'Fat Man' was an implosion device of about 21 kiloton yield.[3]

Blast: The effects of the blast reduced an area of 13 square km in Hiroshima and about seven square km in Nagasaki to rubble.[4] This area was later engulfed by fire and reduced to ashes.

Thermal Radiations: In Hiroshima, at a distance of 500 metres from Ground Zero (GZ), the thermal radiation received in the first three seconds was about 600 times as searing as the sun on a bright day. Even at a distance of three km, the heat in the first three seconds was about 40 times more than from the sun. The heat was sufficient to burn exposed human skin at distances as far as four km. The heat at Nagasaki was even more intense, twice that of Hiroshima. All this resulted in violent fire storms which consumed every combustible object within two km of the GZ.[5]

Nuclear Radiation: Casualties due to radiation exposure in both Hiroshima and Nagasaki were caused by the INR only. There was no evidence to suggest casualties from persistent effects of radioactivity.[6] The effects of induced radioactivity and distribution of fission products was also minimal.

Personnel Casualties: The number of people present at the time of the bombing of Hiroshima and Nagasaki is not very clear. This is due to the presence of thousands of Japanese troops besides forced Korean labour in both the cities. As per some estimates, about 350,000 and 280,000 people were present on that fateful day in Hiroshima and Nagasaki respectively.[7] The personnel casualties at these two places have been a subject of various studies, some carried out within weeks/months of the explosions and others carried out subsequently. However, most of these have been unable to accurately estimate the casualties because of the large floating population and the confusion which reigned after the strike. Data from two such studies is tabulated and presented in Table 1.

Table 1: Estimate of Personnel Casualties in Hiroshima and Nagasaki

Study	Hiroshima (15 Kiloton)			Nagasaki (21 Kiloton)		
	Population	Dead	Injured	Population	Dead	Injured
The US Strategic Bombing Survey[8]	245,000	70,000 - 80,000	70,000- 80,000	Not given	35,000	> 35,000
The Atomic Bombing of Hiroshima and Nagasaki[9]	255,000	66,000	69,000	195,000	39,000	25,000

Cause of Casualties: The immediate cause of major casualties in both the cities was assessed due to flash burns, secondary effects of blast and falling debris and burns from secondary fires. The Hiroshima prefectural health department placed the proportion of deaths from burns (flash or flame) at 60 percent, from falling debris at 30 percent, and from other injuries at 10 percent. It is generally agreed that burns caused at least 50 percent of the initial casualties. Of those who died later, an increasing proportion succumbed to radiation effects. A plausible estimate of the various causes of death would range from flash burns as 20 to 30 percent, other injuries 50 to 60 percent and radiation sickness as 15 to 20 percent.[10]

Material Damage: The number of personnel casualties as a result of pure blast effects alone in both Hiroshima and Nagasaki was negligible as compared to thermal and nuclear radiation. In comparison, the main cause of damage or destruction to material and infrastructure was assessed to be blast effects followed by thermal radiation. Data related to damage or destruction to buildings compiled from the aforementioned studies is presented in Table 2.

Table 2: Material Damage in Hiroshima and Nagasaki

Hiroshima (15 Kiloton)			Nagasaki (21 Kiloton)		
Buildings	Destroyed	Damaged	Buildings	Destroyed	Damaged
90,000	62,000 (69%)	6,000 (6%)	52,000	14,140 (27.2%)	5,441 (10.5%)

The nuclear bombs at Hiroshima and Nagasaki were dropped from similar heights (570 and 500 metres respectively) and the meteorological conditions at the time of bombing were nearly similar, yet there was a disproportionate variation in personnel casualties as well as in material damage despite the Nagasaki bomb having a higher yield. This is because Hiroshima, being a plateau, had relatively flatter areas and was almost circular in shape. As a result, the effects of the explosion were uniformly distributed. In contrast, Nagasaki lay on mountainous terrain. The irregular shape of the city, combined with the fact that a mountain spur ran through the centre of the town, reduced the area of damage. This also ensured that there were no fire storms in Nagasaki.

Casualty Estimation: An immediate analysis of personnel casualties and material damage caused in both the Hiroshima and Nagasaki bombings indicates that the target posture has an important bearing on the extent of damage likely to be suffered in a nuclear strike. Notwithstanding the aforementioned, the nuclear bombing of these two cities are the only empirical models from which a broad estimation of mortality rates can be derived. Tables 3 and 4 give the mortality rates for Hiroshima and Nagasaki as a function of distance from the GZ. The data can be used to make a broad estimate of personnel casualties by multiplying the mortality rates with the population density of the concerned city or town. It needs to be mentioned, however, that in our context, this data needs to be used with caution as not only the exact population of Nagasaki is subject to debate, but extrapolating the data in the case of Indian cities/border towns will be fraught with uncertainties due to differences in layout, architecture and planning from that of Japanese cities. It also needs to be added that both the bombs were detonated as air bursts due to which there was no fallout. This would have had an important bearing on overall casualties if not immediate casualties.

Table 3: Mortality: Hiroshima[11]

Distance from GZ (in km)	Percentage
0.0 - 0.5	96.5
0.5 - 1.0	83.0
1.0 - 1.5	51.6
1.5 - 2.0	21.9
2.0 - 2.5	4.9
2.5 - 3.0	2.7
3.0 - 4.0	2.5
4.0 - 5.0	1.1

Table 4: Mortality: Nagasaki[12]

Distance from GZ (in feet)	Percentage
0 -1000	93.0
1000 - 2000	92.0
2000 - 3000	86.0
3000 - 4000	69.0
4000 - 5000	49.0
5000 - 6000	31.5
6000 - 7000	12.5
7000 - 8000	1.3
8000 - 9000	0.5
9000 -10000	0

Other Studies

In the South Asian context, three independent studies have estimated the damage from a nuclear strike. The primary proposes of these studies may not have been nuclear damage estimation except for the one carried out by M.V. Ramana. There is a need to briefly analyse the purpose of these studies and models used in them for nuclear damage estimation.

S. Rashid Naim: The purpose of the study was to discuss various scenarios for a nuclear exchange between India and Pakistan, with a view to generate awareness amongst decision makers about the known and unknown consequences of the use of nuclear weapons. The techniques used for damage estimation were primarily based on the effects of the blast wave wherein 100 percent people were assumed to be killed or injured in an area affected by an overpressure of 5 and 2.2 pounds per square inch (psi), respectively. The 5 and 2.2 psi circle for a 20-kiloton surface burst was taken as 0.8 and 1.3 miles, respectively. The casualties were estimated by multiplying the affected area with the population density. In addition, two psi circle corresponding to 1.4 miles was used to determine damage to property, which was assumed to be 100 percent. Long-term effects from nuclear fallout were calculated based on people likely to be exposed to 30 and one rad per hour. Wind speeds of 10 mph were assumed to calculate the areas likely to be affected by the fallout.

General K. Sundarji: Nuclear damage estimation was carried out by General Sundarji as an adjunct to his broader argument on nuclear deterrence and force structuring in 'Combat Paper No. 2' and in one of the chapters of his famous book *The Blind Men of Hindoostan.* In both cases, the effects of a 20-kiloton nuclear strike on tactical targets in the Tactical Battle Area (TBA) as well as on a metropolis and a medium-sized border town have been considered. The damage estimation technique followed in *The Blind Men of Hindoostan* is similar to that of Rashid Naim and takes into account blast effects only. In the combat paper, which was written much earlier, nuclear damage estimation for a small-sized border town is based on the premise that within one km radius from the GZ, all buildings will be destroyed and 95 percent of those inhabitants will be casualties (dead or seriously wounded). Between one and two km from the GZ, there will be partial or complete destruction of buildings and 50 percent of those inhabiting the area will be casualties, and finally, about 35 percent of the inhabitants will be casualties in the area between two to three km from the GZ.

M.V. Ramana: *Bombing Bombay,* as the name suggests, is a case study for understanding the effects of nuclear weapons by taking a hypothetical case of a nuclear strike over Mumbai. The study analyses 'blast' and 'thermal' effects of a nuclear explosion to estimate the damage. In addition, the casualties have been predicted based on available mortality rates for Hiroshima (refer Table 3). Casualty estimation for blast effects is based on the Office of Technology Assessment (OTA) model, where mortality rates are further fine-tuned to various overpressure ranges. Casualty estimation for thermal effects is based on Superfires model, where the ranges affected by a thermal flux of 10 and 6 calories per square cm is used to estimate the dead and injured, respectively.

R. Rajaraman, Z. Mian and A.H. Nayyar: This study analyses the feasibility of nuclear civil defence in the South Asian context after estimating the type of damage that will occur in case 10, 20 and 200 kiloton nuclear weapons are used.

The study does not venture into actual casualty estimation but identifies the radius of an area that will be completely destroyed by the said strikes. However, it identifies the criteria taken for calculating fatal and non-fatal casualties and the corresponding ranges till where the effects of blast, thermal and initial nuclear radiation will prevail. The criterion is generally similar to the one used by M.V. Ramana but presented in a graphic form for better comprehension. The findings of this study were more useful in formulating a preparation and response strategy for post-strike consequence management.

The likely casualties from hypothetical nuclear strikes, estimated in the first three studies, are summarised in Table 5.

Table 5: Estimation of Casualties for a Nuclear Strike in Bombay (now Mumbai)

Analyst	Strike Yield	Estimated Casualties for Immediate Effects		Basis of Estimation		Remarks
		Dead	Injured	Dead	Injured	
Rashid Naim	20 kt surface burst	136,900	224,000	Area between 5 psi circle	Area between 5 and 2.2 psi circles	Population of Bombay taken as 11,914,900. Effects of 1 mt strike based on similar parameters also included.
General K. Sunderji	20 kt	165,000	345,000	Area between 5 psi circle	Area between 5 and 2.2 psi circles	Population density taken as 15,000 per sq km.
M.V. Ramana	15 kt air burst	160,000	485,000	OTA Model >12 psi=98% 5-12 psi=50% 2-5 psi=5%	OTA Model > 12 psi=2% 5-12 psi=40% 2-5 psi=45% 1-2 psi=25%	Population density taken as 23,000 per sq km. Figures will increase if population density taken as 100,000 per sq km
		200,000	131,000	Superfires Model Thermal flux of 10 cal/cm^2 = 1.66 km	Superfires Model Thermal flux of 6 cal/cm^2 = 2.14 km	–
		739,000	Not available	Mortality rates of Hiroshima (refer Table 3)	–	–

Damage Estimation in the TBA: Indian writing on the effects of a nuclear strike on purely military targets like missile sites, airfields, naval dockyards and ships or armoured formations in the TBA are practically non-existent. Being a military matter, it probably has been left for the defence services to ponder upon. The armed forces on their part have basically relied on de-classified NATO and

US Army NBC training manuals to derive simplistic tables for assessing damage. Known as Atomic Damage Templates (ADT), these have also been used by General K. Sunderji in Combat Paper No. 2 to derive the likely lethal distance from the GZ, where troops may be killed or injured and equipment may be destroyed during a 20-kiloton strike. The prescribed distances laid out in these ADT for various yields assess the damage on a limited type of targets only. These are as under:

- 100 percent destruction of tanks.
- 100 percent destruction of vehicles.
- 100 or 33 percent casualties among protected troops.
- 100 or 33 percent casualties among exposed troops.

The lack of both scientific and academic literature for assessing damages on military targets could be attributed to a variety of reasons. A military target will always be so disposed that the scale of destruction as compared to a counter-value target like a city will certainly not be as horrendous. The personnel casualties will be far less, not only because of reduced troop densities but also because the troops will be better protected, forewarned and well-trained to take evasive measures. As far as the damage or destruction of equipment like aircraft, helicopters, tanks, infantry combat vehicles, missiles and their transporter erector launcher vehicles is concerned, the criteria for assessing damage will have to be very specific and probably based on empirical data from actual tests. The damage criterion for military equipment included in the study is limited to the extent that is available in open source literature. This remains a major grey area and needs to be addressed because such criteria will also be required to formulate one's own strike options on the potential military targets of adversaries.

ENDNOTES

1. The energy yield of a 1 kiloton nuclear weapon equals the explosive power of 1000 tons of trinitrotoluene (TNT), which releases an equivalent of 4.615 × 1012 joules of energy.
2. Initial Nuclear Radiations are those that are emitted within one minute of the nuclear detonation.
3. John Malik, *The Yields of Hiroshima and Nagasaki Nuclear Explosions*, Los Alamos National Laboratory, 1985, http://www.nuclearpathways.org/Docs/pdfs/00313791.pdf, accessed on 10 July 2008.
4. Frank Barnaby and Joseph Rotblat, "The Effects of Nuclear Weapons," *AMBIO*, Vol. 11, Nos. 2/3, 1982, pp. 84-93.
5. Ibid.
6. The nuclear explosions at Hiroshima and Nagasaki, being Air Bursts, produced no major radioactive fallout.
7. Barnaby and Rotblat, n. 4.
8. The US Strategic Bombing Survey, *Effects of Atomic Bombs at Hiroshima and Nagasaki*, http://ibiblio.org/hyperwar/AAF/USSBS/AtomicEffects/AtomicEffects-2.html, accessed on 20 July 2008.

9. The Manhattan Engineer District of the US Army, *The Atomic Bombing of Hiroshima and Nagasaki* (Pennsylvania, PA: Pennsylvania State University Press, 1946).
10. The US Strategic Bombing Survey, n. 8, p. 15.
11. M V Ramana, quoting The Committee for the Compilation of Materials on Damage Caused by the Atomic Bombs on Hiroshima and Nagasaki, in *Hiroshima and Nagasaki – The Physical, Medical and Societal Effects of the Atomic Bombing* (New York: Basic Books, 1981).
12. US Army, n. 9.

3

Damage from Effects of Blast

In a typical nuclear explosion, about half the energy is released by blast, one third by thermal radiation and the balance by ionising radiation. Most of the material damage caused by a nuclear explosion, especially for a surface burst or a low air burst can be attributed to the blast (or shock wave), which is a mass of compressed air travelling at supersonic speed. The two important determinants of damage from blast are height and the explosive yield of the burst. It may be prudent to examine this phenomenon in some detail.

The blast wave produces what is called static over pressure, accompanied by high velocity winds. The high velocity winds also produce a dynamic pressure front, which along with the moving shock front and accompanying winds, is all part of the blast wave phenomenon. However, the blast wave strength is generally described in terms of peak static over pressure. The dynamic pressure and high velocity winds created by the peak static overpressure are given in Table 6. Wind

Table 6: Overpressure and Wind Velocities[1]

Peak Static Over Pressure (psi)	Dynamic Pressure (psi)	Maximum Wind Velocity (kmph)
200	330	3343
150	222	2859
100	123	2277
50	41	1503
30	17	1076
20	8.1	808
10	2.2	473
5	0.6	262
2	0.1	112

velocities are significant considering the winds accompanying normal cyclones, which regularly strike our eastern coast line, are generally of the order of 200 kmph.

As the shock front passes a particular point, the pressure falls below the ambient atmospheric pressure, which is generally 15 psi at mean sea level. This causes the high velocity winds to flow inwards towards the GZ. However, these winds are not strong enough to be considered militarily significant. The positive and negative pressure phases of the blast wave phenomenon are illustrated with the help of Figure 1.

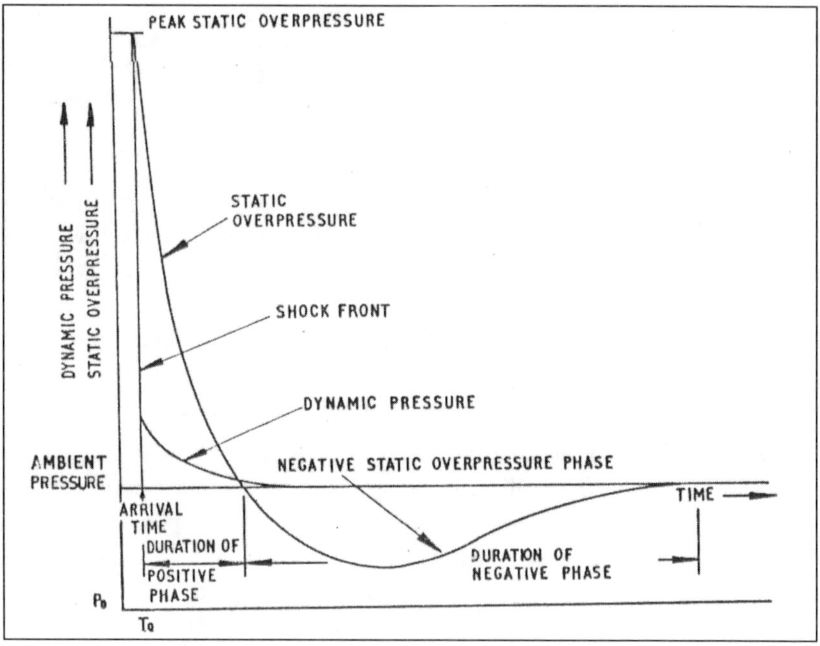

Figure 1: Blast Wave Phenomenon

As the blast (or shock) wave produced by the nuclear explosion accelerates outwards, it strikes the ground, generating a secondary shock wave. The two waves propagate outwards forming a single reinforced front called the Mach front. The point where the original and secondary shock waves meet is called the Triple Point. The Triple Point increases in height as the blast wave travels outwards from the GZ. The over-pressure created by the Mach front is roughly twice that of the primary or secondary shock wave. The formation of the Mach front is explained with the help of Figure 2. In case of an air burst, the formation of the Mach front is dependent on the height of the burst. This has a significant bearing on the damage inflicted on the target. A lower air burst will produce the Mach front closer to the GZ and is hence ideal for the destruction of hardened targets like missile silos or military equipment, tanks, etc.

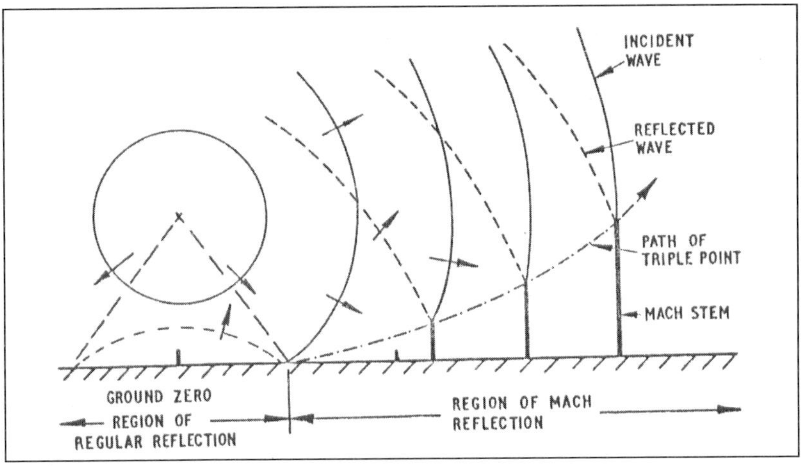

Figure 2: Formation of Mach Effect

Distance, Height of Burst and Overpressure Relationship

Three graphs establishing the relationships between slant range, height of burst and static overpressure for one kiloton yield are given in Appendix A. The corresponding slant ranges or overpressure for other yields can be calculated by the help of these graphs and scaling laws. The scaling laws and their application for calculating the slant range and height of burst for desired overpressures is also explained in the Appendix.

In order to avoid tedious calculations, relevant distances from the GZ for yields from five kiloton to one megaton, have been pre-calculated for pressure ranges of interest, i.e., from one to 30 psi. These are given in Table 7.[2] Since the slant ranges for overpressure are dependent on the height of burst (HOB), these have been calculated separately for likely counter-force and counter-value targets. In

Table 7: Distance and Overpressure Relationship for Specific Yields

Yield	Ideal HOB (in metres)		Distance in Metres for Specific Overpressure											
			30 psi		20 psi		10 psi		5 psi		2 psi		1 psi	
	Counter Force (CF)	Counter Value (CV)	CF	CV	CF	CV	CF	CV	CF	CV	CF	CV	CF	CV
5 kt	314	-	330	-	487	-	734	-	1092	-	1941	-	2917	-
10 kt	396	-	416	-	614	-	925	-	1454	-	2445	-	3675	-
20 kt	500	1000	525	-	774	-	1166	1250	1831	2000	3081	3580	4630	5542
50 kt	-	2952	-	-	-	-	-	1695	-	2712	-	4860		7522
100 kt	-	1708	-	-	-	-	-	2136	-	3417	-	6123		9478
1 mt	-	3680	-	-	-	-	-	4600	-	7632	-	13192		20420
1 kt	184	368	189	GZ	285	GZ	430	460	675	736	1135	1319	1706	2042

the former case, the height of burst which will maximise Mach effect for 30 psi has been considered, especially for lower yields because such yields are likely to be used for counter-force targets. For counter-value targets, the height of burst which will maximise Mach effect for five psi has been taken and higher yields considered as these will be relevant for targeting cities and towns. An intermediate yield of 20 kiloton has been considered for both counter-value and counter-force strikes.

Damage Criterion

Personnel: The human body has a lot of tolerance to withstand overpressure, but at higher ranges, the overpressure from blast wave may crush human bodies, damaging lung and circulatory systems. The thresholds or severe damage criteria due to overpressure are given in Table 8. Since the thresholds are very high, overpressure by itself is unlikely to produce fatalities per se. A more probable cause of death or injury to personnel from blast effects will be from missiles and debris accompanying the high velocity winds or from collapsing buildings in which persons are likely to be trapped. The overpressure ranges for calculation of personnel casualties from blast effects is presented in Table 9.

Table 8: Overpressure Damage Criteria Due to Blast Effects[3]

Effect	Effective Peak Pressure (psi)
Eardrum Rupture	
Threshold	5
50 percent	15-20 (more than 20 years old) 30-35 (less than 20 years old)
Lung Damage	
Threshold	12 (8-15)
Severe	25 (20-30)
Lethality	
Threshold	40 (30-50)
50 percent	62 (50-75)
100 percent	92 (75-115)

Table 9: Relevant Overpressures for Calculation of Personnel Casualties[4]

Overpressure	Dead (percentage of population density)	Injured (percentage of population density)	Possible Survivors (percentage of population density)
12 psi and more	98	2	nil
5 - 12 psi	50	40	10
2 - 5 psi	5	45	50
1 - 2 psi	-	25	75

Buildings: Large targets such as buildings are most vulnerable to diffraction loading and the blast damage will be affected by peak static over pressure. However, the damage at various levels of overpressure is difficult to predict due to the varying standards of construction and the complicated nature of interaction of the blast wave with various terrain features/man-made structures. Nevertheless, rough estimates can be made. These are summarised in Table 10.

Table 10: Overpressure Effects on Buildings[5]

Over pressure	Likely Destruction
5 psi	Light housing like huts and shacks
10 psi	Brick housing and commercial buildings made form reinforced concrete
20 psi	Heavy built reinforced concrete structures
100 psi	Multi-storied buildings with steel frames

Military Equipment: Smaller targets which include military equipment such as tanks, artillery guns and vehicles will be prone to damage due to drag loading in which dynamic pressure and duration of the positive blast phase are important criteria. Table 11 gives the moderate damage criteria for select military equipment from over peak static overpressure generated by 1 kiloton and 1 megaton nuclear explosions. The table clearly shows that due to the longer positive phase produced by a higher yield explosion, the peak static overpressure required for similar damage is lesser by almost half.

Table 11: Moderate Damage to Military Equipment[6]

Equipment	Peak Static Overpressure	
	1 kt	**1 mt**
Tank	45 psi	22 psi
Artillery Gun	30 psi	17 psi
Soft Vehicle	18 psi	9 psi

ENDNOTES

1. Samuel Gladstone and Philip J Dolan (eds.), *The Effects of Nuclear Weapons* (Washington, D.C.: US GPO, 1977), p. 82.
2. The ideal height of burst is more relevant for offensive use of nuclear weapons as this criterion can be manipulated for desired effect as per the target posture. In case of damage assessment from the enemy's nuclear strikes, it will be rather difficult to calculate the exact height of burst. Hence, Table 7 provides the height of burst that is likely to be used for counter-value or counter force strikes. In case of a lower height of burst, the distances will reduce marginally besides higher pressures coming into play.

3. Samuel Gladstone and Philip J Dolan, "Biological Effects", in Christine Cassel, Michael McCally and Henry Abraham (eds.), *Nuclear Weapons and Nuclear War: A Sourcebook for Health Professionals* (New York: Praeger Publishers, 1984), p. 95.
4. Office of Technology Assessment, *Effects of Nuclear War* (Washington, D.C.: Congress of the United States, 1979), p. 19.
5. Compiled from various sources.
6. LW McNaught, *Nuclear Weapons and Their Effects* (London: Brassey's, 1984), p. 83.

4

Damage from Effects of Thermal Radiation

At the instant of a nuclear detonation, there is a sharp rise in temperature and pressure (millions of degrees centigrade and atmospheres). At such high temperatures, electromagnetic waves of very short wavelength called X-rays are generated. These get absorbed by the surrounding air, which re-radiates this energy at higher wavelengths leading to the release of ultraviolet, visible and infrared radiations. This process leads to the formation of the fireball and resultant release of thermal energy into the surrounding atmosphere. Thermal radiation being electromagnetic, it travels at the speed of light and, therefore, its arrival at any distance is instantaneous to the formation of the fireball.

In a typical nuclear detonation, about 35 percent of the total energy yield is emitted in the form of thermal radiation. This thermal radiation is radiated in two pulses – prompt and delayed thermal pulse. Prompt thermal radiation contains less than one percent of the total thermal energy. The latter pulse peaks at about one second after the detonation and is more significant from the point of view of causing damage like secondary fires or personnel casualties like damage to eyes and skin burn. The duration of the latter thermal pulse increases with the yield of the weapon. Table 12 compares the fireball sizes and time taken for 80 percent of the thermal yield to be radiated for one kiloton and one megaton air bursts. The effect of thermal energy delivered at the target is dependent on both the amount of heat delivered and the rate at which it is delivered. From Table 12, it is clear that although from a 1 megaton weapon the thermal energy will be delivered at a much greater range, it will be delivered over an extended period of time and hence will be much less damaging.

Distance and Thermal Energy Deposition Relationship

Thermal radiation decreases in its intensity as it travels outwards because of the spread of radiation over a larger area and attenuation due to scattering by dust

Table 12: Variation in Thermal Pulse Duration[1]

	1 kt	1 mt
Maximum fireball diameter	140 m	2,200 m
Duration of thermal pulse	.25 seconds	8 seconds

and water molecules present in the air. While the distance for decreased intensity of thermal radiation due to spreading over a larger area varies as the square root of the explosive yield, the attenuation due to scattering is dependent upon visibility. The latter takes into account dust and water vapour present in the air that will scatter or absorb the thermal radiation. Hence, during periods of good visibility, the effects of thermal radiation will be felt at greater distances and vice versa, if the target is obscured by smoke, smog, industrial haze, natural fog, mist, etc. The scaling laws for attenuation of thermal radiation are explained in Appendix B.

The damage caused by thermal radiation is dependent upon the amount of thermal energy received per unit area of an exposed surface. This is generally expressed in calories/cm^2. The ranges at which thermal energy of interest will be deposited for various yields has been pre-calculated and presented in Table 13. The technical basis for the calculation is explained in Appendix B.

Table 13: Yield, Distance and Thermal Energy Relationship

Yield	Thermal Energy Deposition Ranges in Metres				
	30 cal/cm^2	20 cal/cm^2	15 cal/cm^2	10 cal/cm^2	5 cal/cm^2
1 kt	254	311	360	441	622
5 kt	568	696	804	984	1392
10 kt	804	984	1137	1392	1969
20 kt	1137	1392	1608	1969	2785
50 kt	1798	2202	2542	3114	4404
100 kt	2542	3114	3596	4404	6228
1 mt	8041	9848	11372	13928	19696

Damage Criterion

Thermal radiation causes primary and secondary burns amongst exposed personnel. Primary burns are those that are caused by direct action of thermal radiation, emanating from the fireball and are also called 'flash burns'. Secondary burns, also called 'flame burns', are caused by secondary fires. The severity of the burn on human skin depends on the amount of heat received and its duration. Skin burns are generally classified as first, second and third degree burns, in increasing order of their severity. The distribution of burns into three groups has certain limitations, since it is not possible to draw a sharp distinction between first and second or second and third degree burns. Mortality due to burns is also dependent on the degree of burn as well as coverage of body area or burns on vital parts.

Personnel Casualties: Fatal and non-fatal casualties from thermal radiation can be considered for distances where exposed personnel will be subjected to third and second degree burns. As a general yardstick, human skin, when exposed to thermal radiation at 10 calories/cm^2, is likely to suffer third degree burns and exposure up to 6 calories/cm^2 will result in second degree burns. However, larger thermal energy will be required at higher yields because heat is dissipated due to longer duration of the thermal pulse. Although under normal conditions, a person suffering from second degree burns will survive, but during times of crisis, especially after a nuclear strike, the provision of special medical care to such a victim will be impossible. It also needs to be considered that such a person will also be subjected to other effects of a nuclear detonation like exposure to radiation or injuries from blast effects. Hence, third and second degree burns can also be associated with immediate and later deaths. The thermal energy required from various yields to produce second degree burns and the distances at which such thermal energy will be deposited are given at Table 14.

Table 14: Thermal Energy Required for Causing Second Degree Burns and Corresponding Distances

Yield	Thermal Energy Calories/cm^2	Distances Metres
1kt	4	760
5 kt	4.2	1500
10 kt	4.3	2100
20 kt	4.5	2900
50 kt	4.8	4500
100 kt	5	6228
1 mt	6.5	17000

Primary and Secondary Fires: The immediate and important physical effects of thermal radiation results in direct charring and ignition of combustible material in the target area. Secondary effects are caused by electrical short circuits, upturned stoves etc and may result in the starting of fires over a large area. Table 15 gives approximate ignition energies from a one kiloton and one megaton air burst due to the direct effect of thermal radiation. Secondary fires are difficult to predict on the basis of thermal energy alone.

Massed Fires: It is possible that secondary fires can coalesce into 'massed fires' which can consume larger areas than ordinary secondary fires. Massed fires can be of two types, a 'fire storm' in which violent inrushing winds create extreme high temperatures but prevent the fire from spreading outwards, and 'conflagration'

Table 15: Ignition Energies for Common Items[2]

Item	Ignition Energy in Calories/cm^2	
	1 kt	1 mt
Cloth khaki drill	5	11
Dark wool flannel	6	13
Combat dress	15	30
NBC suit	15	30
Truck canvas canopy	15	30
Dry grass	2/3	5/7
Cardboard	6	13
Plastic	4/6	9/13

in which a fire spreads along a front.[3] The nuclear strike on Hiroshima resulted in a 'fire storm', whereas there are many examples of a 'conflagration' starting from ordinary fires. A fire storm can kill a larger number of people than a conflagration because people may not have enough time to escape.

The prediction of damage that can be caused by massed fires has largely been ignored in favour of damage from blast effects. This is based on the assumption that massed fires are difficult to predict. In fact some analysts believe that since the armed forces understand explosives and their effects better, they relied on blast effects to codify the damage criterion.[4] The codification of damage criterion based on massed fires was largely ignored because the United States Air Force (USAF), being the initial custodian of nuclear weapons, relied on the doctrine of 'precision strategic bombing' and hence were only interested in 'pinpoint targets' rather than 'area targets'. This emphasis towards blast effects to codify damage criterion reflected more confidence in predictions that looked like those made by 'civil engineers' rather than 'fire protection engineers' who had lesser status.[5] It is now believed that visual analysis of the target area maps and photographs can help make an assessment of the damage caused by massed fires. Such fires, to a large extent, are dependent upon the presence or absence of trees or foliage, type of houses (wooden or concrete), specific areas of the city being targeted like industrial, office or residential, presence of slums which are generally prone to catch fire and presence of inflammable material in the form of gas pipelines or gas stations. Some generalised conclusions made by the OTA are that while an urban fire can be started with 20 calories/cm^2 of direct thermal radiation, an inflammable material density (called fuel loading) of 8 lb/feet^2 or 3.9 gram/cm^2 will be required to convert a secondary fire into a massed fire.[6]

Endnotes

1. LW McNaught, *Nuclear Weapons and Their Effects* (London: Brassey's, 1984), p. 38.
2. Ibid, p. 43.
3. Office of Technology Assessment, "A Nuclear Weapon over Detroit and Leningrad: A Tutorial on the Effects of Nuclear Weapons" in Christine Cassel, Michael McCally and Henry Abraham (eds.) *Nuclear Weapons and Nuclear War: A Sourcebook for Health Professionals* (New York: Praeger Publishers, 1984), p. 135.
4. See Lynn Eden, *Whole World on Fire: Organizations, Knowledge and Nuclear Weapon Devastation* (New Delhi: Manas Publications/Cornell University, 2004).
5. Ibid, p. 6.
6. In the US, it is assessed that combustible material in suburban areas is about 3 grams/ cm^2 and about 10 grams/cm^2 in the city centres.

5

Damage from Initial Nuclear Radiation

A nuclear explosion besides causing destruction by blast and thermal radiation, also produces nuclear radiation. However, the potential of nuclear radiation to cause immediate large-scale casualties has often been considered insignificant when compared to the effects of blast and thermal radiation. It is well established that at lower yields, personnel casualties due to such radiation may exceed casualties caused by blast or thermal effects. The importance given to the shock wave phenomenon to cause destruction is evident as the yield of nuclear weapons continues to be expressed in equivalent tonnage of TNT. It, however, needs to be understood that while the effects or resultant damage from blast and heat will be limited both in time and space, the effect of nuclear radiation can lead to a long-term contamination hazard in areas that lie well beyond the area actually devastated by blast and thermal radiation.

The radiation accompanying a nuclear blast is generally classified as Initial Nuclear Radiation (INR) and residual radiation. INR is that radiation that is emitted up to one minute after the detonation. The intensity and rate of emission of INR is much greater than that of residual radiation and hence the former may contribute considerably in causing personnel casualties, especially among unprotected personnel.

The INR mainly consists of neutrons and gamma rays. While neutrons are particles of appreciable mass, gamma rays are essentially electro-magnetic waves. Both neutrons and gamma rays are harmful to the human body, though they differ in the details of their interaction with cells and tissues. However for military purposes, the acute effects from their exposure can be taken as similar. The effect of both neutrons and gamma rays on exposed personnel will be additive as they will arrive simultaneously, but it will be prudent to consider their effects separately.

Neutrons

Neutrons are emitted, both by fission and fusion reactions. However, for a given explosive yield, the number of neutrons produced in fusion reactions is 10 times greater than in fission reactions.[1] Also, the energy level of the neutrons emitted from a fusion reaction is far more (12 to 14 MeV) than that produced from a fission reaction (2 MeV) and hence, they have a higher potential to cause damage to human cells and tissues. Even in fission explosions of similar yield, the number of neutrons produced will depend upon the method of assembly of the bomb. An implosion device, like the one used in Nagasaki, will produce lesser neutrons as compared to a gun barrel type assembly which was used in Hiroshima. This is because of the large presence of hydrogenous material in the former, which will absorb slow neutrons as well as slow down fast neutrons.

All the neutrons produced as a result of a nuclear explosion experience elastic and inelastic scattering within the weapon itself when they travel through the air. As the neutrons travel away from the source of explosion, they are spread over a larger area and are also absorbed in the air. If the neutrons were to travel in a vacuum, the decrease in neutron activity would follow an inverse square law, i.e., the fluency at a distance of two km would be four times less than at one km. The attenuation of neutron activity is dependent on air density. For normal air density, the energy of neutrons would decrease by a factor of 10 each time a neutron passes through a layer of air 570 metres thick.[2]

When the neutrons reach the human body, they are partially absorbed by it and deliver a dose of radiation. A graph depicting the neutron dose delivered as a function of slant range for a 1-kiloton bomb detonating at 100 metres is given at Appendix C. The data extracted from the graph is presented in Table 16. Since the graph and resultantly the data in the Table applies to an air burst, for surface bursts the dose values should be reduced by half. For higher explosive yields, the neutron dose rate can be obtained by simply multiplying the dosage with the explosive yield.

Table 16: Neutron Dose Rate for 1 kt Air Burst

Radiation Dose in rads/cGys	Slant Range in metres
8000	480
5000	550
3000	610
1000	770
500	850
300	920
100	1090
50	1220
10	1450
5	1550

Gamma Rays

Gamma rays are emitted as part of a nuclear explosion (prompt gamma rays) as well as due to secondary emissions, the latter caused by the interaction of neutrons with the nuclei of the weapon material and air molecules. These rays are attenuated as they travel through air and follow the same laws as for neutrons, except that the rate of their absorption in air is considerably less. Here, a ten-fold decrease in the intensity of gamma rays will occur in an air column of 730 metres thick, as compared to 570 metres for neutrons.[3]

Gamma dose rates at various slant ranges cannot be extrapolated from the standard graph of a 1 kiloton yield due to the hydrodynamic expansion factor.[4] A correction for enhancement factor has to be applied by drawing graphs for specific yields. Graphs giving gamma dose rates from various yields of fission and thermonuclear weapons as a function of slant range are given in Appendix C. Data extracted from the graphs for relevant yields is presented in Table 17.

Table 17: Gamma Dose Rates for Specific Yields

Radiation Dose (rads/cGys)	Slant Range (metres)			
	1 kt (fission)	10 kt (fission)	100 kt (fission)	100 kt (fusion)
8000	400	725	1250	1150
5000	450	800	1325	1250
3000	525	900	1500	1400
1000	675	1125	1750	1650
500	800	1250	1900	1800
300	900	1375	2025	1900
100	1100	1600	2275	2200
50	1225	1750	2425	2350
10	1600	2100	2950	2700

Combined Doses from Neutrons and Gamma Rays

The total dose that a person may receive due to INR will be a combination of neutrons and gamma rays. At shorter distances, neutrons will be a major contributing factor, but as ranges increase, the dose from gamma rays will become the dominant factor. In case of thermonuclear weapons of very high yield, due to hydrodynamic enhancement, the dose that a person may receive at longer ranges will be entirely due to gamma rays.

In order to calculate the acute effects of INR, doses due to neutrons and gamma are simply added, although the long-term biological effects of neutrons may be more severe. Combined dosages at various distances are given in Table 18.

Table 18: Combined Dosage from Neutron and Gamma Rays

Distance (metres)	Radiation Dose in Rads/cGys								
	1 kt			10 kt			100 kt		
	Gamma	Neutrons	Total Dose	Gamma	Neutrons	Total Dose	Gamma	Neutrons	Total Dose
600	1600	3000	4600	Too high to be relevant			Too high to be relevant		
700	850	1500	2350	-do-			-do-		
800	450	700	1150	5000	7000	12000	-do-		
900	270	300	570	3000	3000	6000	-do-		
1000	160	170	330	1800	1700	2500	-do-		
1100	90	80	170	1000	800	1800	-do-		
1200	55	45	100	600	450	1050	-do-		
1300	35	23	58	400	230	630	6500	2300	8800
1400	20	14	34	250	140	390	4100	1400	5500
1500	13	7	20	170	70	240	2700	700	3400
1600	10	4	14	95	40	135	1800	400	2200
1700	Too less to be significant			60	20	80	1200	200	1400
1800	-do-			40	10	50	750	100	850
1900	-do-			28	7	35	590	70	660
2000	-do-			17	4	21	390	40	430
2100	-do-			10	2.5	12.5	200	25	225
2200	-do-			Too less to be significant			150	15	165
2300	-do-			-do-			90	9	99
2400	-do-			-do-			55	4	59
2500	-do-			-do-			35	1	36

Co-relation between Radiation Exposure and Casualties

Exposure to radiation, even in small doses, is harmful to the human body and hence, unwarranted exposure must be avoided as far as possible. Radiation exposure at higher dose levels may result in death due to 'acute effects'. Exposure at medium or lower dose levels is more likely to produce long-term effects, which are further classified as somatic or genetic. The accurate prediction of casualties due to radiation exposure is difficult as the effect of similar doses on two or more persons may not result in similar fatalities or long-term effects. The effects will largely depend upon the health and age of the person, type of exposure (partial or whole body) and response of the person to post exposure treatment. While the effect of radiation exposure on human beings at the lower dose end is still a subject of study, some generalised conclusions can be made at the higher end of radiation exposure.

The 'acute effects' are likely to manifest itself when the whole body or a large part of it is exposed in a short time to a radiation dose of about 20 rads and upwards. The early symptoms of acute effects like anorexia, nausea and headaches, form part of so-called 'radiation sickness'. With doses up to 100 rads, these symptoms soon disappear and recovery is apparently complete. With an increasing dose, mortality increases, reaching close to 100 percent for a dose of about 500 rads and upwards, although in a healthy adult, survival is possible even for somewhat larger doses, if special treatment is provided. Table 19 presents likely mortality rates and time of death due to radiation exposure as well as likely symptoms and time of their onset.

Table 19: Radiation Dose and Time of Death[5]

Dose Range (rads/cGys)	Onset and Duration of Initial Symptoms	Probable Time of Death
8000	30 min to one day. Severe and prolonged nausea, vomiting, fatigability, weakness, headache, disorientation and fluid imbalance.	100 percent death in one day
3000 - 8000	30 minutes to 5 days. Severe nausea, vomiting, fatiguability, weakness, headache, disorientation and fluid imbalance.	100 percent death in 2 to 3 days
830 - 3000	30 min to 2 days. Severe nausea, vomiting, fatiguability, weakness, headache, disorientation and moderate to severe fluid imbalance.	100 percent death in 5 to 10 days
530 - 830	30 min to 2 days. Moderate to severe nausea, vomiting in 80 to 100 percent cases. Severe fatiguability, weakness, in 90 to 100 percent cases.	At lower end of range, death may occur in 50 percent in 6 weeks. At higher end, death may occur for 99 percent
300 - 530	2 hours to 3 days. Transient nausea and vomiting in 50 to 90 percent cases.	At lower end, death in 10 per cent cases and at high end, death in 50 percent cases.
150 - 300	2 hours to 2 days. Transient nausea and vomiting in 20 to 70 percent cases.	At high end, death may occur in 10 percent cases.
70 - 150	2 to 20 hours. Transient mild nausea and vomiting in 5 to 30 percent cases.	–
0 - 70	From 6 to 12 hours. None to slight incidence of transient headache, nausea	–

Neutron Bomb

Enhanced Radiation Weapon (ERW) or neutron bomb,[6] as it is popularly called, is designed to kill by radiation rather than by other effects of a nuclear explosion, i.e., blast and thermal radiation. If such a bomb is exploded at a height of 500 metres, the damage from the blast and thermal radiation will be minimal, but the radiation level will be high enough to deliver a neutron dose between 450 to 1000 rads at a distance of 1300 to 1500 metres. Since such a bomb will cause little collateral damage, the possibility of its use in a counter-force mode is more likely. One of our immediate adversaries already possesses such a capability and hence, the effects of such a strike have also been factored in the study. Table 20 gives the neutron dose as a function of slant range for a 1 kiloton ERW. The data has been extracted from a graph included in Appendix C.

Table 20: Dose Rate from a 1 kiloton Neutron Bomb

Slant Range in meters	Dose (rads/cGys)
800	15,000
900	8000
1000	4600
1100	2800
1200	1800
1300	1000
1400	800
1500	420
1600	280
1700	180
1800	100

Damage Criterion

From the data presented in Table 19, it is evident that while the symptoms of radiation exposure appear almost immediately, death as a result of exposure may not occur for some time. However, for the purposes of the study, estimation of fatal casualties will be based on distances where exposed persons are likely to be subjected to a combined dose of 500 rads or more. This is because at these distances or exposure levels, the victim will be subjected to other effects of the nuclear explosion also, which are likely to worsen his/her medical condition. In addition, the provision of specialised medical treatment to such persons will be difficult in a post-strike scenario. Similarly, for calculation of non-fatal casualties, distances where exposed persons will be subjected to a combined dose of above 100 rads but below 500 rads will be taken as a yardstick. Relevant distances from the GZ where unprotected personnel could be exposed to a combined dose of 500 and 100 rads from nuclear explosions of various yields are given in Table 21.

Table 21: Combined Dose for Predicting Casualties

Yield	Distance for Exposure to	
	500 rads (Fatal)	100 rads (Non-fatal)
1 kt	930	1200
5 kt	1250	1520
10 kt	1350	1650
20 kt	1500	1830
50 kt	1750	2060
100 kt	1950	2300
1 mt	2800	3300

ENDNOTES

1. Stockholm International Peace Research Institute (SIPRI), *Nuclear Radiation in Warfare* (London: Taylor & Francis Ltd, 1981), p. 60.
2. Ibid, p. 61.
3. Ibid, p. 64.
4. Hydrodynamic enhancement occurs in case of higher yields, especially in a typical three-stage thermonuclear bomb. The gamma rays follow the blast wave and hence travel through air that is considerably less dense. Due to this effect, the gamma rays of greater intensity reach larger distances. In case of a 1 Mt weapon, the enhancement of yield for calculating the effects of gamma rays could be as high as ten times.
5. Army Field Manual FM 8-9, *NATO Handbook on the Medical Aspects of NBC Defensive Operations* (Washington, D.C.: Departments of the Army, Navy and Air Force, 1996).
6. The neutron bomb is a thermonuclear device without the tamper and with minimum extraneous material, so that few neutrons will be lost in collision with the nuclei before being emitted. At a given distance, the neutron fluence from a neutron bomb will be much larger as compared to a pure fission or a traditional thermonuclear bomb.

6

Damage from Residual Nuclear Radiation Including Nuclear Fallout

A nuclear explosion, besides producing INR, also emits residual nuclear radiation (RNR). As a general rule, all ionising radiation emitted one minute after the nuclear explosion is termed as RNR. RNR may not contribute significantly in causing immediate destruction or fatalities, but it has the potential to cause long-term radiation hazard in areas well beyond those affected by the thermal and blast effects of a nuclear explosion. Considering the effects of RNR as part of damage assessment is important for making an estimation of the population, which could be exposed to harmful effects of ionising radiations, as well as to calculate the real estate that could be laid waste after a nuclear strike due to nuclear fallout.

The major effects of RNR are witnessed either as part of nuclear fallout or as neutron-induced gamma activity (NIGA). Nuclear fallout is more applicable for a surface or low air burst, whereas the effects of NIGA will be more pronounced during an air burst.

Nuclear Fallout

Nuclear fallout consists primarily of radioactive fission products and un-fissioned uranium or plutonium from the weapon, which gets deposited on the earth's surface after the rising fireball has cooled down sufficiently. During surface or low air burst, huge quantities of earth and debris are also sucked up in the fireball, together with other fission products. As the fireball cools down, the radioactivity condenses on particles of ground material which, depending upon their size, are then deposited at varied time intervals on the earth. This leads to either an early (local) or delayed (global) fallout.[1] In case of an air burst, the deposition of fallout is slow and more widespread as finer fission products reach greater heights, thus leading only to global fallout.

Different kinds of fallout produce different types of radiation hazards. While early (local) fallout will produce a severe radiation hazard in a comparatively smaller area, delayed (global) fallout will affect a larger area and consequently more people, albeit with lesser radiation doses. For the purposes of the study, only early fallout has been considered, as its impact is more significant.

Distribution of Fallout: The distribution of fallout on the earth's surface is dependent upon meteorological conditions[2] including the nature[3] and layout[4] of terrain features. The size of debris sucked up from the earth on which the radioactivity condenses could vary from a few microns to a few millimetres. Larger particles would fall in a faster timeframe and will generally get deposited in and around the GZ, causing local fallout. As a rough yardstick, about 60 percent of the radioactivity is deposited during local fallout. The smaller, micron-sized particles remain suspended in the air for a longer duration and consequently are carried for longer distances by prevailing winds. Not only are these lighter particles deposited farther away from the GZ, the intensity of their radioactivity also decreases due to radioactive decay.

Since the size and the formation of a nuclear cloud are dependent upon the yield and height of the burst, these factors directly influence fallout predictions. Several methods have been developed for predicting the fallout dose rates and total dose at various distances from the GZ.[5] The idealised fallout pattern is one such method which is based on determining fallout distribution, based on effective wind speed rather than considering wind speed for all height bands of the radioactive cloud. This method postulates that under conditions of steady winds with no shear, the fallout is likely to be deposited uniformly on the ground and will be in the form of highly elliptical and concentric contours, shaped somewhat like cigars. Each of the contour lines would denote a particular dose rate line as shown in Figure 3. However the dose rate at a particular place will initially increase due to the arrival of fallout and after reaching a peak value, will gradually decrease due to radioactive decay.

There will always be a variation in the idealised pattern of fallout and the actual pattern. Nevertheless, an idealised pattern is useful to make an approximate estimate of possible radiation hazard from early fallout. Tables 22 to 24 give the likely downwind distances, GZ width and maximum fallout width for specific dose rates. The Tables are based on formulae that are explained in Appendix D. The dose rates are expected once the fallout has ceased and are applicable for wind speeds of 24 kmph. The downwind distances for other wind speeds can be calculated with the help of the multiplication factors presented in Table 25.

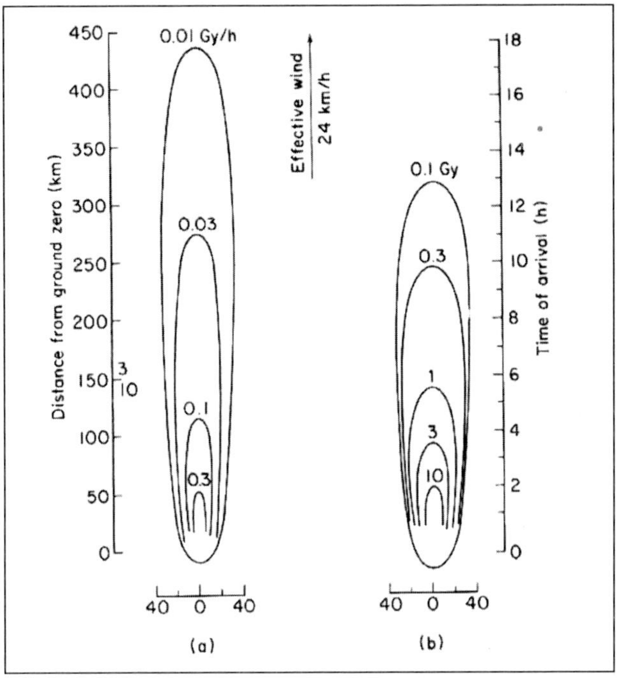

Figure 3: Idealised Fallout Contours

Table 22: Maximum Downwind Distance for Specific Dose Rates

Dose Rates (Rads/hour)	5 kt (km)	10 kt (km)	20 kt (km)	50 kt (km)	100 kt (km)	1 Mt (km)
3000	3.2	4.3	5. 9	8.9	12.1	34.21
1000	6.0	8.2	11.1	16.8	23.0	64.83
300	15.0	20.4	27.9	42.1	57.5	162.1
100	29.5	40.4	55.1	83.3	113.7	320.6
30	53.1	72.6	99.1	149.7	204.5	576.3
10	79.7	108.8	148.7	224.6	306.7	864.5
3	99.6	136.0	185.8	280.7	383.4	1080.6
1	139.5	181.4	247.8	374.2	511.2	1440.8

Table 23: GZ Radii for Specific Dose Rates

Dose Rate (Rads/hour)	5 kt	10 kt	20 kt	50 kt	100 kt	1 mt
3000	0.11	0.16	0.24	0.40	0.60	1.42
1000	0.24	0.36	0.53	0.90	1.33	4.95
300	0.7	0.97	1.36	2.10	2.93	8.86
100	1.23	1.65	2.20	3.24	4.34	11.42
30	1.65	2.19	2.91	4.24	5.63	14.48
10	2.11	2.81	3.74	5.44	7.23	18.58
3	2.77	3.68	4.9	7.12	9.46	24.32
1	4.67	6.2	8.24	12.00	15.95	40.98

Table 24: Maximum Fallout Width for Specific Dose Rates

Dose Rate (Rads/hour)	5 kt	10 kt	20 kt	50 kt	100 kt	1 mt
3000	0.048	0.089	0.16	0.35	0.64	4.65
1000	0.196	0.34	0.56	1.13	1.92	11.03
300	0.605	0.96	1.51	2.76	4.37	19.98
100	1.61	2.43	3.69	6.4	9.7	38.58
30	3.01	4.44	6.55	10.93	16.12	58.52
10	5.29	7.63	11.02	17.91	25.86	87.64
3	7.91	11.2	15.83	25.03	35.4	111.94
1	11.49	16.03	22.36	34.71	48.4	146.24

Table 25: Dependence of Fallout Distance on Wind Velocity[6]

Wind Velocity (kmph)	Multiplying Factor
12	0.75
24	1.00
36	1.13
48	1.25
60	1.38
72	1.50

Time of Arrival: The time of arrival of the fallout at any location is dependent on the wind speed and the distance of that location from the GZ. Since the fallout will commence from the extremities of the radioactive cloud and not from the centre of the GZ, the radius of the mushroom cloud is normally subtracted from the distance the cloud is required to travel. Fallout arrival timings of some common yields for wind speeds of 24 kmph are presented in Table 26. Since the deposition of fallout is time dependent, in certain circumstances, like in open areas where the armed forces are likely to operate, fallout can be avoided. However, fallout avoidance may not be possible in cities and towns which have limited exit routes that may be destroyed or clogged.

Table 26: Arrival of Fallout

Distance	5 kt	10 kt	20 kt	50 kt	100 kt	1 mt
25 km	57 m	55 m	53 m	49 m	45 m	20 m
50 km	120 m	118 m	116 m	111 m	107 m	82 m
100 km	245 m	243 m	241 m	236 m	232 m	207 m
150 km	NA	368 m	366 m	361 m	357 m	332 m
200 km	NA	NA	491 m	486 m	482 m	458 m
250 km	NA	NA	NA	611 m	608 m	582 m
300 km	NA	NA	NA	737 m	732 m	707 m
400 km	NA	NA	NA	NA	983 m	956 m
500 km	NA	NA	NA	NA	1232 m	1208 m

The fallout predictions based on U.S. Army Field Manuals are of a conical configuration (refer Figure 4) rather than the usual cigar shape of an idealised fallout pattern. This is because in the latter half of the cigar, radioactivity would have decreased considerably by the time the fallout arrives, so as to be of any significance to protected troops. The conical pattern also represents three areas where radiation exposure[7] will not exceed specified doses, as given below:

- **Zone 1** – This zone delineates the area of primary hazard and is called the zone of immediate operational concern. In this zone, exposed and unprotected personnel may receive doses of 150 rads or greater in less than four hours after arrival of fallout.
- **Zone 2** – Zone 2 is called the zone of secondary hazard. In this zone, the total dose received by exposed, unprotected personnel is not expected to reach 150 rads within four hours after arrival of fallout; but personnel may receive a total dose of 50 rads or greater within the first 24 hours after the arrival of the fallout.
- Outside Zone 1 and Zone 2, exposed, unprotected personnel may receive a total dose that does not reach 50 rads on the first day (24 hours) after arrival of the fallout.

Neutron Induced Gamma Activity (NIGA)

Neutrons are produced in all nuclear explosions. While some of these will interact with the construction material of the bomb, like iron and nitrogen present in the air, most of these neutrons are captured by various elements present in the soil directly below the burst.[8] As a result of the latter activity, the soil becomes radioactive and starts emitting secondary gamma radiations for extended periods of time. This phenomenon is known as NIGA and is more prominent during an air burst. The phenomenon is also witnessed during a surface or low air burst but the soil affected by induced activity would be sucked up as part of the mushroom cloud. The area affected by NIGA is always circular in pattern and

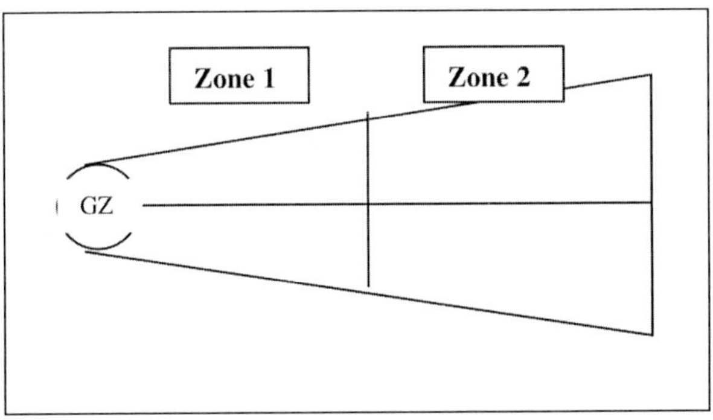

Figure 4: Fallout Predictions of the US Army

located around the GZ. Weather conditions have no influence upon the location and size of the affected area.

Estimating that the area affected by NIGA would be an important pre-requisite before inducting personnel in contaminated zones. This will assist in reducing undue exposure of personnel to radiation. Table 27 shows the boundaries of a NIGA-affected area for air bursts of various yields. The distance given is maximum horizontal radius, up to which a 2 rad dose rate will extend one hour after the burst.

Table 27: Radii of Induced Contamination[9]

Estimated Yield	2 rad Dose Rate at H plus 1 (metres)
1 kt	700
10 kt	1000
100 kt	1600
1000 kt	2000

Decay of Radioactivity

A fission reaction splits Uranium^{235}, Uranium^{238} or Plutonium^{239} atoms present in the bomb core in more than one manner. Most of the fission products are radioactive and decay as per their half-life to form stable atoms. The decay of each of the radioactive nuclides among the fission products follows a simple exponential decrease with time, but for a whole mixture of fission nuclides, the variation of activity with time is highly complex. The decay for the first six months, however, follows the 7/10 rule, as per which for every seven-fold increase in time, the dose rate decreases by a factor of 10. Table 28 gives the average dose rates

Table 28: Dose Rate from Fallout at Various Times After the Explosion[10]

Time (Hours)	Relative Dose Rate (rads/hour)
1	100
2	40
4	15
6	10
12	5
24	2.4
36	1.6
48	1.1
72	0.62
100	0.36
200	0.17
500	0.05
1000	0.023

due to gamma rays from early fallout at different times after the explosion. The dose rates in the Table are with reference to the dose rate at H plus 1 hour, at which time the dose rate was assumed to be 100 rads per hour. The Table can be used to derive dose rates at desired times if the dose rate in that area from any time or situation is known. The process is explained in Appendix D.

ENDNOTES

1. Early fallout is deposited within 24 hours, whereas delayed fallout may take years for deposition. This is also called 'global fallout'.
2. In case of precipitation conditions, a rainout or snowout may occur, in which case, a smaller area will be more severely affected. Such areas are called radiation hotspots.
3. Since fallout is dependent upon particle size of sucked-up earth, a nuclear explosion in deserts with finer sand particles will produce more widespread fallout as compared to mud clay flats of, say, Punjab.
4. The undulations in the terrain will produce uneven fallout patterns. For example, the leeward side of a hill may receive very little fallout as compared to the windward.
5. The basic models for hazard prediction, as per Gladstone and Dolan, are the Mathematical Fallout Model, Analog Model, Danger Sector Forecast and Idealised Fallout Pattern. Samuel Gladstone and Philip J Dolan, "Biological Effects," in Christine Cassel, Michael McCally and Herry Abraham (eds.), *Nuclear Weapons and Nuclear War: A Sourcebook for Health Professionals* (New York: Praeger Publishers, 1984).
6. Stockholm International Peace Research Institute (SIPRI), *Nuclear Radiation in Warfare*, (London: Taylor & Francis Ltd, 1981), p. 90.
7. Army Field Manual FM 3-3, *Chemical and Biological Contamination Avoidance* (Washington, D.C.: Department of the Army, 1992), p. D2.
8. Important substances induced by neutrons in the soil are Aluminium^{28}, Manganese^{56}, and Sodium^{24}.
9. Army Field Manual 3-3, n. 7, p. L1.
10. SIPRI, n. 6, p. 81.

7

Yield Estimation and Locating Ground Zero

Earlier chapters have established some sort of a relationship between all the three major effects of a nuclear explosion, i.e., blast, thermal and nuclear radiation and corresponding ranges where these effects are likely to produce fatalities among personnel and damage or destruction of property and equipment. The relationship is, however, closely dependent on the yield of the explosion and hence, there will be an inescapable need to establish the likely yield of the nuclear strike before any assessment of damage can be attempted. Yield estimation, besides assisting in damage assessment, will also be of help in predicting the area likely to be affected by radioactive fallout. In addition, there will also be a need to determine the GZ of the strike so that the radii of damage can be plotted to assess it. This chapter deals with various techniques for estimating the yield of a nuclear strike and the mythology for assessing the GZ.

Yield Estimation

Cloud Morphology: The yield of a nuclear strike can be estimated by studying the morphology of the cloud, whose formation succeeds the rapidly cooling fireball. Depending upon the height of burst, a spherical cloud would be formed in the case of an air burst and a mushroom cloud with a stem, in the case of a surface or low air burst. This nuclear cloud continues to grow in height and size till the stabilisation of both these parameters. Depending upon the yield of the explosion, a stabilised cloud is formed between 4 to 14 minutes after the explosion.[1]

- The first measurement that is normally taken for yield estimation is the annular width of the mushroom cloud (shown in Figure 5) at H plus 5 minutes. The nomogram used to estimate the yield using 'Cloud Width' parameters at H plus 5 minutes and the procedure for yield estimation is given in Appendix E.

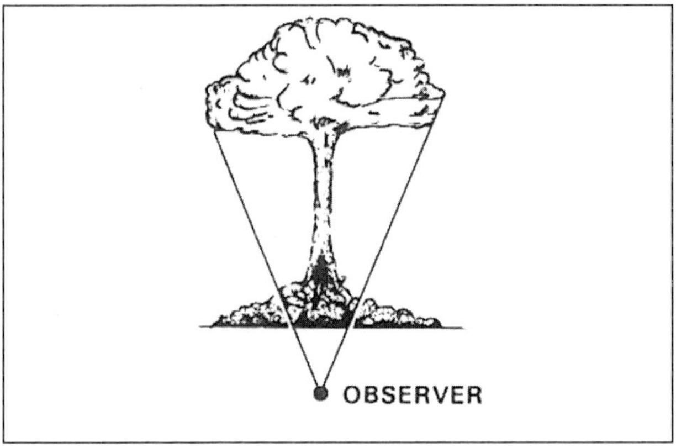

Figure 5: Cloud Width

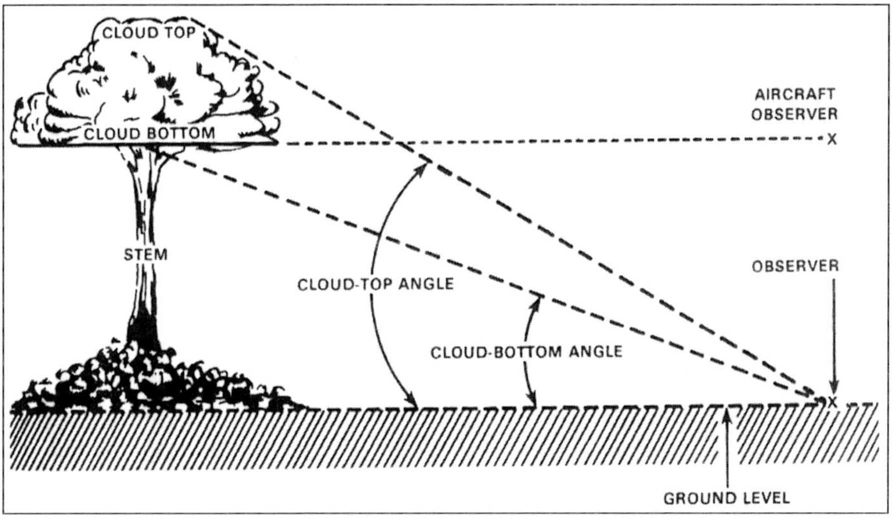

Figure 6: Cloud Top and Bottom Angles

- The angles sustained by 'Cloud Top' and 'Cloud Bottom' (Figure 6) at H plus 10 minutes from the known location of an observer can also be used to estimate the yield. The nomogram which uses this technique to estimate the yield is also placed at Appendix E. The methodology of using this nomogram is the same as for annular cloud width nomogram.
- 'Cloud Top Height', 'Cloud Bottom Height', '2/3rd Stem Height' or 'Cloud Radius' at H plus 10 minutes can also be used to estimate the yield. The third nomogram given in Appendix E uses these parameters to estimate the yield. The cloud parameter data extracted from the nomogram of certain yields of interest are given in Table 29.

Table 29: Stabilised Cloud Parameters at H Plus 10 Minutes

Yield	Cloud-Top Height (m)	Cloud Bottom Height (m)	2/3 Stem Height (m)	Cloud Radius (m)
1 kt	3800	2100	1400	1000
5 kt	7300	4500	2900	2000
10 kt	9500	6400	4200	2700
20 kt	10900	7300	4800	3500
50 kt	12900	8400	5600	5300
100 kt	14500	9500	6200	7000
1 mt	21500	13500	9000	17000

Crater Examination: The dimensions of the crater produced by a sub-surface, surface or low air burst depends upon the yield, height (or depth) of the burst and the soil characteristics. In case of surface bursts, a rough idea of the yield can be obtained by analysing the crater dimensions for a known type of soil. For one kiloton yield, the apparent crater radius for wet soft soil will be 82 feet; for dry soft soil 61 feet; wet hard rock 58 feet and dry hard rock 49 feet. Similarly, the depth of the apparent crater will also vary. Table 30 shows the typical dimensions of crater radius and depth for yields.

Table 30: Crater Dimensions

Dimensions	Yield						
	1 kt	5 kt	10 kt	20 kt	50 kt	100 kt	1 mt
Radius (metres)	18.5	30	36.9	45.4	59.8	73.6	147
Depth (metres)	8.5	13.7	17	20.8	27.5	33.8	67.5

Illumination Time: The study of cloud morphology to estimate the yield can only be undertaken during the day and periods of good visibility. During the night or conditions of poor visibility, the yield may be estimated by measuring the illumination time. The technique is not very accurate and may give an error of plus or minus 10 percent. The illumination times for various yields is presented in Table 31.

Adversaries' Capability: Cloud morphology, illumination time or crater examination techniques can be used independently or in combination to predict the yield. The conclusions of this analysis can also be corraborated with the known capabilities of the adversary. These are discussed in some detail in the next chapter.

Table 31: Nuclear Explosion Yields and Illumination Time[2]

Illumination Time (seconds)	Approximate Yield (kt)
Less than 1	2
1	2.5
2	10
3	22
4	40
5	60
6	90
7	125
8	160
9	200
10	250
11	285
12	325
13	400
14	475
15	550
16	700
17	750
18	800
19	900
20	980

Seismic Sensors: Over the years, a range of methods and technologies for monitoring of nuclear tests have been developed. Some of these technologies can also be used to estimate the yield of nuclear tests. Seismic sensors have been used in the past to estimate yields of tests conducted by India, Pakistan and North Korea. In fact, the monitoring system proposed during the Comprehensive Test Ban Treaty (CTBT) consisted of an International Data Centre and Monitoring stations based on various technologies including seismic sensors to detect nuclear tests. India has about 212 seismic stations functional under various organisations and educational institutions. Many of these are in research mode, and do not take observations continually. The operational network, known as the National Seismological Network (NSN) is manned and operated by the Indian Meteorological Department (IMD). It consists of 55 observatories. Of these 55 stations, 30 are equipped with state-of-the-art broadband sensors, high dynamic range digitizers, GPS time synchronisation and facility to access the data remotely through satellite communications and telephone mode. The remaining 25 stations are equipped with older analog seismograph systems. With the help of the digital

OTHER TECHNOLOGIES FOR DETECTION

1. The International Monitoring System (IMS) proposed to be established as part of the Comprehensive Test Ban Treaty (CTBT) plans to use four technologies for detecting nuclear tests. Its monitoring stations were to be based on seismic, infrasonic and hydro-acoustic technologies to detect signals from underground, atmospheric and underwater nuclear explosions, respectively. In addition, radionuclide stations were to be established to detect radioactive debris from atmospheric explosions or those vented by underground or underwater nuclear explosions. These stations were to be linked through satellite links to the International Data Centre (IDS), which was to be located in Vienna.
2. **Infrasonic** – One of the means of detecting a nuclear test is based on infrasound, which is ultra-low noise from an explosion below the range of human hearing. This can travel up to 1,000 kilometres (620 miles) depending on wind direction. Sensors based on infrasonic technology detect the pressure produced by the nuclear explosion or a high-explosive conventional test, using acoustic methods. These generally use infrasound microbarographs (acoustic pressure sensors) that detect very low-frequency sound waves in the atmosphere produced by natural and man-made events.
3. **Hydro-acoustic** – Water is a remarkably efficient medium for the transmission of sound energy. Hydro-acoustic sensors are underwater microphones that detect the presence of additional pressure waves in water to make an estimate of any nuclear explosion. The hydro-acoustic network of IMS was to be composed of eleven stations, of which six stations were to be equipped with hydrophoneic sensors and the remaining five with seismic sensors to detect waterborne energy.

network, it is now possible to determine the location and magnitude of any seismological event within 15 to 30 minutes. These seismic stations could also be used to estimate the yield of nuclear explosions and need to be networked with stake holders like the Department of Atomic Energy (DAE), National Disaster Management Authority (NDMA) and the armed forces. However, in field conditions, the armed forces will have to continue to rely on existing techniques and methodologies for estimation of the yield and the GZ.

Ground Zero (GZ)

The GZ of a nuclear strike can be obtained by a variety of methods. Seismological analysis, which is normally used to pinpoint the epicentre of an earthquake, can be used to locate the GZ. Aerial photography of the crater could be another technique. However, for the armed forces, with their system of designated nuclear observers, a reliable and effective method would continue to be based on field readings of the mushroom cloud. The designated nuclear observers take the forward bearings of the mushroom cloud centre and pass it on to their HQs. Here, the back bearings of three or more readings are then plotted on a map for estimation of the GZ.

ENDNOTES

1. Army Field Manual FM 3-3, *Chemical and Biological Contamination Avoidance* (Washington, D.C.: Department of the Army, 1992), p. A1.
2. Ibid, p. B6

PART II

NUCLEAR STRIKE SCENARIOS

8

Introduction

Indians and Pakistanis fight war by the textbook. The same textbook

Moshe Dayan[1]

During the height of the Cold War, when the spectre of a nuclear holocaust really haunted the West, a large number of think tanks, both private and government funded, were engaged in scenario building for a nuclear war between the two super powers, besides predicting the immediate after-effects and long-term consequences of such a war. Some of these studies led to fearful conclusions like the 'nuclear winter' which would severely damage, if not completely destroy, human life and other habitation on planet earth. Most of these studies were based on scenarios of large-scale nuclear exchange, involving de-capacitating first strikes followed by retaliatory second strikes. Even the scenarios involving limited tactical nuclear strikes in Europe, more often than not, also ended in a full-scale nuclear exchange between the two super powers. Consequently, there is a lack of literature on the consequences of a limited nuclear exchange from which relevant lessons for the South Asian context could be either culled or extrapolated. Probably scenarios involving a limited nuclear exchange were left out because if the consequences of multiple strikes over a number of targets have been taken into account, then studying the effects of single or limited strikes can easily be extracted. However, the analysis of single or limited strikes has its own pitfalls. Such an analysis cannot be generalised and has to dwell into details. Since this study analyses the effects of single strikes, it should in no way lead the reader to a conclusion that a nuclear exchange in the South Asian context will be limited to two or three nuclear weapons. Such an exchange has portents of escalation, in which case, the consequences will be graver. Single strikes have been considered in most of the scenarios to keep the damage assessment simple and as accurate as possible. Hopefully, the predictions would assist decision makers, all of whom may not have the time and inclination to go into the intricacies of damage assessment techniques but only into the possible consequences and mitigation efforts.

The effects of nuclear weapons, as was covered in the previous part, are either enhanced or minimised due to terrain and meteorological conditions. The US and former Soviet Union did not share a common land border. In fact, the distance between the Soviet Union and the US varied between approximately 2,500 kilometres from Alaska to Vladivostok in Eastern Russia and 7,500 to 10,000 kilometres from central US to the heart of Russia over the North Pole. Such large distances would have ensured that other than the global effects of a nuclear explosion, the impact of nuclear strikes on one would have no adverse effect on the other. Obviously this paradigm does not hold true in an Indo-Pakistan or Sino-Indian equation. In the Indo-Pakistan context, demography may also influence the selection of targets for a nuclear strike. Hence, an analysis of geographical, meteorological and demographic factors as prevailing in our subcontinent may provide useful indicators as to which areas can be engaged, without its consequences having adverse spill-over effects on the targeting nation. Such an analysis can assist the armed forces and civil defence planners not only in locating the resources and specialised units for dealing with such a disaster, but also in effective crisis management, if they were faced with such a situation.

It is also important to add that the 'hair trigger' alert nuclear posture of the Cold War era, existing between the US and former Soviet Union, does not exist in the South Asian context because our threat perceptions are entirely different. While this saves both the countries from false alarms of a nuclear attack due to computer generated errors, which have happened on more than one occasion in the US and former Soviet Union, it also throws up unique scenarios for the possibility of commencement of a nuclear conflict in the region. The absence of a reliable warning system due to geographical proximity may give rise to a perception that nuclear assets are vulnerable, leading to a dispersed and decentralised command and control system. This raises the risk of accidental or unauthorised use of nuclear weapons. Accordingly, this part of the study initially analyses the various scenarios, albeit briefly, which may lead to a nuclear exchange between India and Pakistan. Thereafter, based on geographical, meteorological and demographic factors, it examines India's vulnerabilities so that the likely areas and targets for counter-value and counter-force nuclear strikes by Pakistan and China can be deduced and then prioritised. Finally, the damage assessment of two such targets is be analysed in detail to broadly identify the scale of disaster that will occur in the aftermath of a nuclear strike.

Conflict Scenarios

A major problem with the incipient nuclear capabilities of both India and Pakistan is the continued reliance of both the nations on dual use vectors like short-range ballistic missiles and fighter aircraft. This enhances the chances of a conventional conflict spiralling into the nuclear domain very rapidly. In order to overcome the problems of limited range afforded by these vectors, both India and Pakistan will be tempted to deploy them as far forward as possible to get maximum targets within their coverage area. The air assets will be mobilised to their forward airbases and missile units would be deployed almost in the shadow of the tactical battle area, if not within it. Such forward basing of these dual use vectors during a conflict will send wrong signals to the politico-military leadership of either country and may be construed by them as an act of belligerence. Between India and Pakistan, all this is likely to take place in a distrustful atmosphere surcharged with emotions, almost bordering on hysteria, duly aided and abetted by an ill-informed public, media and the political leadership. Any action, even if carried out with an honest intent, has chances of being misread, misinterpreted and misjudged. The problem may get obviated to some extent as and when reliable long-range delivery vectors are developed by both nations. However, as far as Pakistan is concerned, given the political turmoil in Baluchistan and the Federally Administered Tribal Areas, the number of long-range missile assets that can be safely deployed west of the Indus will always be limited.

In any conventional conflict, one of the immediate tasks of the Indian Air Force will be to establish a 'favourable air situation' and, if possible, to graduate, in the earliest time frame, towards achieving 'local or limited air superiority' over the Tactical Battle Area (TBA). The operation will involve targeting of Pakistan's air assets including the airfields. Similarly, ballistic missiles and their support infrastructure, once spotted, will become legitimate targets for air and missile attacks in order to reduce the damage they might cause, even if armed with conventional warheads over populated towns and cities. What if a large number of these dual use vectors are lost in the first few days of the campaign. The act can be interpreted as pre-emptive attacks to destroy the adversary's nuclear capability. If such a scenario does not raise the spectre of a nuclear exchange, what if some of these airfields or missile sites were also being used to store nuclear weapons without the attacker having knowledge of this fact? If the nuclear weapons are held in a disassembled state, due to the war being in its opening stages, these may spill out radioactivity from fissile cores that have been accidentally targeted. Such a situation may also lead to a faulty interpretation of being hit with a nuclear weapon which did not explode. Finally, during any stage of the conflict, if vectors armed with assembled nukes, on being struck with conventional weapons, go up in prominent mushroom clouds, these will be certainly interpreted as nuclear strikes.[2] Such accidents or incidents during war may take place in the TBA or on airfields which are located reasonably close to the international border and will always have chances of being construed as counter-force nuclear strikes and may unleash a retaliatory response.

Apart from nuclear weapons and their delivery vectors, another important component of the nuclear capability of any nation is its nuclear command, control and communication infrastructure. Hence, protection of the nuclear decision makers and maintaining their communication links with units entrusted with the custody of nuclear weapons is essential so that release orders can be communicated, when required. In the case of Pakistan, it is well known that the Pakistan Army maintains an 'iron clad' control over both the development and employment of nuclear weapons.[3] Hence, it would be logical to conclude that command and control functions of both conventional and nuclear capabilities of Pakistan are closely intertwined, notwithstanding the fact that the General Staff Headquarters (GHQ) of the Pakistan Army is located at Rawalpindi and HQ Army Strategic Forces Command (ASFC) at Thalian, a suburb of Islamabad. During a conflict with Pakistan, the command and control centres become legitimate and lucrative targets for air strikes. Such strikes may well be viewed as an attempt to degrade, if not destroy, the nuclear response capability of Pakistan.

The degradation of the command control and communication systems of Pakistan's nuclear command authority cannot be viewed in isolation. It will be fair to assume that the strategic assets of Pakistan, during a conflict, will be dispersed at select locations with reliable communication arrangements including multi-layered backups. The shorter range assets will be deployed closer to the border and the safety and security of such assets will be delegated to the local commanders. In certain cases, the authority for the release of nuclear weapons could also be delegated. Without the benefit of being aware of the overall strategic situation, a local commander may view the ongoing conflict in isolation and as restricted to his area. If the operational situation deteriorates rapidly in such an area, the commander may be tempted to launch these weapons before facing the prospect of losing them.

In most of the scenarios mentioned above, confusion exacerbated due to the fog of war may lead to accidental release of nuclear weapons by Pakistan's National Command Authority (NCA). The reverse is also possible. India's nuclear doctrine states that its nuclear deterrent will be based on a triad. The only missing link of the triad is the nuclear submarine, which is presently under sea trials. Since this Advance Technology Vehicle (ATV) will be armed with nuclear-tipped missiles, it brings out yet another contingency of a nuclear conflagration starting accidentally. What if this ATV is targeted without the attacker knowing that it is a nuclear-armed submarine? What if the submarine meets with an accident during a conflict or even during peace time? India may consider it as an act of taking out of its second strike capability.

Besides an inadvertent exchange, a deliberate nuclear exchange of nuclear weapons is also possible between the two nations. The disparity in conventional capabilities between India and Pakistan has often been cited by the latter as the *raison d'être* for its acquisition of nuclear weapons. During any future conflict, if Pakistan starts feeling the heat due to this disparity in conventional capability, it may be tempted to use nuclear weapons.[4] In fact, most analysts from Pakistan justify their 'first use' policy on the grounds of conventional asymmetry, which they claim may not be able to stymie an Indian offensive. The scenarios of deliberate escalation of a conventional conflict into the nuclear domain by Pakistan and its manifestation in the types of threat are discussed subsequently as part of nuclear targeting.

Some nuclear exchange scenarios also speculate upon the possibility of nuclear weapons being stolen by terrorists or renegade military commanders in Pakistan. Thefts or armed attacks on likely weapon storage sites in such scenarios can be carried out by terrorists either independently or with the help of insiders who have been subverted. An extreme version of such a scenario is the partial loss of territory, including some strategic enclaves, by the failing state of Pakistan to extremist elements. Such nightmarish scenarios pose equal danger to India as to the rest of the world, including Pakistan, and hence lie in an entirely different domain.

ENDNOTES

1. General Moshe Dayan, former Israeli Defence Minister, quoted in Randeep Ramesh, 'Turning to a new textbook,' *The Guardian*, 25 July 2006.
2. It is often believed that accidents involving assembled nuclear weapons may not lead to detonation. US B-52 bombers carrying nuclear weapons on two occasions have crashed overseas – in 1966, near Palomares in Spain and in 1968, near Thales Air Base in Greenland – without the weapons actually detonating, but requiring large-scale environmental cleanup, due to the spillage of fissile material. US weapons are very sophisticated, with 4 to 5 interlocks called Permissible Action Links, along with the use of insensitive high explosives and fire resistant pits. Pakistan's inventory of nuclear weapons may not have similar safety standards. The warhead's electrical arming and fusing system could get activated, leading to an accidental detonation of explosive lenses placed around the core.
3. The National Command Authority of Pakistan has Development and Employment Control committees chaired by the head of the government. The Chairman COSC and the other two service chiefs are members, but the real authority lies with the COAS. The third important arm of the NCA is the Strategic Plans Division (SPD), which acts as a secretariat for the NCA.
4. Nuclear thresholds of Pakistan are discussed subsequently in Chapter 10.

9

Areas Vulnerable to Nuclear Strikes

Nuclear Targeting

Targets for a nuclear strike are generally classified as counter-value and counter-force. Counter-value targets are those that are 'valued' more. These generally consist of major population centres and industrial installations and are the ones that exemplify terror in the 'balance of terror' equation.[1] The threat of its destruction, or even a portion thereof, may not be acceptable to any government. In fact, the roots of the deterrence theory are entwined around this core issue, that such targets cannot be put to risk under any circumstances. During the initial years after the invention of the 'bomb', the focus on counter-value targeting led to development of doctrines like 'Massive Retaliation' and once a similar capability was available to the adversary, it graduated to 'Mutually Assured Destruction'. The latter also ensured 'strategic stability' between the two super powers during the Cold War.

Counter-force targets focus on the nuclear capability of the adversary so that the danger of retaliation is minimised by targeting them as part of a calibrated 'first strike'. Counter-force targets primarily consist of nuclear weapons, their delivery vectors and associated command, control and communication systems. Large mechanised military formations in the field, particularly when concentrated before or during employment, are also classified as counter-force targets.[2] Counter-force targeting strategies led to the development of 'tactical nuclear weapons' including doctrines for their possible use like 'Flexible Response'. It also promoted concepts like 'Nuclear War-fighting' which envisaged conventional operations in a battle field where nuclear weapons are being exchanged by both the belligerents over an extended time and space horizon.

Pakistan: Vulnerability Assessment

Counter-value and counter-force targeting, although Cold War terms, have relevance to South Asia also because the possibility of our potential adversaries restricting their targeting options to only one type of target looks remote. In the regional context, not only is the development of nuclear weapons, their delivery vectors and command and control systems in a state of infancy but also the doctrines for their employment. Due to the existing uncertainty and ambiguity on a host of nuclear issues including nuclear targeting, it may be prudent to analyse India's vulnerabilities across the entire range of potential targets. A cursory examination of the issue will indicate that all targets cannot have the same vulnerability to nuclear strikes. The location of the target may be one of the considerations that may decide its vulnerability. As far as counter-value targets are concerned, India's major urban population centres, located across the length and breadth of the country, would be potential targets for nuclear strikes. Counter-force targets, on the other hand, could either be located in the hinterland or near border areas. Counter-force targets in the hinterland, like major airbases, naval dockyards and strategic enclaves or assets are by and large located within cities. Hence their vulnerability should be accessed along with counter-value targets. The counter-force targets near the border areas will include aircraft squadrons located in forward airfields, short-range missile units either in their hides, mating bays or launch pads, and the Indian Army's strike formations located in military cantonments or in their concentration areas, TBA or after a few days of the war, in the adversary's territory. Some scenarios speculate on the last possibility that Pakistan may target India's mechanised forces once they are deep inside its territory.[3]

Pakistani Territory

Any major thought on a nuclear exchange scenario in the South Asian context generally commences with a conventional war being fought between India and Pakistan under a nuclear backdrop. This conventional conflict generally graduates into a nuclear one when Indian mechanised formations are on the threshold of making a major breakthrough, which may result in either the destruction of Pakistan's military potential or a substantial loss of territory. Pakistan's politico-military leadership at this stage is depicted to be caught on the horns of a major dilemma of either making good their oft-repeated threat of 'first use' or face capitulation and subsequent loss of face. In order to caution India, control the level of escalation and widen its response options, one of the choices available to Pakistan is to target the Indian armed forces with tactical nuclear weapons. A fair number of these scenarios result in Pakistan nuking advancing Indian forces in its own territory. The scenario pre-supposes that Pakistan, fearing an Indian retribution, will like to control the escalation at the lowest ebb and will commence its nuclear gamble with the lowest stakes.

The credibility of such a scenario, from an Indian point of view, is strengthened by the fact that the Indian government, while approving the draft nuclear doctrine prepared by the National Security Advisory Board (NSAB) on 04 January 2003 has amended a key line in it to say that "nuclear weapons will only be used in retaliation against a nuclear attack on the Indian territory or on Indian forces *anywhere*"[4] (emphasis added). The word 'anywhere', it is often alleged, was included to forestall the possibility of Pakistan nuking the Indian Army in its own territory. The scenario of Pakistan using nuclear weapons in its own territory also gains credence from similar views held by some senior strategic analysts in India.[5] Such a scenario has also gained some popularity in the Indian Army, which has held a series of exercises for 'fighting conventional operations under a nuclear or NBC backdrop'. How many of these exercises actually played up the scenario of Pakistan nuking India's mechanised formations on its own territory, is not very clear from open source literature, but it is possible that some did war-game such a possibility. The May 2001 issue of *India Today* carried a lucid article on such an exercise where "India's ace strike corps moved swiftly across the Rann of Kutch in a major offensive to capture large swathes of Pakistani territory. Suddenly the sky was lit up by a brilliant and blinding flash. Those coming up from the rear saw the forward row of over 2,000 men reduced to ashes in a flash of a second."[6]

A conflict scenario where Pakistan chooses to exercise its nuclear option on Indian strike formations in its own territory is not the brainchild of Indians alone. Some Pakistani analysts have also speculated on such a possibility. Lieutenant General (retired) Sardar FS Lodhi visualises that "Pakistan could use an option enhancing policy. This would entail a stage-by-stage approach in which the nuclear threat is increased at each step to deter India from attack. The first step would be a public or private warning, the second a demonstrative explosion of a small nuclear weapon on its own soil, the third step would be the use of a few nuclear weapons on its own soil against attacking Indian forces. The fourth stage would be used against critical but purely military targets in India across the border from Pakistan—probably in thinly populated areas in the desert or in semi-desert, causing little collateral damage."[7] Another Pakistani analyst, Zia Mian, suggests that "Pakistan may seek to use the threat of nuclear weapons as a way to incite intervention to terminate the war before it lost more ground. This would be done simply by moving some nuclear armed missiles into the open for US satellites to be able to detect them. Failing appropriate intervention, it is imaginable that Pakistan would consider the battlefield use of nuclear weapons against advancing Indian tanks, for instance, as a way to signal desperation."[8]

A strike on the Indian armed forces, even in Pakistani territory, as per India's enunciated doctrine, will invite 'massive retaliation'. Such a 'disproportionate response' has often put the credibility of India's nuclear threat, especially in Pakistani eyes, suspect of being carried out to its logical end. This, in turn, makes the possibility of Pakistan targeting Indian armed forces more likely than counter-value targeting of densely populated cities. This logic can also be turned around to say that any advocacy of 'proportionate response' which will limit the Indian response to counter-force targeting only, will in any case lower the threshold of a Pakistani 'first strike', whose target in the first place would have been the Indian Army. So in all likelihood, if Pakistan is forced to make the hard choice of using its ultimate weapon, it might be employed on counter-force targets, but where and when is a major question.

Guesstimation of counter-force strikes, whether they will take place in Indian or Pakistani territory, is dependent upon our understanding of how Pakistan perceives this whole issue, including the long-term effects of such a strike on Pakistani soil. The issue is important for Pakistan because the terminal objectives of any major Indian offensive will be politically sensitive towns or economically important centres. The issue is also important from the Indian Army's point of view, so that it remains mentally, physically and materially prepared to deal with such a crisis, especially if it has to face it deep inside Pakistan. Grouping of specialist NBC units and provisioning of additional capabilities will be necessary to overcome such a challenge. However, there are sufficient indicators to rule out the possibility of Pakistan nuking India's mechanised formations in its own territory. It would be unwise for Indian defence planners to presume that Pakistan would not have taken into their calculations the impact of long-term radioactive contamination from certain live examples which are available openly and freely. One only has to read the detailed IAEA reports on the following incidents to rule out the oft-repeated argument that Pakistan will nuke the Indian Army on its own territory.

- **Goiânia, Brazil** – The accident occurred in 1987 due to an act of scavenging of a radioactive source containing Caesium-137, which was being used for radiotherapy in a local hospital, by poor and innocent people. In spite of the small size of the source (2 × 1.8 inches), the incident not only exposed to harmful radiation many people of which several died, but also led to the spread of radioactivity over a select but large area. The decontamination and waste disposal operations involved a colossal effort including removal of topsoil, demolition of contaminated buildings and carriage of about 275 lorry loads of radioactive waste to a specially constructed waste disposal site.[9]
- **Chernobyl** – The overall cost of the Chernobyl disaster estimated at today's prices is about $200 billion US dollars,[10] making it the costliest disaster in modern history. Besides the financial aspects, its impact on ecology and environment can be gauged from the fact that although the accident occurred in 1986, even today, a 30 km area around the nuclear plant, including the city of Pripyat, remains as a 'Zone of Exclusion' and is still out of bounds for people.

- **Bikini Atoll** – The last nuclear test on Bikini Atoll was conducted by the US in 1958. By the mid-1970s, some locals were resettled on the atoll but were removed in 1978 as medical tests indicated that the Strontium-90 level in their bodies was beyond acceptable levels. Based on the request of the government of Marshall Islands, IAEA had sent an environmental monitoring team to Bikini Atoll in 1995 to perform a limited programme of environmental measurements and sampling. In 1998, it was recommended by the IAEA that Bikini Atoll should not be permanently resettled under present radiological conditions. This recommendation was based on the assumption that persons resettling on the island would consume a diet of entirely locally produced food. The radiological data support that if a diet of this type were permitted, it could lead to an annual effective dose of about 15 millisivert (mSv),[11] which as per IAEA standards, was bordering on the dangerous levels.

In order to understand the long-term effects of a nuclear detonation on terrain, let us carry out a back-of-the-envelope type of calculation to find out how much real estate will be laid waste and for how long by a typical counter-force strike. A 10 kiloton low or surface burst will produce a fallout, whose 30 rad/hour dose rate contour will approximately cover an area of 75 by 5 kilometres. The safe radiation exposure limits laid down by the International Commission for Radiological Protection (ICRP) for persons employed in the nuclear industry is 20 mSv per year.[12] When converted into an hourly dose rate, this works out to 23×10^{-4} mSv per hour. In case we consider one Sivert equivalent to one Gray or 100 rads, the 30 rads per hour will decay to a dose rate of 23×10^{-4} mSv per hour in 49,000 hours or about five and a half years. This implies that while people can transit through the contaminated area or even stay there temporarily, any stay beyond one year will have harmful effects as per ICRP guidelines.

The likelihood of contaminating its territory, the effect of which will last for years if not decades, will play in the minds of the Pakistani leadership before considering the option of targeting Indian Army formations inside Pakistani territory. The effect of such long-term contamination cannot be quantified in terms of fatalities among personnel or livestock, which can easily be prevented by restricting their entry into severely contaminated areas. The effects will be by and large social, economic and psychological. A large number of people will have to be re-located, the cost of decontamination, if attempted at all, will be colossal and periodic monitoring of the area and the environment will be required. In fact, the local economy of the area will be severely affected as the sale of agricultural produce and dairy products, even from relatively safer areas will be viewed with suspicion by non-locals.

It can however be argued that Pakistan, when faced with such a dilemma, may use sub-kiloton yield tactical nuclear weapons to avoid a nuclear fallout or even of medium yields and need not use them in a surface or low airburst mode. It can always select the height of burst, so that the possibility of fallout is eliminated. Such a targeting option will limit contamination to a much smaller area, affected only by induced radiation, the effect of which is short-lived. After all, people continue to live in Hiroshima and Nagasaki, where nuclear weapons were detonated in an airburst mode. The use of low yield nuclear weapons on dispersed and advancing armoured columns can be ruled out due to their limited damage potential but adjustment of height of burst is a compelling argument and needs to be debated further from the point of view of practical application.

A large number of strategic analysts believe that Pakistan's preferred vector for delivery of nuclear weapons will be a ballistic missile, preferably its most tested missile, the Ghaznavi, also called as the Hatf III. The use of aircraft is an option but the chances of such a strike package[13] penetrating the umbrella of 'local air superiority' that will be ensured over the TBA by the Indian Air Force will be difficult. The option of using the cruise missile, 'Babur', which is still under an extended flight test programme, could also be exercised. However, engaging a moving target with a cruise missile, which normally uses 'terrain and counter matching' during its terminal phase of guidance is rather farfetched an idea. Such missiles are normally used to carry out surgical strikes over pinpoint targets. Hence, the chances of using a ballistic missile remain high.

The terminal velocity of the short-range Ghaznavi missile, even by conservative estimates, would be of the order of 1,000 to 1,500 metres per second. The longer range Ghauri or Shaheen will have higher terminal velocities. On the other hand, the 99 percent 'fallout safe' height of a 10 kiloton nuclear bomb is about 178 metres, a distance that will be covered in a fraction of a second by a missile, leaving very little margin for error. Whether the environmental sensing devices that are normally placed on the nose cone of the missile, will be able to arm and initiate the fuze of the weapon, at the exact height, is a major challenge that could be well beyond the present technological capability of Pakistan. To detonate the weapon at a greater height remains an option but this option will significantly reduce the effects of blast, which is a major criterion that is considered for destruction of hardened targets like armoured vehicles. For example, if a 10 kiloton weapon is detonated at a height of 500 metres, the area affected by the 30 psi circle would be only 32 metres. The number of armoured vehicles in a circle of such a small radii will be miniscule. The area affected by induced contamination from such a strike will be 100 metres around the GZ, which can also be easily bypassed. The point is that such a strike will not pay desired dividends. A large number of soldiers, who would not have witnessed the phenomenon of a nuclear detonation earlier, will be dazzled, even affected mentally or psychologically, but there will be no major attrition in the combat potential. A surface or low airburst, besides maximising the effects of blast, also produces nuclear fallout over large areas, which creates problems for mechanised forces and does not allow them to operate freely. A realistic analysis of the risks and payoffs that will accrue to Pakistan by using nuclear weapons on its own territory indicates that the chances of such an option being exercised are remote.

Border Areas: Geographical Aspects

An Indian offensive, in the perception of Pakistan's military strategists, could also be foiled by targeting areas just across the border with nuclear weapons. After all, this would be the next best option, in case the use of nuclear weapons in Pakistani territory is ruled out. Some of these areas would be under the use of the Indian Army to support its operations inside Pakistan. In order to exploit the full potential of such a strike as well as to ensure its success, such a strike will again be a surface or low airburst. The drainage system along the Indo-Pak border will play a significant role, because such strikes will result in nuclear fallout. Radioactivity is likely to be deposited into the rivers or their tributaries and will eventually travel due southwest following the natural drainage pattern of the region. However, the network of irrigation canals, which has come up over a period of time on both sides of the border, may deposit such radioactivity in agricultural fields, both in India and Pakistan, rather than washing them down into the Arabian Sea.

The Indo-Pak border is served by six major rivers. Starting from the north, these are the Indus, Jhelum, Chenab, Ravi, Beas and Sutlej. As per the Indus Waters Treaty, the waters from the three northern rivers are meant for Pakistan. Apart from the Uri hydel project on Jhelum and the Baglihar dam on the Sutlej, these rivers flow freely into Pakistan. Any major nuclear strike in their catchment areas or tactical nuclear strikes along the international border north of Chicken Neck – Akhnoor, is likely to deposit waterborne radioactivity into Pakistan. Even between the Chenab-Ravi corridor, a large number of perennial and seasonal rivers like Tawi, Degh, Basantar and Bein will ensure that some part of the radioactive fallout travels into Sialkot and Sakargarh bulge areas of Pakistan.

The catchment areas of the three southern rivers have important military cantonments like Pathankot, Gurdaspur, Amritsar, Jalandhar and Ferozepur as possible targets for a nuclear strike. Any tactical nuclear strike along the international border on the Indian side, north of Ferozepur, is also likely to deposit nuclear fallout on these rivers. In addition, after the first monsoon, some of the surface radioactivity present in the topsoil will also collect in these water bodies. India has constructed major barrages on these rivers very near the border to divert their water into Punjab and Rajasthan for irrigation purposes. These are Madhopur Headworks on the Ravi and Harike and Hussaniwala on the Sutlej. In the case of any nuclear strikes in areas which fall south of the Ravi but north of the Sutlej, which results in a major nuclear fallout, India could and must allow the waters to flow into Pakistan. Depending on the residual surface radioactivity in these areas after the conflict, India could also allow the waters after the first monsoon

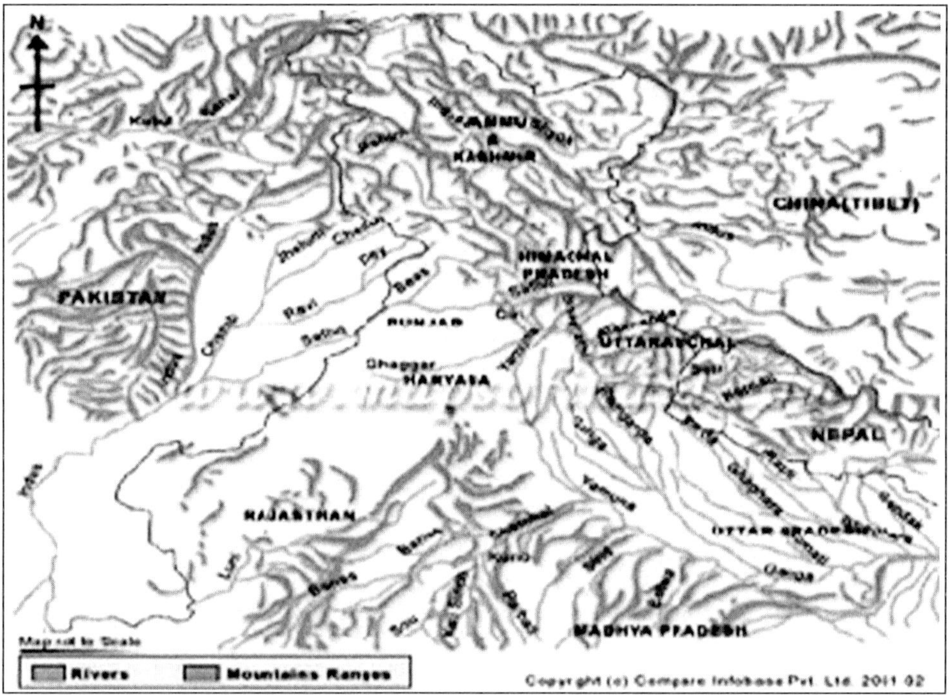

Map 1: Rivers along the Indo-Pakistan Border

to flow into Pakistan. There is no reason for India to risk the flow of contaminated waters into the Bikaner-Gang Canal or the Indira Gandhi Canal. In the post-war scenario, if India is forced to carry out comprehensive decontamination operations due to heavy contamination of the terrain including selected removal of topsoil, its actions will be guided by the advice of the international community including that of the IAEA but one of the easier options will be to deposit the radioactive waste in the rivers and water bodies that eventually flow into Pakistan. Most Indians may see no justification whatsoever in transporting this contaminated soil through peninsular India for safe dumping into the sea.

It can be argued that the fear of residual radioactivity may not deter Pakistan because it will be looking for immediate gains in a do-or-die type of situation. The effect of residual radioactivity will have no impact on the outcome of the immediate battle or indeed the complete war, because traditionally all Indo-Pakistan wars have been of very short duration. However, Pakistan will have to consider the fact that the areas that are likely to suffer most from long-term contamination are those that are considered to be the 'bread basket' of the nation. Besides, some important cities like Lahore, Bahawalpur and Hyderabad may also suffer to some degree, howsoever minor, as they are located on the banks of either the Ravi or the Sutlej.

Areas south of Ferozepur, in Punjab and the border areas of Rajasthan and Gujarat are devoid of any natural water bodies that flow into Pakistan. Hence, these border areas become comparatively more vulnerable as potential target areas for nuclear strikes. However, they may have other considerations which may need to be factored for a comprehensive assessment of vulnerabilities.

Border Areas: Meteorological Aspects

Two major factors that will influence the size and location of the area over which nuclear fallout will be deposited are wind speed and wind direction. Surface winds will influence local fallout produced from surface and low airbursts. The upper atmospheric winds will come into play for distribution of delayed fallout from megaton yield low airbursts or lower yield airbursts. The impact of local nuclear fallout as compared to delayed fallout will be more severe and hence it will be a major factor for consideration during selection of targets for nuclear strikes. The movement of the fallout will depend upon local meteorological conditions over the target area, which changes very frequently, especially wind speed and direction. However, some conclusions can be drawn from general meteorological conditions prevailing in the region.

Surface Winds: Pressure and wind conditions over the Indian subcontinent are unique. During winters there is a high pressure area north of the Himalayas due to which cold dry winds move from the northeast to low pressure areas over the Indian Ocean to the south. This phenomenon is also referred to as the northeast monsoon and is effective from December to March. In summers, a low pressure area develops over interior Asia as well as over northwest India. This causes a complete reversal of direction of the winds during the summers. Air moves from a high pressure area over the southern Indian Ocean, crosses the equator and turns east towards low pressure areas over the Indian subcontinent. These southwest monsoon winds, effective from June to September, bring widespread rainfall over the mainland of India.

Upper Atmosphere Winds: The upper air circulation in South Asia is dominated by the subtropical westerly jet streams. These streams are located over 27 to 30 degrees north latitude blowing south of the Himalayas throughout the year from Sindh in Pakistan to Rajasthan in India. During summers, an easterly jet stream called the subtropical jet stream, blows over the Indian peninsula approximately 14 degrees north latitude but this pertains to the southern states of Tamil Nadu and Karnataka and hence may not be a relevant factor in the movement of a nuclear fallout into Pakistan.

Analysis of Meteorological Aspects: A broad analysis of the prevailing wind patterns with the layout of the Indo-Pakistan border indicates the following:

- In the event of a nuclear attack by Pakistan into the Indian hinterland, the local fallout is likely to be contained within Indian territory. Even

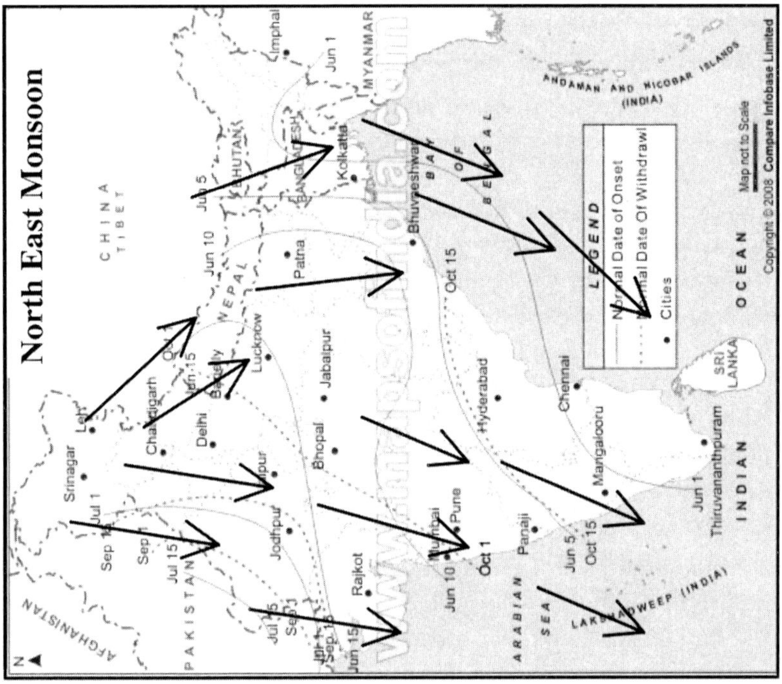

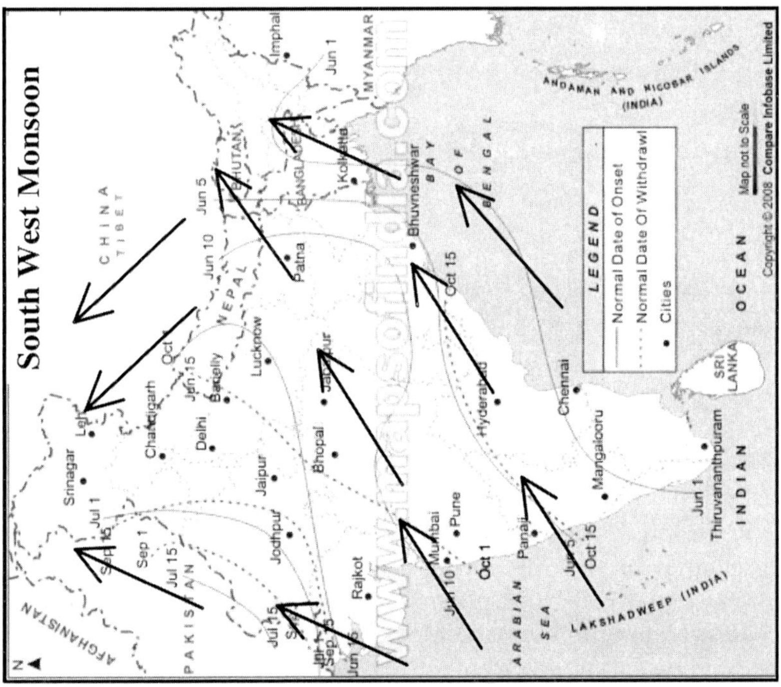

Maps 2 & 3: Showing SW and NE Monsoons

the danger of a delayed fallout (or global fallout) moving into Pakistani territory with the help of upper atmosphere winds seems remote during summers and negligible during winters.

- Any tactical nuclear strike along the border areas, especially in north Gujarat (Bhuj, Raan of Kutch, etc.), south Rajasthan (Jaisalmer, Barmer, Ramgarh, Tanot, etc.) and in areas immediately north of Gurdaspur in Punjab and J & K (Chicken Neck area) has portents of a portion of the local fallout spilling back into Pakistani territory irrespective of the time (season) of the strike. Similarly, in any Indian strikes into Pakistani territory opposite these areas, the local fallout may travel into Indian territory irrespective of the season.
- Any tactical nuclear strike by Pakistan during winters (northeast monsoon) along the international border in areas south of Gurdaspur till opposite Bikaner will contain the local fallout in Indian territory and hence, is advantageous from Pakistan's point of view.
- As far as nuclear targeting by India is concerned, the summer and monsoon months between April to October seem to be suitable. During these months, surface winds will contain most of the early fallout within Pakistani territory and the absence of the westerly jet stream will ensure that portions of delayed or global fallout do not cross over into Indian territory.
- Prevailing wind conditions over the Indian subcontinent by and large favour Pakistan as its targeting options are not foreclosed during certain seasons.

Wind Speed: While wind direction may have a bearing on the selection of targets for a nuclear strike, wind speed will have an important bearing on ranges up to which deposition of radioactive fallout may take place. A wind and cyclone map of India has been prepared by an expert group on 'natural disaster prevention, preparation and mitigation' and included by them as part of 'Vulnerability Atlas of India'. It is shown in Map 4. While the wind speeds in the map represents peak gust velocities averaged over a short time interval of three seconds, there is also a need to prepare average wind velocities and wind direction maps of the border areas so that they are readily available to the armed forces and the National Disaster Management Authority (NDMA), both for assessment of vulnerabilities and to facilitate informed discussions on nuclear targeting. Average wind speed and flow patterns over vulnerable cities are also recommended to be used to assess their vulnerabilities during various months of the year.

Border States: Demographic Aspects

The demographic profile of India's border states as well as towns and cities located in the hinterland may be an important factor during selection of potential targets

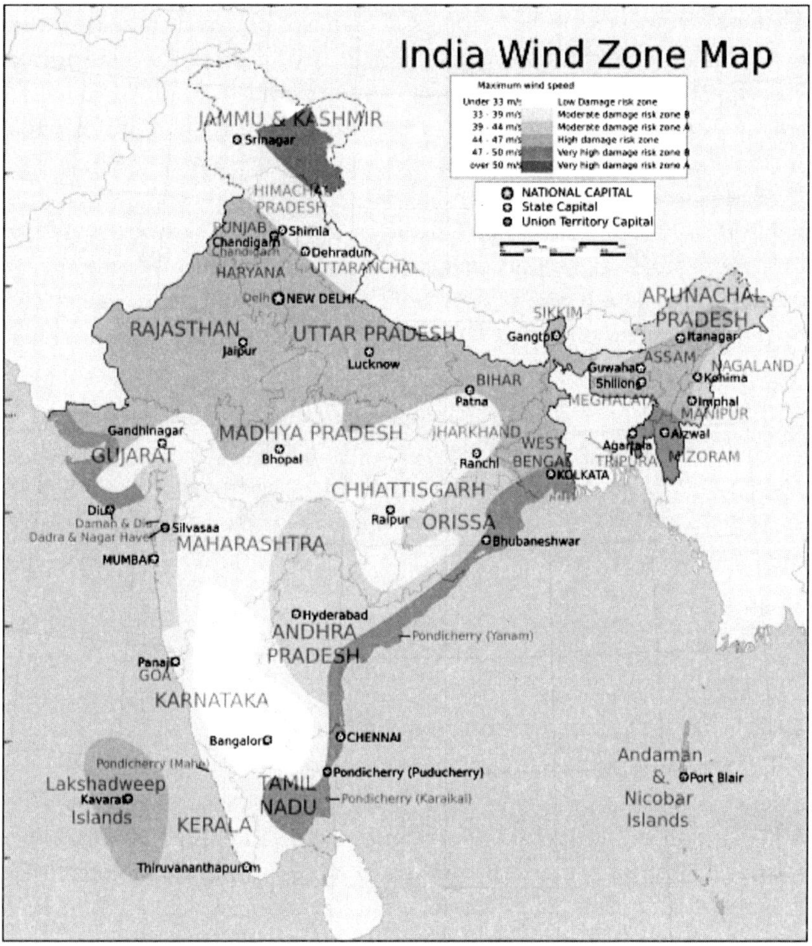

Map 4: India Wind Zones

for nuclear strikes, as far as Pakistan is concerned. Most of the major urban centres of India have a fairly large Muslim population residing along with citizens of other religious denominations. Pakistan has, on many occasions in the past, picked up cudgels for Indian Muslims and has attempted to become their spokesperson, much to the discomfit of India. Such support comes from the basic ideology behind the creation of Pakistan. Even today, its leadership is inclined to think that a nuclear strike on India may cause a backlash against local Muslims. Accordingly, it can be assumed that Islamabad is mindful that a Pakistani attack on an Indian city would, of course, bring a response fatal, not only against itself, but also endanger the future of the Muslim community in India.[14] The use of the 'Islamic bomb' on Indian cities which also kills thousands of Muslims would also dilute the role of Pakistan in the Muslim world, besides Indian Muslims distancing themselves from Pakistan once and for all.[15] Hence, the demographic profile may become one of the factors, if not a major one, as far as nuclear targeting is concerned.[16] In case the demographic profile becomes a matter for consideration for Pakistan, then cities with substantial Muslim population will be put on a lower priority. Among cities in northern India that have a substantial Muslim population, with close links with their families in Pakistan, i.e. the Mohajir population, may even be put on the lowest priority. Similar considerations may put Karachi and Hyderabad in Pakistan on a lower priority, as far as India is concerned. However, among the border states, Indian Punjab, with the lowest density of Muslim population, stands out as the most vulnerable for counter-value strikes. The demographic profiles of Indian states bordering Pakistan are given in Table 32.

Table 32: Demographic Profile: Border States

State	Population in 2001[17]	Muslim Population		Projected Population in 2008[18]
		Numbers	Percentage	
J & K	10,143,700	6,793,240	67	12,366,000
Punjab	24,358,999	382,045	1.56	26,591,000
Rajasthan	56,507,188	4,788,227	8.47	64,541,000
Gujarat	50,671,017	4,592,854	9.06	56,408,000

Vulnerability Assessment: Counter-force Strikes

Whether the next Indo-Pakistan conflict will spiral into the nuclear domain or not, will remain an enigma that will continue to baffle strategic planners on both sides of the border. While Pakistan has laid down some thresholds for the use of nuclear weapons, India, especially its armed forces, thinks that there is 'space for conventional operations' and disregards the Pakistani 'red lines' as 'red herrings'. So while there remains some ambiguity about the 'whether' and 'when' aspects of the threat, the 'where' aspects can be deduced with somewhat lesser ambiguity. The assessment of the vulnerability of the Indian states bordering Pakistan to counter-force tactical nuclear strikes based on geography, demography and meteorological conditions is summarised in Table 33.

Table 33: Vulnerability Assessment: Border States

State	Various Considerations			Overall Vulnerability
	Demography	Geography	Meteorology	
J & K	Unlikely	Unlikely	Possible	Priority 4
Punjab	Most Likely	Most Unlikely	Unlikely	Priority 3
Rajasthan	Likely	Likely	Likely in north Rajasthan	Priority 1
Gujarat	Likely	Likely	Unlikely	Priority 2

The data in Table 33 indicates that all the border states will not share the same vulnerability during a nuclear stand-off between India and Pakistan. Among the Indian Army's pivot corps, those deployed in Rajasthan are more vulnerable to those located in Punjab or J & K. Depending upon their area of employment, similar conclusions can be drawn about the strike corps. The vulnerability analysis could be taken as additional input while deciding upon the inter-se priority for equipping of formations to undertake operations in a nuclear environment, placement of reserve stocks of NBC stores including drugs and medicines, raising of specialist units, their subsequent orbating, etc. The analysis also provides a basic framework for building realistic scenarios for the conduct of exercises and war-games 'under a nuclear backdrop' and training of troops.

The effects of nuclear strikes, if at all they take place, on Indian Army or Indian Air Force units, will not limit the damage and destruction to the armed forces alone. They will also affect the civilian population residing in or nearby areas. Since such nuclear strikes may take place when a full-fledged war is on, it may not be possible for the armed forces to come to the aid of civilian authorities. Most of their NBC equipment and specialised NBC units will be engaged in combat operations. The NDMA and the concerned state governments should be aware of such an eventuality and prepare accordingly.

Counter-Value Targets

From an attacker's point of view, counter-value targeting has its own advantages. It is free from the incumbencies of counter-force targeting. Passive defensive measures like camouflage and concealment, deception, reducing the overall vulnerability of targets by re-locating of assets, reducing of troop density, etc., that are possible in case of tactical targets, cannot be practically undertaken in the case of cities. In fact, for counter-value strikes, the delivery vectors can be selected in advance for each target and strike parameters like weapon yield, coordinates of the GZ and ideal height of burst, can be pre-calculated. There are very few practical ways to defend a city that is being held hostage to the threat of nuclear weapons. The inability of the defender to undertake practical defensive measures for its cities is the key to deterrence.

In all the major wars fought between India and Pakistan till date, both the sides have taken extraordinary precautions to prevent collateral damage by avoiding bombardment of cities. This has been referred to by some analysts as 'fighting honourably by following certain codes of conduct'. This code recognises the political infeasibility of waging wars of annihilation and hence indicates the 'non-total character' of the wars fought so far.[19] Demographic factors alone cannot be said to have prevented both the nations from targeting each other's civilian population during war. In the words of Jaswant Singh, "India, Pakistan and Bangladesh are born out of the same womb. It is not just that we understand

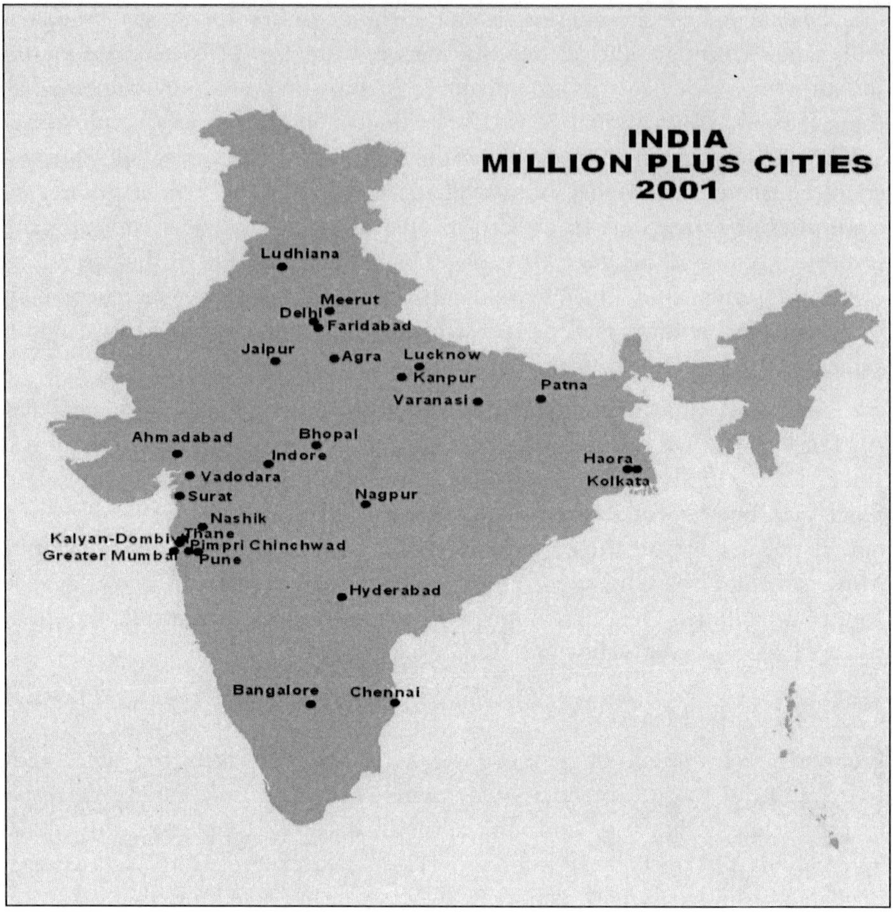

Map 5: Million Plus Cities

each other's language, our intestines are inter-twined. That is the reality."[20] However, if the deteriorating politico-military situation in the next war comes to such a pass that Pakistan is forced to exercise the nuclear option, it could also put India's major population centres in its nuclear cross-hairs. Such a situation may arise out of gradual escalation following counter-force strikes or as part of a 'first strike' strategy.

As per the 2001 census, India has 27 cities with a million plus population.[21] These are Greater Mumbai (11,914,398), New Delhi (9,817,439), Kolkata (4,580,544), Bengaluru (4,292,223), Chennai (4,216,268), Ahmedabad (3,515,361), Hyderabad (3,449,878), Pune (2,540,069), Kanpur (2,532,138), Lucknow (2,531,078), Surat (2,433,787), Jaipur (2,324,319), Nagpur (2,051,320), Indore (1,597,441), Bhopal (1,433,875), Ludhiana (1,395,053), Patna (1,376,950), Vadodara (1,306,035), Thane (1,261,517), Agra (1,259,979),

Kalyan-Dombvili (1,193,266), Varanasi (1,100,748), Nashik (1,076,967), Meerut (1,074,229), Faridabad (1,054,981), Haora (1,008,704) and Pimpri-Chinchwad (1,006,417). In case of a nuclear crisis, any one or a few of these can be held hostage to a threat of counter-value strikes by Pakistan. The bigger the city and more densely packed population in it, the greater will be its vulnerability. However, the importance of these cities, especially from a defender's point of view, cannot be judged on the sole yardstick of population alone. Even if the population was the sole criteria, the loss of a literate, skilled and trained workforce, say in a city like Bengaluru or Hyderabad will be far greater than Bhopal or Patna. In addition, factors like the industrial, commercial or financial importance of the city, location of strategic enclaves and assets, military cantonments and politico-military importance are some other factors that will also come into play while assessing their vulnerability.

Counter-value nuclear strikes on cities and towns are likely to be airburst so that the area affected by the effects of blast and thermal radiation is maximised. Such a targeting strategy is also likely to be adopted because the attacker would not like a 'tit-for-tat' type of retaliatory strike that can lay its cities to waste. Air burst nuclear strikes will produce no local fallout and hence geographical location and meteorology will not be a major consideration for assessing vulnerability. The demographic profile and economic importance of the cities may, however, be a factor in deciding potential targets by Pakistan. The vulnerability assessment of the eight most populated cities is summarised in Table 34. The analysis indicates the priority areas where we must focus aspects related to NBC defence, including nuclear disaster management.

Table 34: Vulnerability Assessment: Major Indian Cities

City	Population Total	Strategic Assets	Military Importance	Economic Importance	Miscellaneous Factors
Greater Mumbai	11,914,398	BARC, Naval Docks	Western Naval Command	Stock exchanges, Banking hub, Important ports	Overseas communication hubs
New Delhi	9,817,439	Politico-military leadership	MoD, Service HQs, Western Air Command	Ministry of Finance and RBI	Diplomatic Missions
Kolkata	4,580,544	Naval docks	HQ Eastern Command	Industrial manufacturing	–

(Contd.)

City	Population Total	Strategic Assets	Military Importance	Economic Importance	Miscellaneous Factors
Bengaluru	4,292,223	Aircraft industries, DRDO Labs, ISRO	–	IT Industry	–
Chennai	4,216,268	Nuclear power plants	–	Industrial manufacturing	–
Ahmedabad	3,515,361		–	Chemical and fertilizer plants	–
Hyderabad	3,449,878	DRDO labs, Missile manufacturing units	–	IT Industry	–
Pune	2,540,069		HQ Southern Command	Industrial manufacturing	–

China: Vulnerability Assessment

Nuclear Threat: China is a full-fledged nuclear power since 1964 and officially recognised as a nuclear weapon state after it joined the Nuclear Non-proliferation Treaty in 1992. It possesses a complete spectrum of warheads, ranging from sub-kiloton tactical nuclear weapons to megaton yield strategic weapons. Its triad of delivery systems can target any region within the Indian sub-continent. India's unresolved border dispute with China and China's efforts, both overt and covert, to limit India's strategic horizon to South Asia, makes China a major threat. The nuclear dimension of the threat is evident from the deployment of nuclear weapons in Tibet, which are primarily aimed at India. In fact, the nuclear threat from China was cited as one of the main reasons for the 'Shakti' series of nuclear tests conducted by India in May 1998.[22]

As an emerging global player, China will be seeking to enhance and match its strategic capability with that of the US and Russia. One can already see the counters of an incipient arms race emerging between the US and China as witnessed from the latter's effort to develop underwater nuclear submarine bases, the conduct of the much debated anti-satellite missile test, and its desire to acquire longer range ballistic missiles with Multiple Independently targetable Re-entry Vehicle (MIRV) capability. Any augmentation in China's strategic capability has serious security implications for India. However, India's immediate concern remains the deployment of nuclear weapons in Tibet and the reported upgradation of nuclear infrastructure in Tibetan Autonomous Region (TAR).[23]

Geography and Meteorology

Geography or meteorology is unlikely to play a major role as far as the nuclear targeting of India by China is concerned. Although the Himalayan watershed and the Tibetan plateau divide the two countries into separate geographical and climatic entities, they remain as a source of major rivers in India as well as China. The Indus and the Sutlej which flow into northern India and the Tsangpo, which flows as the Brahmaputra in eastern India, actually originate in Tibet. The rest of the Indian rivers originate in the Himalayan watershed. The use of nuclear weapons by China or India in the Himalayan region makes no sense. The glaciers of the region, already receding from the effects of global warming, may vanish altogether. This will be a major environmental disaster for both India and China as it will affect the fragile eco-system of the area and affect the long-term availability of water. The long-term effect of use of nuclear weapons on the Himalayan watershed needs to be studied by both China and India so that some kind of a non-targeting agreement is reached as part of nuclear Confidence Building Measures (CBMs) as and when they are initiated.

Counter-force Targets

The vulnerability of the Indian Army in states bordering China to counter-force nuclear strikes does not stem that much from geographical considerations as from aspects of China's nuclear doctrine. Although China professes a No First Use (NFU) doctrine, its military strategists do not consider the use of nuclear weapons on their own territory as a violation of the NFU doctrine.[24] This leeway has ostensibly been left with reference to Taiwan but has serious implications for India as well. Since China has not renounced its claim over Arunachal Pradesh, the use of nuclear weapons by China in any future war in Arunachal Pradesh, to tide over a conventional stalemate cannot be ruled out. Such nuclear strikes are likely to be tactical in nature and may target Indian Army strongpoints like Tsela in Tawang sector or important roadheads like Migging, Menchuka, Neelu Basti and Kibuto in the rest of Arunachal Pradesh (RALP), which are well south of the Himalayan watershed.

A closer look at the Chinese nuclear arsenal suggests that 96 percent of its weapons are of the non-strategic variety, which have relevance only for China's immediate neighbours.[25] These tactical weapons are more suitable for counter-force targeting. In fact, China's preoccupation with the miniaturisation of their nuclear warheads and the development of mobile, solid fuel, MIRVed missile systems explains its change in priorities from counter-value to counter-force strikes.[26] This gradual shift in the development of nuclear assets for counter-force application is backed by subtle changes in China's nuclear thinking. China has traditionally followed a minimalist approach towards the possession of nuclear weapons and accordingly, it has always subscribed to a policy of 'minimum deterrence'. Such a policy would primarily rely on counter-value targeting.

However, in July 2000, during the Central Military Commission conference on strategic military equipment, Jiang Zemin had outlined the 'five musts' that China must possess with regard to nuclear weapons. It is from these 'five musts' that a large number of analysts have inferred that China may be graduating towards a doctrine of 'limited deterrence'. Limited deterrence entails the development of adequate capabilities to deter conventional and strategic war, the ability to suppress escalation during a nuclear war as well as to fight a limited nuclear war. China is also known to have developed operational doctrines and tactics that will allow troops to operate effectively in a contaminated environment and is also known to have conducted large-scale exercises with troops on such scenarios.

Counter-value Targets

A limited nuclear attack by China on select Indian cities is unlikely to adversely affect the Chinese mainland. However, China may be constrained to choose counter-value targets deeper in the Indian peninsula to avoid the adverse effects of nuclear strikes transgressing into third countries like Bangladesh, Myanmar, Bhutan or Nepal. Hence Mumbai, Bengaluru, Hyderabad and, to a lesser extent, New Delhi are relatively more vulnerable as compared to Kolkata, Lucknow, Guwahati or Chennai. Demographic considerations will not influence nuclear target selection by China, but as far as India is concerned, it should and must avoid targeting of areas inhabited by Tibetans. This perception is shared by most strategic analysts in India and exemplified in the writings of Gurmeet Kanwal, who goes on to say that, "India may not be inclined to even think of retaliatory nuclear strikes on Lhasa, even if the whole Chinese politburo was directing war against India from that city."[27] If sympathy for the Tibetan people influences India's selection of nuclear targets, then we may have to exclude areas much beyond the Tibetan Autonomous Region as ethnic Tibetans continue to reside in large numbers in certain prefectures of Gansu, Yunnan, Chengdu and Qinghai provinces.

Both China and India have a very strong commitment towards the doctrine of NFU. Hence, it may be fair to conclude that the chances of a nuclear conflagration or even conventional conflict spiralling into the nuclear domain remain very low. However, the nuclear threat cannot be ruled out altogether because of certain caveats being attached with China's NFU commitments from time to time by China's strategic analysts and military leadership. Hence, China can always use the nuclear threat to extract political, diplomatic or military advantage from India. In case the threat manifests in actual use, then it is most likely that although it may be initiated in Arunachal Pradesh, it may not remain restricted to it.

SINGLE INTEGRATED OPERATIONAL PLAN (SIOP)

- The SIOP is the central strategic nuclear war operations plan of the US, which was first drawn up in 1960. It is a blueprint which specifies how nuclear weapons would be used in the event of a nuclear war. The plan integrates the nuclear capabilities of the 'triad', i.e., the bomber aircrafts, land-based intercontinental ballistic missiles and sea-based submarine-launched ballistic missiles held in the inventory of the US.
- The SIOP is not a one plan or one attack option, but a set of plans and series of options constructed from a single set of targets contained in the National Target Base and based upon a single set of forces. During the Cold War, the target list reportedly contained about 12,500 targets.
- The SIOP planning process is a series of stages. The major functional areas are target development, desired GZ construction, assignment (weapon allocation, weapon application and timings), reconnaissance planning, analysis, and document production.
- SIOP plans are named after the fiscal year in which they come into effect. For example, SIOP-93 would have been approved and operational with effect from 1993. A new SIOP is approved every year, although the plan may well be unchanged. SIOP has since been replaced by one or more CONPLANs (Contingency Plans).

Conclusion

Vulnerability assessment is a two-way path. The broad parameters used to assess the vulnerability of India to nuclear strikes can also be used to identify potential targets in Pakistan and China. This is a major task which will require expertise from various government departments like the Department of Atomic Energy (DAE), Defence Research and Development Organisation (DRDO), the three Service HQs, and Indian Meteorological Department (IMD), to be pooled. The US is believed to have a Single Integrated Operational Plan (SIOP), a plan that accounts for the nuclear weapons of all the three branches of the US military and integrates all the nuclear contingency plans of regional commands. In case India has to develop an SIOP, at the very onset, it will have carry out a detailed risk and cost benefit analysis of possible areas and targets that can be engaged with nuclear weapons without adverse affects impacting upon our territory. This task must be done by the Strategic Forces Command (SFC) with assistance from all the three services and members from the DAE, DRDO and IMD.

The defensive aspects of a nuclear conflict will include preparation for post-strike disaster management which will require a multi-disciplinary response from various organs of the government. While these issues will be discussed in detail in Part III, at the macro level, some of the important issues that could be addressed are the correct disposition of National Disaster Response Force (NDRF) battalions that are trained for handling NBC emergencies,[28] division of responsibility between the NDMA and the state governments, especially in states where such a disaster is more likely to take place, tasks that will be allotted to specialised Army units that may be called upon to handle the disaster, placement of resources in terms of drugs and medicines for prophylaxis and post-exposure treatment of the population.

From the analysis presented, it is obvious that New Delhi and Mumbai stand out as possible targets for counter-value nuclear strikes. Cities in Rajasthan are also vulnerable to such strikes, in case Pakistan assumes that it will be able to control escalation and keep India's retaliatory retribution at a low ebb. Tactical nuclear strikes are in all probability going to be limited to border areas of Rajasthan, especially areas north of Ramgarh and South of Bathinda as far as nuclear targeting by Pakistan is concerned. In the case of China, the Sino-Indian border along Arunachal Pradesh in the eastern sector stands out higher in order of vulnerability as compared to the western and central sectors. Accordingly, the following scenarios for nuclear strikes are discussed in subsequent sections as part of counter-value and counter-force targeting.

- Nuclear strikes on counter-value targets, with New Delhi being considered as the primary example.
- Tactical nuclear strikes on Army formations deployed in the desert and semi-desert sector of Rajasthan, with a brigade-sized defensive node as the prime example.

ENDNOTES

1. Gurmeet Kanwal, *Nuclear Defence: Shaping the Arsenal*, (New Delhi: Knowledge World/ Institute for Defence Studies and Analyses, 2001), p. 75.
2. Ibid.
3. General Khaild Kidwai, the Director General of the Strategic Plans Division of Pakistan, has laid down certain thresholds for the use of nuclear weapons against India. The 'space threshold' visualises that Pakistan will be forced to use the nuclear option, in case India captures a large part of Pakistani territory.
4. Ministry of External Affairs, "The Cabinet Committee on Security Reviews Operationalisation of India's Nuclear Doctrine," 04 Jan 2003, http://meaindia.nic.in/pressrelease/2003/01/04pr01.htm, accessed on 17 November 2008.
5. Kanwal, n. 1, p. 98.
6. Harinder Baweja, "Readying for Nukes," *India Today*, 28 May 2001.
7. Sardar FS Lodhi, "*Pakistan's Nuclear Doctrine,*" *Pakistan Defence Journal* (Karachi), 1999, quoted in Kanwal, n. 1, p. 58.
8. Zia Mian, "A Nuclear Tiger by the Tail: Some Problems of Command and Control on South Asia," *PU/CEES* Report No. 328, p. 19, http://www.princeton.edu/sgs/publications/articles/report328.pdf, accessed on 17 November 2008.
9. International Atomic Energy Agency (IAEA), "The Radiological Accident in Goiânia,"

http://www-pub.iaea.org/MTCD/publications/PDF/Pub815_web.pdf, accessed on 16 November 2008.

10. "Chernobyl Disaster," http://en.wikipedia.org/wiki/Chernobyl_disaster, accessed on 17 November 2008.
11. IAEA, "Radiological Conditions at Bikini Atoll and the Prospects of Resettlement," http://www-ns.iaea.org/appraisals/bikini-atoll.htm, accessed on 17 November 2008.
12. The safe radiation exposure limit laid down for the general public by ICRP is 1 mSv per year.
13. A strike package for delivery of nuclear weapons will consist of about six to eight aircraft.
14. Bharat Karnad, *Nuclear Weapons and Indian Security* (New Delhi: Macmillan, 2005), p. 566.
15. The terrorist strikes in Mumbai in November 2008, which included Muslim casualties, drew sharp condemnation, but also requests to 'leave us alone' from the Indian Muslim clergy and intelligentsia.
16. The demographic factor will certainly come into play when a hard choice is to be made between two closely competing choices for targeting.
17. "Population by religious communities," http://www.censusindia.gov.in/Census_Data_2001/Census_data_finder/C_Series/Population_by_religious_communities.htm, accessed on 20 November 2008.
18. "Projected population for 2008," http://www.censusindia.gov.in/Census_Data_2001/Projected_Population/Projected_population.aspx#2008, accessed on 20 November 2008.
19. Karnad, n. 14, p. 565.
20. Strobe Talbot, *Engaging India: Diplomacy Democracy and the Bomb* (Washington, D.C.: Brookings Institution Press, 2004).
21. "Million plus cities," http://www.censusindia.gov.in/Tables_Published/Admin_Units/Admin_links/slum1_m_plus.html, accessed on 20 November 2008.
22. Prime Minister AB Vajpayee to US President Bill Clinton, in a letter dated 12 May 1998, had mentioned the threat from China, among many other reasons, while justifying the need for nuclear tests.
23. Hans M Kristensen, "Extensive Nuclear Missiles Deployment discovered in Central Tibet," http://www.fas.org/blog/ssp/2008/05/extensive-nuclear-deployment-area-discovered-in-central-china.php, accessed on 15 December 2008.
24. Swaran Singh, "China's Nuclear Weapons and Doctrine," in Jasjit Singh (ed.), *Nuclear India* (New Delhi: Knowledge World/The Institute for Defence Studies & Analyses, 1998), p. 152, quoting Tai Ming Chen, "New Bomb Makers," *Far Eastern Economic Review*, 16 March 1989, p. 27.
25. Jasjit Singh, "A Nuclear Strategy for India," in Jasjit Singh (ed.), *Nuclear India* (New Delhi: Knowledge World/Institute for Defence Studies & Analyses, 1998), p. 306.
26. Singh, n. 24, p. 151.
27. Kanwal, n. 1, p. 103.
28. Kounteya Sinha, "Elite Force ready to Combat Disasters," *The Times of India*, 17 November 2007. The NDRF battalions are currently located at Kolkata, Pune, Chennai and Greater Noida.

10

Counter-value Targeting: New Delhi and ...

The capital of India since 1911, New Delhi, due to its strategic location and commercial-cum-cultural importance, has the ignominious distinction of being subject to numerous aggressions since it was first established as Lal Kot near present day Mehrauli by Tomar Rajputs in the 8th century. Historically housing about seven ancient capital cities of its former rulers,[1] the city is now called as the National Capital Territory (NCT) of Delhi, after the passage of the National Capital Territory of Delhi Act, 1991.

Presently, the NCT is spread over 1,483 square km, of which 924.68 sq km is classified as urban and the balance as rural area. The projected population of NCT of Delhi as on 01 March 2008 was 16.96 million[2] and the average population density was 11,436 persons per square kilometre. The latter would be an important factor for determining the likely casualties, in case the city is subjected to a nuclear strike. However, the population of Delhi is not uniformly distributed. Since 1997, Delhi has been divided into nine districts and 27 sub-divisions. The population densities of the nine districts are presented in Table 35. Depending on the GZ, these densities must be taken into account while estimating the likely casualties. However, an important question that comes to mind is why New Delhi has been considered as a potential target and how have the various strike parameters been arrived at.

Why Delhi? Among the four metros, New Delhi and Greater Mumbai, as compared to Chennai or Kolkata, seem to stand out as lucrative targets at both ends of the conflict spectrum. In the low intensity spectrum of the conflict, both these metros have the ignominious distinction of being targets of several bombing and terrorist strikes, which have resulted in mass disruption and destruction accompanied by near paralysis of the civil administration. Even in the less likely scenario of a nuclear conflict, both these cities stand out as most vulnerable for

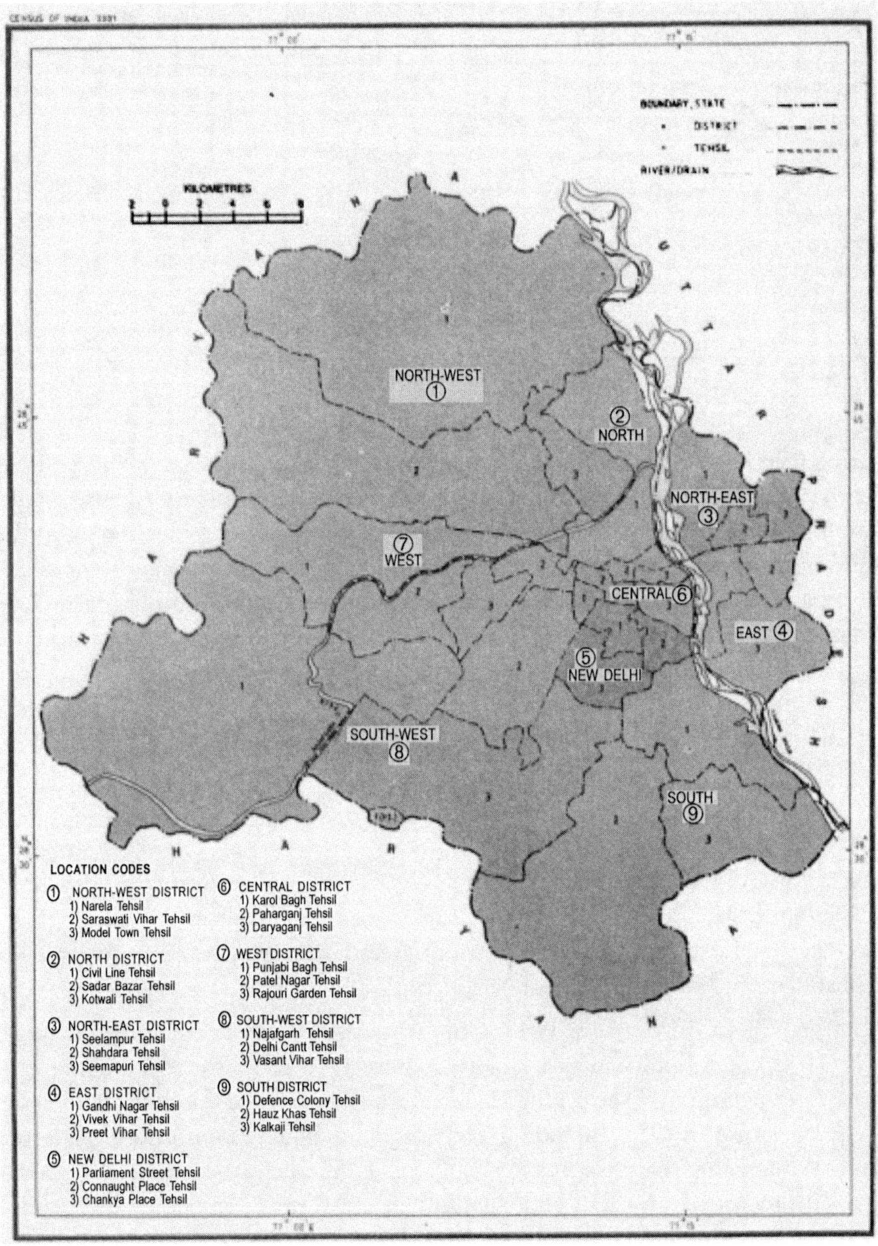

Map 6: Administrative Districts of NCT

Table 35: Population Density of Delhi[3]

District	Area (sq km)	Population in 2001	Population Density (sq km)
North West	440	2,847,395	6,472
North	60	779,788	13,019
North East	60	1,763,712	29,397
East	64	1,448,770	22,638
New Delhi	35	171,806	4,909
Central	25	644,005	25,759
West	129	2,119,641	16,431
South West	420	1,749,492	4,166
South	250	2,258,367	9,034
Total	**1483**	**13,782,976**	**9,296**

being held hostage to nuclear threats. However, Delhi was chosen because, firstly, it is the political, military and diplomatic nerve centre of the country. Its paralysis would delay, if not rule out a retaliatory nuclear strike, besides the attendant difficulties in the mounting of post-strike defensive operations. Secondly, in comparison to other cities, it is more accessible to a larger number of delivery platforms, both from Pakistan and China, and lastly, because people are more familiar with the layout and hence one can easily correlate the names and places being mentioned. The only reason which may deter the targeting of New Delhi is the presence of a large number of foreign diplomatic missions, but then careful selection of the GZ can avert damage to these institutions.

Strike Parameters

Yield: In order to asses the damage to New Delhi from nuclear strikes, yield's of 20 kiloton, 50 kiloton and one megaton have been taken into account. These yields, though selected arbitrarily, are to a certain extent, based on the nuclear capabilities of both our immediate adversaries.

- **China:** In terms of yield, China's inventory of nuclear weapons ranges from sub-kiloton to tens of megaton. Its delivery vectors include long, medium and short range ballistic missiles, bomber aircrafts, land attack cruise missiles including their air launched version, and submarine-launched ballistic missiles. The yields of nuclear weapons that can be mounted on these vectors, summarised from open source literature, is presented in Table 36.
- **Pakistan:** In the case of Pakistan, nothing definitive can be said about their inventory of nuclear weapons, because of the lack of sufficient data in the open domain. Even if this data was available, the nuclear weapons that could be used by them may not detonate with their accessed yields.

Table 36: China's Nuclear Weapon Inventory[4]

Vector	Warhead	Remarks
DF 3/3 A	1 × 2 to 3.3 mt OR 3 × 50 to 100 kt	Deployed facing India
DF 4/4 A	1 × 2 to 3.3 mt	Deployed facing India
DF 5	1 × 4 to 5 mt	Not deployed facing India
DF 21/21 A	1 × 200 to 300 kt	Deployed facing India
DF 31/31 A	3 × 200 to 300 kt	Not deployed facing India
Bombers Hong 6/Qian 5	20 to 200 kt glide bombs	Can be deployed against India
JL 1/JL 2	1 × 200 to 300 kt	Nuclear submarines currently not deployed facing India

Such doubts arise due to Pakistan's sheer lack of experience in conducting nuclear tests. The nuclear tests conducted by Pakistan in May 1998 were proclaimed as one detonation of between 25 to 36 kiloton, two detonations of 12 kiloton and three sub-kiloton tests. The nuclear tests included at least one assembled weapon of 12 kiloton yield. The proclaimed yields of the tests have been disputed by several scientists and seismologists. However, it can be assumed that in future, Pakistan will have the capability to field boosted fission weapons of up to 50 kilotons, a capability it already professes to possess.

Air Burst: New Delhi, in spite of housing the country's top political leadership, the three Service HQs, Advance HQ of SFC and other important ministries, does not have any structures or buildings that are nuclear hardened. The only structure in Delhi that may afford some protection from a nuclear strike is the underground section of the Delhi Metro, whose underground stations have been considered by the Delhi government to serve as nuclear shelters.[5] However, it is too meagre a resource to be counted as an asset. Due to the absence of any hardened structure or shelter, any nuclear strike which is an air burst has the potential to cause maximum damage. A surface burst or a low airburst will produce a long-term contamination hazard which will render the affected areas of the capital uninhabitable for a long time to come. Such a strike will be avoided by even an insane adversary, not because of any love for Delhi, but for the fear of being paid back in the same coin.

GZ: The prediction of a likely GZ from an adversary's perspective is fraught with uncertainty. The GZ selection would depend upon the nature of destruction being contemplated. Likely aims and the possible GZ are summarised in Table 37.

Table 37: Likely GZ in Delhi

Likely Aims (destruction of)	GZ location and corresponding Delhi district	Remarks
Politico military leadership	Vijay Chowk/Raisina Hill (New Delhi)	One of the least population densities
Population	Shahadra Station (Northeast Delhi) OR Connaught Place (Central Delhi)	Maximum population density
Commercial Hub	Connaught Place (Central Delhi)	A day attack may produce highest fatalities
Modern City/IT hub	IFFCO Chowk (Gurgaon)	–
Transportation hub	IG International Airport (Southwest Delhi)	Southwest Delhi has the least population density
Symbolic heritage	Red Fort (Central Delhi) OR India Gate (New Delhi)	–
Power plants	Vikas Minar/ITO Crossing (Central Delhi) OR Badarpur (South Delhi)	Will affect north-east Delhi which has the highest population density

Time of Strike: One of the factors on which the time of strike would depend is the vector being selected by the adversary for the delivery of the nuclear weapon. While a missile strike can be mounted at any time, in the case of aircraft, the possibility of a strike during night time is more. The second factor that would influence the time of strike is the requirement of post-strike damage assessment by the adversary. This aspect assumes importance during scenarios of single or limited nuclear strikes, since the decision to launch follow up strikes will depend upon an assessment of the initial strike's ability to inflict the desired damage or destruction. Needless to add that such an assessment will be easier during the day. The consequences of a nuclear strike during the day will be somewhat different from that of a strike during the night. During the day, the morning and evening rush hours could be worst case scenarios from the point of view of larger casualties and its accurate damage estimation and mounting of relief and rescue operations. The broad consequences or implications of a day and night strike are given in Table 38.

Table 38: Day versus Night Strike

Factor	Day	Night
Estimation of personnel casualties	Difficult due to floating population.	As per population density of the district.
Number of casualties	More as people will be caught in the open	Since people will be indoors, casualties from flash (burns and retinal damage) and direct exposure to radiation (thermal and nuclear) will be less.
Nature of casualties	More due to direct exposure to radiation (thermal and nuclear)	More due to blast effects as most people will be indoors.
Effect on the population	More panic	Relatively calm as unaffected people can be instructed on TV or radio.
Organising of relief and rescue	Difficult as feeder roads to affected areas will be choked with traffic	Less traffic will assist crisis management.
Damage to Infrastructure	-do-	-do-

The armed forces generally consider the worst case scenario while planning their operations. However, for a case of nuclear strike, there is need to be pragmatic and consider the most possible scenario. These imponderables for the purpose of further analysis are fixed as follows:

- **GZ** – Vijay Chowk.
- **Time** – 2300 hours.
- **Yield** – 20 kiloton, 50 kiloton and one megaton.
- **Strike** – Single.
- **Type of Burst** – Air Burst.
- **Mode of Delivery** – Ballistic missile.
- **State of Warning** – War time civil defence measures in place.

Casualty Prediction

To arrive at an estimate of fatal and non-fatal casualties, the area affected by all the three major effects of a nuclear explosion has to be multiplied with the density of the population residing in it. The affected area is assumed to be circular and derived from various damage radii given in Tables 7, 13 and 21 by using the formula πr^2, where π is 3.1428 and r is the damage radius. The circular area affected by a larger radius has been calculated after deducting the area of a smaller circle when it is located within it. The population density has been aggregated by a visual analysis of the affected districts, after plotting the affected area on a 1:50,000 map of New Delhi. The map showing the various damage radii for all the three yields is placed separately as Map 7 for ready reference. The estimation of fatal and non-fatal casualties for all the three strike scenarios is summarised in Tables 39 to 41 respectively.

Table 39: Estimation of Fatal and Non-Fatal Casualties: 20 kt

Effect	Damage Radii (m)	Affected Area (sq km)	Places Affected in Percentage of Overall Affect	Average Population Density	Casualties	
					Dead	Injured
Blast						
(a) 12 psi	1200	04.53	Only N D ie 100%	4,909	21,793	444
(b) 5 psi	2000	08.04	Only N D ie 100%	4,909	19,734	15,787
(c) 2 psi	3580	27.71	ND - 90, C - 10%	6,994	09,690	87,211
(d) 1 psi	5542	56.25	ND - 50, C-25, S-20, SW-5	10,918	–	153,534
					51,217	256,976
Thermal						
10 cal/cm^2	1969	12.18	ND - 100%	4,909	59,791	–
06 cal/cm^2	2900	14.25	ND - 100 %	4,909	–	69,953
Radiation						
500 rads	1500	07.07	ND - 100%	4,909	34,706	–
100 rads	1830	10.18	ND -100%	4,909	–	49,973

Table 40: Estimation of Fatal and Non-Fatal Casualties: 50 kt

Effect	Damage Radii (m)	Affected Area (sq km)	Places Affected in Percentage of Overall Affect	Average Population Density	Casualties	
					Dead	Injured
Blast						
(a) 12 psi	1650	9.03	Only ND ie 100%	4,909	43,441	887
(b) 5 psi	2712	14.09	Only ND ie 100%	4,909	34,583	27,667
(c) 2 psi	4680	45.72	N D - 85, C -15 & S -5 %	8,488	19,403	174,632
(d) 1 psi	7522	109.00	ND - 50,C-25, S-20, SW-5%	10,918	–	297,515
					97,427	5,00,701
Thermal						
10 cal/cm^2	3114	30.45	ND - 100%	4,909	149,479	–
06 cal/cm^2	4500	33.20	ND - 85, C-15 & S-5	8,488	–	2,81,801
Radiation						
500 rads	1750	11.34	ND - 100%	4,909	55,668	–
100 rads	2060	09.91	ND - 100%	4,909	–	48,648

There is still a wide variation in estimated casualties from all the three major effects especially when all of them were assumed to be occurring independent of each other. This variation can be explained because at higher yields, especially in the thermonuclear range, fatalities from thermal effect are expected to exceed fatalities from other effects. In the above tables, the non-fatal casualties from thermal radiation would have been higher if one were to take into account first-

Table 41: Estimation of Fatal and Non-Fatal Casualties: 1 mt

Effect	Damage Radii (m)	Affected Area (sq km)	Places Affected in Percentage of Overall Affect	Average Population Density	Casualties	
					Dead	Injured
Blast						
(a) 12 psi	4,600	66.5	ND - 85, C-15 & S-5	8,488	553,162	11,289
(b) 5 psi	7,632	116.6	ND - 50, C-25, S-20, SW-5	10,918	636,519	509,215
(c) 2 psi	13,192	364.5	ND,C,S,SW,&E -20% each	7,940	144,706	1,302,358
(d) 1 psi	20,420	760.3	Almost complete Delhi	11,436	–	2,173,697
					1,334,387	3,996,559
Thermal						
10 cal/cm^2	13,928	607.2	ND,C,S,SW,&E -20% each	7,940	4,821,168	–
06 cal/cm^2	17,000	301.0	Almost complete Delhi	11,436	–	3,442,236
Radiations	very little ranges	Not relevant	Not estimated	–	Not estimated	Not estimated

degree burns, the threshold of which in terms of thermal fluence will be much lower. For example, if the threshold for first degree burns is taken as 4 calories, the damage radius for a 50 kiloton strike will be 5,400 metres and the affected area will increase by 26 square kilometres, where about 219,648 persons are likely to be affected. Notwithstanding the above argument, since all the three effects are occurring together and resulting in fatalities, it can be said with a higher degree of assurance that the projections will be correct at ranges where at least two effects are occurring together.

The projected casualties will show a downward trend if there is a slight variation in the height of burst, because the most effective height of bursts for counter-value strikes have been considered. In case the GZ or the time for the 20 kiloton strike is changed, there is likely to be an upward trend in projections made, because the revenue district of New Delhi has the least population density.

Damage Estimation

The radius of the area that will be affected by an overpressure of 10 psi will be 1.25 km for a 20 kiloton, 1.7 km for 50 kiloton and 4.6 km for a one megaton strike (refer Table 7). This area is likely to be completely devastated. For a 50 kiloton strike, the outer limits of destruction will include Rashtrapati Bhawan, North & South Blocks, Sena Bhawan, Air Headquarters, Nirman Bhawan, Yojana Bhawan and Rail Bhawan. The official residences of the prime minister and the three service chiefs and other important government servants will also be destroyed. On the northern periphery of this devastation, the multi-storied buildings at Connaught Place may survive but will be badly damaged. On the southern extremity, areas almost up to the boundaries of Nehru Park, which includes Teen Murti and certain foreign embassies, will be destroyed.

The portion of the ridge west of Rashtrapati Bhawan and the commercial areas of Gole Market and Connaught Place may be subjected to secondary fires. The presence of gas filling stations, both CNG and petrol, and the underground domestic gas pipe line in the area, may become the cause of a major fire hazard, but the phenomenon of massed fires may not occur as inflammable material may not be distributed evenly in all the areas.

Impact of Fallout

Surface or low air burst strikes are also possible over counter-value targets like New Delhi, due to some miscalculation in the 'fallout safe height of burst', error in fuze setting, etc. In such a case, the areas affected by fallout will depend upon the prevailing wind speed and wind direction. The average speeds of surface winds for Delhi are given in Table 42. As per available data, the worst time for such a strike would be between February and June. The downwind distances and the approximate area that will be affected by fallout dose rates of 300, 100 and 30 rads per hour for wind speeds of 12 kmph are presented in Table 43. People who cannot be evacuated in time from the area enclosed by the contours of these dose rates can be related with 50 percent long-term fatalities, 50 percent cases of acute radiation sickness and 100 percent re-location of people, at least for a few days, respectively. Areas closer to the GZ will have to be abandoned for years, if not decades. The exact area of Delhi that will be affected will depend upon the wind direction and for a particular day can be plotted on a map.

Table 42: Wind Speeds and Fallout

Months	Average Wind Speeds[6]
January	9 kmph
February, March, April, May & June	12 kmph
July & August	6 kmph
September	9 kmph
October & November	6 kmph
December	8 kmph

Table 43: Downwind Distance and Fallout Affected Area for 12 kmph Wind Speed

Dose Rate	Downwind Distance (km)			Affected Area (sq km)		
	20 kt	50 kt	1 mt	20 kt	50 kt	1 mt
300	20.8	31.5	121.2	18.6	51.5	1,427
100	41.2	62.3	240	91.2	238	5,534
30	74.2	112	431.3	288	484	14,928

Other Counter-value Targets

Greater Mumbai: Some readers may visualise a bigger threat to Mumbai in comparison to Delhi, due to its strategic importance, as India's premier nuclear installation, the Bhabha Atomic Research Centre (BARC) is located there. Any attack on a nuclear reactor that destroys or severely damages it, will leak radioactivity that is far more dangerous than the fallout from a nuclear detonation. However a nuclear attack on BARC[7] or for that matter any other nuclear power plant in the country can be ruled out because of the agreement for 'prohibition of attack against nuclear installations' signed between India and Pakistan in December 1998. Mumbai's greater population density and its economic and financial importance to the nation makes it an alternate target to New Delhi. Ramana in his study 'Bombing Bombay' has subjected Mumbai to a hypothetical strike of 15 kiloton and estimated that about 1.6 to 2 lakh people may die as a result of the strike. The startling variation in New Delhi and Mumbai casualty estimation from nuclear strikes of comparable yields is because the population density of Mumbai has been taken by Ramana as 23,000, as compared to around 6,000 of New Delhi, in the current study. Mumbai, no doubt, has a higher population density, as compared to New Delhi, but it is also elongated in its layout. The elongated layout of the city will reduce estimated casualties, especially from megaton range nuclear weapons because the larger damage radii will cover the adjoining sea as well. This may make Mumbai lucrative for single or multiple strikes from smaller yield nuclear weapons. Delhi, like Hiroshima, has a circular layout and the effects are more likely to be distributed evenly.

Border Cities and Towns: Counter-value strikes can also take place on smaller cities and towns located in states bordering Pakistan, as part of planned escalation control or due to the limited range of delivery vectors. Cities that are located at a fallout-safe distance from the Indo-Pakistan border and have some significance due to the presence of military cantonments or airfields are more vulnerable. The most likely cities and their spread (in kilometres), as seen from hybrid maps available in the open domain like Google Earth are Bathinda (2.8), Bikaner (5), Jodhpur (6.2), Udaipur (4.5), Jaisalmer (2.3), Jamnagar (3.5) and Ahmedabad (10). While the damage to these cities from lower yield weapons will be catastrophic, megaton yield weapons may obliterate them completely.

Conclusion

In terms of fatalities among the unprotected population, displacement of survivors and destruction of dwellings and infrastructure, a 20 kiloton nuclear strike will replicate the devastation that will be equivalent to about three or four natural disasters occurring together. The devastation caused by four natural disasters that have hit India in the recent past is presented in Table 44, for comparison with a 20 kiloton nuclear strike data given in Table 39. The impact of a 50 kiloton strike will be several times more severe. Nuclear disaster management plans for our metros being prepared by NDMA and other civil defence planners will have to take into account the problems associated with such a large number of casualties occurring instantaneously.

Table 44: Casualties from Natural Disasters[8]

Disaster Year and Location	Number of Personnel		Houses		Live Stock Perished
	Dead	Injured	Destroyed	Damaged	
Latur, 1993	7,928	16,000	30,000	211,000	15,854
Bhuj, 2001	19,727 –	166,000 –	348,000 –	844,000 –	More than 20,000
Orissa, 1999	9,887	2507	NK	NK	4.44 lakh
Tsunami, 2004	12,709	647,599 (displaced)	157,383	NK	31,755

In case New Delhi is targeted with megaton range nuclear weapons, the astronomical number of people that will be killed or injured, including the destruction that will be caused, can create a catastrophe of unimaginable proportions, much beyond the comprehension of any rational mind. A 20 kiloton strike may paralyse a city for months but there is hope for recovery. In the case of thermonuclear weapons of megaton yields, the situation becomes virtually hopeless. Smaller cities and towns, as brought out earlier, will cease to exist. Hence, the deterrent potential of a megaton yield nuclear weapon is infinitely more than the weapons in the lower rung of the kiloton range. The importance of possessing thermonuclear weapons by India clearly stands out especially in relation to China. It may be noted that China may have a larger population than India but the average population density of Chinese cities is far less when compared to Indian cities. Hence, relying on fission weapons of small yields for deterrence will be a folly, especially when we know that these have to be delivered over vast distances, much beyond TAR, and any error in the planned GZ or height of burst will reduce their impact.

The immediate lesson that can be drawn from the casualty estimates is that everything possible must be done to ensure that the nation, especially its major cities, is never held hostage to the threat of thermonuclear weapons. The only sure and time tested solution available is to rely on 'deterrence' and hope that it holds even in the most provocative scenarios. Such deterrence based on thermonuclear capability has been advocated by many strategic analysts in India. Deterrence based on kiloton range of nuclear weapons (referred to as petards), is what Bharat Karnad has called "deterrence by half measures". He goes on to state that "a relatively large force of megaton thermonuclear armaments will also ensure that while India may not win a nuclear war with even the biggest powers, it will certainly not lose it because of the sheer levels of destruction that Indian forces would be capable of wreaking."[9] One more method which ensures that the threat of thermonuclear weapons never manifests on our cities lies on the other extreme of the nuclear calculus. The threat can become non-existent if the world is able to achieve global and universal nuclear disarmament, leading to a nuclear weapon-free world.

ENDNOTES

1. The seven ancient cities located in Delhi are Lal Kot, Qila Rai Pathora, Tuglakhabad, Ferozabad, Siri, Jahanpanah and Shajahanabad.
2. "Economic Survey of Delhi, 2007-2008," http://delhiplanning.nic.in/Economic%20 Survey/ES2007-08/T4.PDF, accessed on 20 December 2008, p. 18.
3. The population and population density figures are as of 2001 and taken from "Economic Survey of Delhi, 2007-2008," ibid, p. 21.
4. Compiled from various sources.
5. Kota Neelima, "Learning to live with the Bomb," *The Indian Express*, 30 June 2000.
6. "Average data base for 19 years," http://www.weatherbase.com/weather/weatherall.php3?s=28124&refer=&units=metric, accessed on 17 October 2008.
7. The main complex of BARC is naturally protected by hills on three sides and the sea on the fourth. Any attack that is a near miss will not be able to destroy it.
8. Data compiled from various sources.
9. Bharat Karnad, *Nuclear Weapons and Indian Security* (New Delhi: Macmillan, 2005), p. 627.

11

Counter-force Targets: Indian Armed Forces

Counter-force targeting means the employment of strategic air and missile forces in an effort to destroy, or render impotent, selected military capabilities of an enemy force under any of the circumstances by which hostilities may be initiated. In the lexicon of nuclear warfare, counter-force is a targeting strategy wherein the principal targets during a 'first strike' are those targets that provide the opponent its offensive nuclear capability, like missile complexes, bomber aircraft and their supporting bases, and submarines and supporting facilities. In the Indo-Pakistan context, counter-force targets, if considered in the true sense of the definition, would include air assets and ballistic missile units only.

The selective targeting of Indian airfields by Pakistan with nuclear weapons is unlikely to reduce the danger of retaliatory second strikes on it. The holding of a large number of nuclear-capable aircraft and the choice of using a still larger number of airfields, combined with the inherent flexibility of an air force which permits rapid concentration and dispersal of air assets, rules out a first strike of a decapacitating nature. A similar analogy is true for missile units. Missile regiments equipped with short-range, road mobile Prithvis, on being mobilised, can disperse these anywhere between their permanent locations, storage and integration areas, mating bays or hides near the launch locations. Once these missile units or their batteries are deployed in the field, tactical nuclear strikes to take out dispersed launchers will no longer remain a cost-effective option. In the case of the longer range Agni, its operational locations, as far as Pakistan is concerned, can only be obtained through strategic reconnaissance or periodic monitoring of satellite imagery, both of which are outside Pakistan's current capabilities.

Classical counter-force targeting is carried out as part of a calibrated first strike to reduce the possibility of retaliation, or if it is still launched with residual capability, its obvious effectiveness. Though not articulated officially, the option of 'first strike,' remains part of Pakistan's nuclear thinking. The first strike strategy will always have an element of surprise inbuilt into it, depending upon 'when' it can be unleashed during the course of the conflict. During the Cold War, the problem of timing was exacerbated due to the 'hair trigger' alert status of the deployed missile arsenal, due to which the very survival of either super power was at stake. It led to the development of counter strategies like 'launch on warning' and 'launch under attack', besides the creation of a sea-based deterrent. No such strategies exist or are being contemplated by India or Pakistan. In the South Asian context, in spite of latent animosities and a host of unresolved issues, there has to be a fresh *casus belli* for a conflict to flare up, and even that may or may not lead to the outbreak of an all-out war, as was evident from the Kargil crisis of 1999 and Operation Parakram in 2001. Even if this process of escalation leads to war, it is believed by most analysts that it is unlikely to jump straight away into the nuclear domain and commence with conventional war fighting. In such a case, the list of counter-force targets gets enlarged to include areas that may witness large concentrations of armoured or infantry formations massed by both sides as part of 'force posturing' before the war, or for the conduct of decisive engagement once hostilities break out. Such targets may include concentration areas, assembly areas, bridgeheads, important nodes, etc. It is with such a scenario in mind that General Sundarji, in 'Combat Paper No. 2' had included a 'division-sized bridgehead', a 'brigade defended sector in the plains' and a 'divisional-defended sector in the mountains' for assessment of damage by 20 kiloton nuclear strikes. The conventional war fighting strategies have since undergone major changes but the 'factoring in' of the nuclear threat in war-games and tactical exercises by the Indian Army is generally restricted to 20 kiloton nukes being dropped on familiar targets, as envisaged by General Sundarji some 20 years ago. There is, hence, a need to rationalise, both in time and space, the lucrativeness of tactical targets in the TBA to possible nuclear strikes, in the light of our current military doctrines.

Cold Start and Nuclear Thresholds

The inability of the Indian Army to prosecute operations in the absence of clear-cut aims and guidelines set out by the government during some recent conflict situations[1] or even during the wars of 1965 or 1971 has led to the emergence of the doctrine of 'Cold Start'. In the Indian Army, it is popularly termed as 'hit—mobilise—and hit harder'. The 'trigger or incident-based scenario' to commence hostilities with minimum warning and rapid mobilisation has been expounded to counter Pakistan's deniability factor on the one hand, and to ward of international pressure for conflict avoidance between two nuclear powers on the other. The leadership in the Indian Army assumes that the Cold Start strategy will finally call the Pakistani bluff by putting a caution on its policy of waging a proxy war and finally expose its policy of brinkmanship. The new paradigm takes into account 'no warning or a very short warning time' for commencement of operations and assumes a 'short duration war' with the possibility of 'early conflict termination'. Accordingly, it propounds two important issues. First, is the application of maximum combat potential by ensuring that 'no one should sit out the war' and securing of worthwhile 'conflict termination objectives' at every stage of the conflict escalatory ladder. Accordingly, it proposes to use integrated battle groups, suitably composed from defensive and offensive formations, at an early stage of the conflict to secure important areas along the international border or seize launch pads across existing water bodies for further offensive operations, in case the need so arises. A schematic layout of the concept is given in Diagram 1.

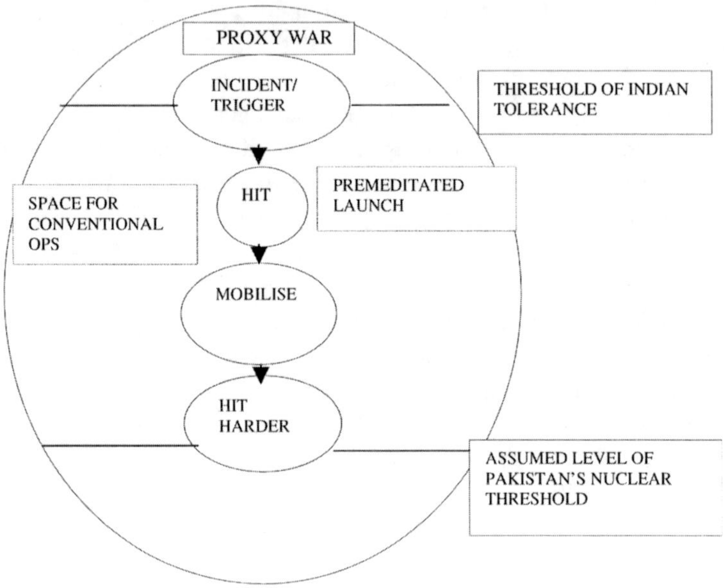

Diagram 1: Cold Start

Some analysts have labelled 'Cold Start' as 'strategically regressive' because it denies the Indian armed forces the time for gaining air superiority; preparation of a joint services action plan, enforcement of an economic blockade by the Navy; exploitation of the Revolution in Military Affairs; and lastly, the creation of information dominance.[2] However, a Cold Start by India does pose major decision dilemmas, both in the conventional and more importantly in the nuclear sphere, for Pakistan's strategic planners. It denies Pakistan the justification for the launch of nuclear strikes because the integrated battle groups would strike at shallow objectives that do not necessarily compel Pakistan to cross its nuclear threshold. These groups would lack the punch to go for Pakistan's innards, the erstwhile role of the 'strike corps'. Therefore, 'military necessity' would not be of the order to permit Pakistan morally and legally to 'go nuclear'.[3] Smaller battle groups would also be more survivable, presenting smaller fast moving targets, even if Pakistan were to contemplate the nuclear option against them. Several of these moving into Pakistan would also pose Pakistan the problem as to which one to tackle and with what weaponry. The idea is to paralyse the Pakistani leadership with this decision dilemma while making quick territorial gains, to be bartered post conflict, on the negotiation table, in return for Pakistan's promise of good behaviour with regard to Kashmir.[4]

Pakistan has repeatedly stressed that its nuclear weapons capability is entirely India-centric and that it has laid some thresholds for use on nuclear weapons in the Indo-Pakistan context. Lieutenant General (retd) Khalid Kidwai, the Director General of Pakistani Army Strategic Plans Division, in an interview to Landou Network, an Italian arms control organisation, in 2002, while explaining the thresholds, had stated that Pakistan might be forced to use nuclear weapons if India attacks Pakistan and takes a large part of its territory (space threshold); India destroys a large part of Pakistan's armed forces (military threshold); India imposes an economic blockade or limits access to river waters (economic strangulation); or India creates political instability or large-scale internal subversion in Pakistan (political destabilisation).[5]

The enunciated 'red lines' drawn by Pakistan, when seen in the light of Cold Start, brings out two important deductions. First, it demonstrates India's resolve to engage Pakistan in an all-out war if its 'threshold of tolerance', already reduced due to the ongoing proxy war in Kashmir and repeated terrorist strikes in the rest of the country, is breached. Second, it will do so without crossing Pakistan's nuclear threshold, which in any case, most of the military considers as a Pakistani bluff. Whether Cold Start permits or actually expands the space for conventional operations, in view of Pakistan's enunciated 'red lines', will remain a matter of academic debate, but it has managed to sow some seeds of doubt and confusion amongst the strategic thinking community of Pakistan. Basically, these relate to 'when, where, and how' to respond. The higher leadership of the Indian Army by and large rejects the concept of nuclear thresholds and does not desire to get tied down with the nitty-gritty. Notwithstanding the rejection of the concept, since their forces may be the first to be targeted as part of the first strike, it would be wise to analyse the threat in detail and prepare accordingly.

Possible Targets

Nuclear targets in the battlefield, also called tactical nuclear targets, are normally those that are either located within the tactical battle area or have a direct bearing on it. Some tactical military nuclear targets, identified by Brigadier (retd) Gurmeet Kanwal in *Nuclear Defence*[6] include the following:

- Bridgeheads established by a 'break-in' force on a defensive obstacle system to facilitate a 'break-out'.

- Leading 'combat groups' forming spearheads of an 'operational manoeuvre group' or an Indian or Pakistani strike corps.
- Defence fortification and nodal/strong points to facilitate a break through.
- Locations of headquarters and adjacent communication centres.
- Mechanised forces—deployed for defence, assaulting, lying off a harbour or being transported to the tactical battle area.
- Surface-to-surface missiles and rocket artillery positions.
- Self-propelled and towed medium artillery regimental gun areas.
- Logistic support areas.

Bridgeheads: The previous chapter had deduced that the fear of contaminating its agricultural lands with radioactivity, the effect of which may last for decades, will prevent Pakistan from nuking the Indian Army on in its own territory. While considering the possible targets for nuclear strikes by Pakistan, it needs to be noted that most of the 'bridgeheads' that will be established by Indian strike formations, either as part of the earlier strategy of 'deep penetration' or seizure of 'launch pads' by integrated battle groups as part of Cold Start, will be on irrigation canals or ditch-cum-bunds (DCB) within Pakistani territory. Most of the major irrigation canals are linked to smaller distributaries, which canalise the waters for purposes of irrigation. Any tactical nuclear strike, which is most likely to be a low air burst, has portents of spreading radioactive contamination through aerial distribution of fallout and water flowing through radioactivity induced areas, in Pakistan's fertile areas. In addition, such a bridgehead, during a conventional battle, will be keenly contested by troops of both sides leading to a very fluid tactical situation. In fact, there will be an intermingling of attacking, defending and counter-attacking units, leading to a situation where the bridgehead will never be of the desired hemispherical shape. Unfortunately, the nuclear strike on such an irregularly shaped bridgehead will still distribute its damaging effects in perfectly circular patterns. Any nuclear strike on such a bridgehead is fraught with the possibility of Pakistan not only nuking its own territory but also its troops. The chances of such a situation being perpetuated by a rational mind are very remote. The nuking of six or seven such launch pads, as envisaged in Cold Start, is out of the question. This deduction should hold true even for any tactical nuclear strike being contemplated by India as part of its second strike response strategy on any bridgeheads established by Pakistan's strike formations in Indian territory.

Concentration and Assembly Areas: Having relegated the possibility of nuclear attacks on leading combat groups or combat commands in Pakistani territory, as well as bridgeheads and launch pads, which also lie in the adversary's territory, to a lower priority, there is a need to identify areas in Indian territory that could be potential targets for counter-force nuclear strikes by Pakistan. This is important for upgrading India's defence preparedness to deal with such contingencies. From the point of view of causing maximum damage to the strike corps, which remains the most potent conventional deterrent with the Indian Army, its concentration area would have been an ideal target for a nuclear strike. These areas are generally located about 150 to 200 km on their own side of the international border to broaden the employment options of the strike corps as well as to avoid detection by reconnaissance aircraft mounted with sideways-looking radars. However, striking the concentration areas would be tantamount to escalating the conflict continuum to the extreme end of the conflict spectrum, without hostilities having actually commenced. This is because the concentration of forces per se on their own side of the border cannot be viewed as an act of war.[7] However, the current doctrine of Cold Start rejects the traditional concentration areas of the erstwhile 'deep thrust' strategy, where mobilisation and concentration of offensive formations would take place weeks before the actual conflict. As per the current strategy, combat potential is generally applied as and when it arrives in the tactical battle area from the hinterland. Since launch pads seized by defensive formations would be contested by the adversary, there may be bunching up of 'follow on forces' in areas east of the initial launch pads, especially as the latter poise to exploit the avenues created by one or more launch pads. Theoretically, these areas can be targeted, but the shortening of the OODA (Observe-Orient-Decide-Act) loop and the fog of war may not allow the adversary to read the battle either correctly or accurately. The former will affect the locating of the target and the latter, timing of the strike. Nevertheless, areas in the vicinity of likely launch pads and the force levels therein can be identified by concerned pivot and strike formations and studied for nuclear damage estimation and the conduct of post-strike operations. The actual locations of the launch pads and the force levels that will be applied through them would be classified information and would be part of approved operational plans. Nuclear damage assessment of such sites cannot be carried out, but needs to done in-house by the respective formations.

Battle Support and Logistic Support Areas: The battle support areas will be located immediately behind the launch pads seized by the integrated battle groups and will primarily consist of artillery and combat engineer support units. Further behind would be the logistic and support areas. These areas, especially the latter, could again be considered as potential targets for counter-force nuclear strike by Pakistan. The Indian Army would do well to identify these and upgrade the NBC preparedness of units that would be occupying these areas or passing through them during the conduct of active operations.

Nodal Points: An Indian offensive, apart from being contested by local reserves, may draw out the Army HQ reserves of Pakistan.[8] These reserves, if they don't get fully committed to draw out the weight of an Indian offensive, could also be used to launch a counter-offensive or riposte in adjoining areas or in an entirely different sector. Such an offensive by Pakistan leads to another interesting postulation on nuclear weapon employment options available to Pakistan. In such a scenario, tactical nuclear strikes can be designed to unhinge the defender from key communication nodes, destabilise adjoining areas, and thereafter, exploit the temporary instability of the defender to seize important objectives in depth areas. A nodal point or a strong point in the desert or semi-desert terrain is an ideal target for a nuclear strike, due to the almost circular configuration of its defensive layout. Any strike on such a defensive position will be a surface or low air burst of a low yield nuclear weapon to maximise the effects. Whether such an option can be used by Pakistan for furthering its offensive operations into Indian territory will depend upon the Pakistani Army's ability to conduct operations in a radiologically contaminated environment. This ability will be a function of the availability of NBC protective equipment (both individual and collective), detection and decontamination equipment, NBC training of troops and availability of NBC units for specialist tasks like radiological reconnaissance, monitoring and survey. Since such operations will also be contested by the Indian Army, there is a need to identify possible nodes that can be targeted and the areas that are likely to be affected by the nuclear fallout. In order to cull some important lessons from the after effects of a nuclear strike on a node, a hypothetical brigade-sized node along the Indo-Pakistan border has been randomly selected for further analysis.

Counter-Force Targets: China

The Sino-Indian border runs along a watershed in most places. The previous chapter had identified that Indian Army units deployed for the defence of Arunachal Pradesh are more vulnerable to tactical nuclear strikes. The state can be geographically divided into Kameng division and RALP. While Kameng is connected by road from Assam to Tawang and further on to the passes on the international border, RALP remains under-developed with roadheads located 50 to 100 km short of the international border. Scenario building or war gaming on nuclear aspects during a Sino-Indian conflict is often neglected both by the strategic community and the armed forces. This is because even a conventional threat from China is considered a few decades away, as the Chinese, it is assumed, are currently focusing on building their comprehensive national power and would hence, desire peace and tranquillity on their borders. Nuclear scenario discussions are limited to the availability of a nuclear triad with China, range and coverage areas of their delivery vectors and an increasing range of Indian missiles like Agni III, under the overall philosophy that the nuclear deterrence between the two countries will hold. No discussion or writings are forthcoming on the ramifications of nuclear deterrence breaking down and nuclear weapons being used, because the chances of it occurring are very low. What if China uses tactical nuclear weapons in Arunachal Pradesh to overcome a tactical stalemate and then holds our cities to threat from thermonuclear weapons, the differential in effects of which from fission weapons we have seen in the previous chapter? How will India respond to such a situation? Can we risk escalation with fission weapons by targeting Chinese cities?

While considering the possibility of tactical nuclear strikes, the targets that will immediately come to mind, even of a layman, is Tsela. The passes on the watershed or the town of Tawang are generally ruled out because of the simple reason that the Chinese would like to possess them after the conflict is over and hence, factors like local support and radioactive contamination will come into play. However, a dispassionate and detailed consideration of the whole issue, from the Chinese point of view will make Bomdila stand out as a more lucrative target as compared to Tsela for a nuclear strike. A 10 kiloton surface burst at Bomdila will not only affect the morale of the forward troops but will make the place impassable for reinforcements and supplies to be moved forward. Such a strike will also obviate the danger of a fallout affecting Chinese troops. Similarly, roadheads in RALP and communication choke points leading to the roadheads may also become potential targets for Chinese tactical nuclear strikes.

Damage Assessment

Targets: A brigade-size node located in the semi-desert terrain in Rajasthan has been randomly selected to analyse the effects of a nuclear strike on a military target. During offensive operations, the targets that seem to be lucrative as well as safe for engagement with tactical nuclear weapons are the battle and logistic support areas, in the vicinity of the bridgeheads or the launch pads seized by integrated battle groups. The damage assessment for these targets can be extrapolated by superimposing the damage radii data being presented on envisaged deployment.

Strike Parameters: Three yields are being considered in a mix of surface and low airburst for counter-force strikes. These are 5 and 10 kiloton low airbursts and 1 kiloton air burst of a neutron bomb. The GZ is assumed to be the centre of the node. The relevant radii for assessment of damage from individual effects of a nuclear detonation are presented in Table 45.

Meteorological Parameters: The essential meteorological parameters required for the calculation of fallout are wind speed and wind direction as applicable during the strike. Meteorological conditions generally change every 6 hours. Hence, there will be a need for army formations to obtain local met conditions every four hours from the Indian Meteorological Department. Air Traffic Controls of the Indian Air Force generate their own meteorological data from the DIGICORA system held with Surveillance and Target Acquisition (SATA) of artillery units. The meteorological data for case has been assumed to be 24 kmph of average wind speed[9] and average wind direction of 45 degrees.

Table 45: Damage Criteria for Select Yields

Effect	10 kt		5 kt		1 kt		Remarks
	Radii (m)	Area (sq km)	Radii (m)	Area (sq km)	Radii (m)	Area (sq km)	
Blast – Equipment							
(a) 30 psi	416	–	330	–	190	–	Tanks and artillery guns destroyed
(b) 20 psi	614	–	487	–	285	–	Soft vehicles destroyed
Blast – Personnel							
(a) 12 psi	925	2.7	734	1.7	430	0.58	–
(b) 5 psi	1454	3.9*	1092	2.04*	675	0.85*	*Area between 12 and 5 psi
(c) 2 psi	2445	12.1*	1941	8.1*	1135	2.6*	*Area between 5 and 2 psi
(d) 1 psi	3675	23.6*	2917	14.9*	1706	5.1*	*Area between 2 and 1 psi
Thermal							
(a) 30 Cal/cm^2	804	–	568	–	254	–	Vehicles catch fire
(b) 10 Cal/cm^2	1392	6.1	954	2.8	441	0.6	Third degree burns – fatal
(c) 6 Cal/cm^2	2100	7.7	1500	4.2	760	1.2	Second degree burns – non-fatal
Radiation							
(a) 500 rads	1350	5.7	1250	4.9	1450	6.6	–
(b) 100 rads	1650	2.8*	1520	2.3*	1800	3.6*	Area between 100 and 500 rads circle

Estimated Damage

Brigade Node: Most of our border downs that need to be defended, typically have a built-up area of about 1.2 kilometres from the centre of the town. This forms the inner core of the defences. The outlying defences, depending on the tactical situation, may be constructed a few kilometres away from the outer periphery. It is also assumed that the town has a peace time population of around 30,000 people and even during a war situation, about 1,000 adults will remain behind to look after their property, belongings, cattle etc. In case the town is defended as a brigade node, it will have inside its perimeter elements of infantry, tanks, artillery and logistic support. The average density of the node during active hostilities will be about 100 people per square kilometre. As far as equipment is concerned, the B vehicles are likely to be distributed uniformly, the artillery concentrated in the centre and some tanks on the outer periphery supporting the infantry while some are held as reserve. The assessment of damage from the three scenarios involving the use of tactical nuclear weapons of different yields is summarised in Tables 46 to 48.

Table 46: Damage Assessment on Brigade Node-10 kt Fission Bomb

Effect	Personnel 5,000		Equipment Destroyed		
	Killed	Injured	Tanks 14	Artillery 12	Vehicles 200
Blast	519	1,296	4	4	6
Thermal	610	770	6	8	8
Radiation	570	280	-	-	-

Table 47: Damage Assessment on Brigade Node-5 kt Fission Bomb

Effect	Personnel 5,000		Equipment Destroyed		
	Killed	Injured	Tanks 14	Artillery 12	Vehicles 200
Blast	308	821	2	3	3
Thermal	280	420	4	5	4
Radiation	490	230	-	-	-

Table 48: Damage Assessment on Brigade Node-1 kt Neutron Bomb

Effect	Personnel 5,000		Equipment Destroyed		
	Killed	Injured	Tanks 14	Artillery 12	Vehicles 200
Blast	112	280	-	1	2
Thermal	60	120	1	2	2
Radiation	660	360	-	-	-

Personnel Casualties: The immediate inference that can be drawn from Tables 46 to 48 is that a 10 kiloton nuclear strike will render a brigade node non-effective for combat due 30 to 40 percent casualties. A 5 kiloton strike may result in 8 to 15 percent casualties. However, actual fatalities among the combatants would be less than the estimates presented in the above mentioned tables. This is because the bulk of the infantry will be deployed on the outer periphery and at least some of them will be inside their dugouts and bunkers at the time of the strike. In case of a strike from a one kiloton neutron bomb, personnel who have survived the effects of blast and thermal radiation will be exposed to lethal doses of radioactivity. A neutron bomb will affect only personnel, while causing very little material and infrastructure damage and hence, in terms of personnel casualties, it may cause more damage than a 5 kiloton fission weapon. An important aspect to be noted is that in case troops are located in underground bunkers, their chances of survival from a neutron bomb will increase dramatically.

Material Damage: The built-up area of a small border town around which the node has been sited is likely to be completely flattened by a 10 kiloton fission weapon, because most of the houses, being made of brick and masonry, will not be able to withstand the overpressure of 10 psi. Troops and equipment located inside the built-up area or in its immediate vicinity will suffer casualties from flying debris. Bunkers and dugouts made on the outer periphery of the node will survive as they are located almost four kilometres away from the GZ, where the overpressure will be less than one psi.

Equipment Damage: As far as damage to military equipment is concerned, there is no clear cut criterion available in the open domain for calculating the damages with certainty. In the instant case, the damage assessment to B vehicles has been carried out based on the assumption that 200 vehicles will be evenly distributed inside the node, thus having a vehicle density of four vehicles per square kilometre. Tanks and artillery guns have been assumed to be concentrated near the centre of the node. An accurate deployment will be of some help, but in the absence of a definite criterion, the damage assessment will lack accuracy. Accurate damage assessment from the effects of blast and thermal radiation is important from the defensive aspects of nuclear warfare as well as the offensive use of nuclear weapons. This criterion, in the opinion of this author, can be developed without resorting to actual nuclear testing by subjecting the equipment to actual pressures and temperature.

Nuclear Fallout: One of the significant aspects of surface or low airburst nuclear strikes is the local fallout. This will have a major bearing on the conduct of further operations. The idealised fallout pattern and the fallout prediction for conduct of military operations are plotted on Map 7 for the 10 kiloton strike. The idealised fallout contours has been plotted from data given in Table 49 for dose rates of 30 and 100 rads per hour. The militarily significant fallout prediction

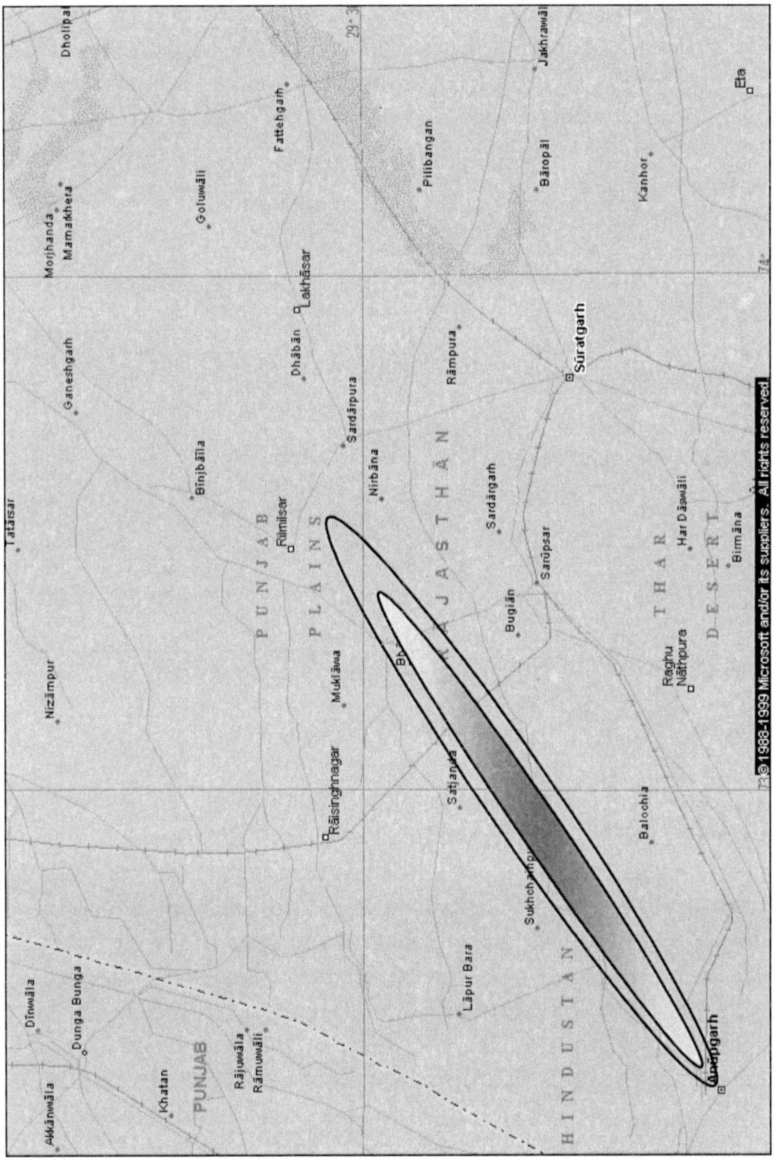

Map 7: Idealised Fallout and Military Significant Fallout

is based on Maximum Zone 1 and Zone 2 distances for specified yields. For a 5 kiloton surface or low airburst, this works out to 13 and 26 kilometres and for a 10 kiloton strike as 17 and 34 kilometres respectively.

The techniques and methods used for estimation of personnel casualties and damage to equipment due to a nuclear strike on a brigade node can be used on other targets like battle support and logistic support areas, mountain passes or any other targets that a military commander thinks can be subjected to a nuclear strike. However, the actual fatalities during a conflict will depend upon how many such strikes take place in a theatre.

Table 49: Idealised Fallout Parameters

Distances	Distance - Dose Rates (rads/hour)				
	3000	1000	300	100	30
1 kt Low Airburst					
(a) Downwind distance	-	-	-	-	-
(b) Maximum width	-	-	-	-	-
(c) GZ radius	-	-	-	-	-
5 kt Surface Burst					
(a) Downwind distance	3.2	6	15	29.5	53.1
(b) Maximum width	0.05	0.2	0.6	1.6	3.0
(c) GZ radius	0.1	0.2	0.7	1.2	1.7
10 kt low Airburst					
(a) Downwind distance	4.3	8.2	20.4	40.4	72.6
(b) Maximum width	0.09	0.34	1.0	2.4	4.4
(c) GZ radius	0.2	0.4	1.0	1.6	2.2

Counter-force nuclear strikes, if carried out by the adversary, will be a part of a well thought out grand strategy. Such a strike will not be carried out in isolation, merely for warning, or as part of the first step in the escalatory ladder. Hence, not one, but a series of targets could be engaged in a theatre, with the aim of exploiting the temporary imbalance of the opponent and seizing the initiative from him. The idea will be to either capture large amounts of territory which can be used as a bargaining chip after the hostilities or the destruction of combat potential. Hence, in such an eventuality, the task of armed forces would be two-fold. First, is the mitigation effort in the area of the nuclear strike and second, is to contest the enemy, if need be, in areas contaminated by nuclear fallout. So when nuclear weapons are used on a field force, one of the major criteria dictating the future course of action of commanders at all levels, would be an early estimation of damage suffered by own troops and equipment and the prediction of nuclear fallout. The former would assist in arriving at critical decisions like evacuation of casualties, gearing of medical echelons in rear areas, limiting the spread of radioactive contamination, relief or replacement of affected units, etc., and the latter in hazard avoidance or, if need be, employment of troops in contaminated areas.

Conclusion

NBC Defence: The mitigation effort in the strike-affected area and conduct of operations in areas contaminated by fallout will require specialist equipment and trained manpower so that the field force is able to survive and fight in a post-strike scenario. Here, the requirement is not to equip the complete field force but only a few selected units. Since NBC equipment has a short shelf life and is also very expensive, a brick system of equipping rather than across the board equipping would be a preferable option. The analysis carried out in this section provides sufficient inputs for equipping formations depending upon their traditional area of deployment and operational role. Strike formations, especially the combat commands would be vulnerable only when they are in Indian territory. After they have entered Pakistan, their support and logistic tails could be targeted. States earlier assessed as vulnerable, namely, Rajasthan, Gujarat and Arunachal Pradesh, are most vulnerable, followed by Punjab and finally Sikkim and J & K. The placement of NBC bricks, the priorities for equipping and further replacement, could be made in the light of the aforementioned findings.

Medical Planning: In the Indian Army, medical support for war is planned by the General Staff and is generally based on 'casualty planning data'. The present planning figures are archaic and do not take into account the possibility of the use of weapons of mass destruction. In order to successfully fight the next war under a 'nuclear backdrop', medical preparedness will need to be upgraded. Static military hospitals in the western theatre will need to be upgraded on a priority basis to handle nuclear casualties that are likely to occur during a war with Pakistan. On the second priority should be hospitals in the eastern theatre. Similar considerations may affect the stocking of drugs and medicines, which again must be based on the brick system of equipping.

Equipment Damage: Like vulnerability analysis, damage assessment is also a two-way path. The damage criterion for all types of equipment, if known, can also assist in nuclear strike planning. However, unlike the criteria for estimation of personnel casualties, about which a lot of information is available in scientific literature including the open source media, there is a corresponding lacuna about the damage criterion for military equipment. What if a nuclear strike was to be launched on DF-4 silos or a battery of DF-21 deployed in the open stretches of TAR or a missile factory located in Fatehjung or on the Sargoda airfield? If the aim of such a strike is to destroy only these targets, then not only precision strikes, but accuracy in the weapon yield will also be required to avoid collateral damage. There is no damage criterion available to the Indian Army for, say, aircraft, missile launchers, helicopters etc. Will such a damage criterion be required by the Strategic Forces Command (SFC) for planning purposes or not? We may presently not subscribe to the philosophy of counter-force nuclear strikes, but we came of foreclose our options for all time to come. When atmospheric testing was allowed, the US and other nations conducted physical trials on a range of military equipment. This is not possible now. Can such data be generated for select equipment from non-nuclear testing or from available scientific literature? There is, in the opinion of the author, a need for identifying the equipment for which damage criterion should be made available to the armed forces by the scientific community. The SFC should act as a lead agency to undertake this initiative.

VNTK CODES

- The US has developed a coded system for nuclear target analysis in which blast wave effects and structural response is embedded in a four letter code referred to as VNTK.
- The code provides nuclear strike planners three types of information. The VN number indicates the rating for target hardening given in terms of psi. T stands for type of target. A 'P' type target would be sensitive to static overpressure (generally point targets) whereas 'Q' type targets would to drag pressure (extended target). The K factor from 0 to 9 is related to the sensitivity of the structure to yield.
- In case a missile silo of a particular type had a VNTK code of 35P7 and had to be destroyed by a 10 kiloton bomb, the targeting officer would read a chart which gives the required overpressure (P chart) to cause the designated level of damage (destruction, severe or moderate).

The scale of immediate destruction that will be caused by counter-force strikes on the army's field formations will be much smaller than counter-value strikes on towns and cities of comparable yields. The impact of counter-force strikes on mechanised formations whose battle arrays are more dispersed than the compact defensive deployment of the infantry and would generally be engaged in offensive manoeuvres in close proximity of the enemy will be even lesser. In such fluid situations, selecting the desired GZ and accurately engaging it will be difficult. Such a conclusion should, however, not lead to a sense of complacency, that a nuclear strike situation can be handled or managed. There is also a need to understand that post-strike operations in the TBA will be focused towards denying the enemy tactical or operation advantage following the use of nuclear weapons, whereas post-strike operations in the cities will aim at limiting the scale of disaster and saving as many people as possible.

ENDNOTES

1. Operation Vijay (Kargil War) in 1999 and Operation Parakram in 2001.
2. K Raja Menon, "Cold Start under the Nuclear Shadow," IPCS/IDSA Workshop on Nuclear Disarmament Issues, 17 November 2008.
3. Firdaus Ahmed, "The Calculus of Cold Start," http://www.indiatogether.org/2004/may/fah-coldstart.htm, accessed on 05 December 2008.
4. Ibid.
5. "Nuclear Safety, Nuclear Stability and Nuclear Strategy in Pakistan," http://www.pugwash.org/september11/pakistan-nuclear.htm, accessed on 06 December 2008.
6. Gurmeet Kanwal, *Nuclear Defence: Shaping the Arsenal*, (New Delhi: Knowledge World/Institute for Defence Studies and Analyses, 2001), p. 96.
7. The mobilisation of the Indian Army during Operation Parakram did not lead to war.
8. Pakistan's AHQ reserves. Army Reserve North (ARN) is located at Mangla and Army Reserve South (ARS) is located at Multan.
9. Surface winds may be moving at different speeds in various atmospheric layers. The aggregate takes into account wind speeds from the bottom to the top of a mushroom cloud, for a specified yield at a height interval of 2000 metres. Average wind direction is also aggregated in a somewhat similar manner by making a wind vector plot.

PART III

POST-STRIKE OPERATIONS IN THE AFTERMATH OF A NUCLEAR ATTACK

12

Introduction

The surviving will envy the dead

—**Nikita Khrushchev**

The possibility of a nation facing a nuclear attack can be the most daunting crisis for the political leadership of any country, especially if the nation is unprepared for it. Such a situation probably arose for the first time in 1989, when after the nuclear crisis, Prime Minister VP Singh, on the suggestion of VS Arunachalam, the scientific advisor to the Minister of Defence, formed a secret committee to review India's plans to respond to a nuclear attack. The committee was entrusted with the task of developing plans for ensuring that in the event of a nuclear attack on India, the government continued to function and was also able to deliver nuclear retaliation.[1] Management of the disaster following a nuclear strike, it was assumed, would follow the established procedures already prepared for handling natural disasters. Obviously some sort of analogy was being drawn between the large-scale devastation that would be caused by a natural disaster and the destruction that would follow a nuclear strike. However, as we have seen in the previous chapter, a single nuclear strike of megaton yield on a bustling metropolis can cause far more destruction than two or three natural disasters occurring simultaneously. Apart from the difference in the magnitude of the calamity, a post-strike response will require specially trained and equipped personnel.

India has come a long way from 1989 and has created both institutional mechanisms and response elements to deal with large-scale disasters including those caused by WMDs. On 23 December 2005, the Government of India enacted the Disaster Management Act, which created the National Disaster Management Authority (NDMA), headed by the Prime Minister, and State Disaster

Management Authorities (SDMAs) headed by respective chief ministers, to spearhead and implement a holistic and integrated approach to disaster management in India. The NDMA is now responsible for the management of all disasters, including chemical, biological, radiological and nuclear (CBRN) disasters. As part of national capacity building, a National Disaster Response Force (NDRF) has also been created. The NDRF has eight battalions for disaster management, of which four are specially mandated to handle CBRN disasters. However, considering the scale of the disaster that would follow in the wake of a nuclear strike, even from a weapon of modest yield, the resources for 'immediate response' seem to be quite inadequate. Such a scenario will require a multi-disciplinary response. While the operations will be conducted under the overall supervision of the NDMA, the actual response elements of the NDRF will have to be assisted and supplemented by the armed forces and Department of Atomic Energy (DAE) personnel. In addition, other ministries and departments of the Government of India and NGOs will also have a significant role to play in mitigating the effects of the disaster, especially during the rehabilitation and reconstruction stage.

Nuclear disaster management in the country, till recently, was the responsibility of the DAE. The DAE is primarily concerned with nuclear emergencies occurring in facilities being run by them and operates about 18 Emergency Response Centres (ERCs) for such contingencies. Although a nuclear attack is in a totally different league than a nuclear emergency, the institutional knowledge and expertise of the DAE to deal with a nuclear disaster will come in handy for overall employment of resources, guidance etc. The armed forces, as an institution, have been involved in the management of all natural disasters that the nation has faced till now. They have a wealth of knowledge and experience in the management of natural disasters. As an organised and disciplined force, they are quick to respond in times of emergency. The armed forces have also created a capability to 'conduct operations in a NBC environment', although it is still in its incipient stage. The resources of the armed forces, in terms of specialised units and equipment, can be diverted to the aid of the civil administration, if not committed to their primary task. Hence, there is an overarching need to analyse the strengths and weaknesses of various response organisations, forecast their availability at a time when the nation will be faced with such a crisis and evaluate their employment options under the framework of the type of operations they will need to perform in the aftermath of a nuclear strike. Consequent management requires detailed coordination during peace time because both 'preparedness' and 'response' will be essential in saving lives and lessening disruption during a nuclear attack. There is, therefore, a need to give a holistic look to the issue.

This part of the study deals with a suggested methodology for a post-strike response to a nuclear attack based on the assessment of personnel casualties and material damage on the counter-value and counter-force targets discussed in Part II of the study. The scale of disaster during a counter-force strike being less and actions of the military somewhat easier to spell out, post-strike military operations are discussed in the beginning. The focus of this section is on the operations that the military will have to undertake to survive, fight and win in a nuclear scenario and not on typical disaster management aspects. Civil disaster management after a nuclear strike on a metro like Delhi is discussed in the subsequent section. Both these scenarios are analysed with a view to draw out some useful lessons for capacity building for the preparatory stage. In order to put the 'post-strike operations' in the correct perspective, there is a need to identify measures being undertaken globally and in India to reduce the risk of use of nuclear weapons and aspects of nuclear defence. Since both these issues precede the threshold of actual use being breached, these are discussed very briefly in the beginning.

Reducing the Risk

Nuclear weapons, if used even on a limited scale, can result in a catastrophe of unimaginable proportions. Besides immediate fatalities, the economic burden of large-scale medical management, environmental clean-up, rehabilitation of displaced people, reconstruction etc., would be colossal. To any rational mind, such a disaster must be prevented at all costs. The US and the former Soviet Union were able to prevent a nuclear war for 40 long years through 'deterrence'. In fact, they had taken the concept to an absurd level by not only deploying an obscene inventory of nuclear weapons that could have destroyed the world many times over, but also agreeing not to undertake measures for active nuclear defence. The Anti-Ballistic Missile Defence (ABM) treaty signed between the US and the former Soviet Union in 1972[2] envisaged both the belligerents agreeing on not to deploy missile defences except at one agreed location. In other words, both nations had tacitly agreed to hold their population, cities and economic centres at the risk of nuclear attack by the other in the hope that such a threat will provide strategic stability and thus avoid a nuclear conflagration. This was deterrence being practised in its extreme manifestation through 'mutually increased vulnerabilities'. However, the merits of a defensive strategy based on a threat of mutual annihilation is questionable because such a strategy will always promote suspicion and is contrary to the philosophy of mutual trust for building confidence and risk reduction. Did a treaty like ABM actually eliminate the risk of a nuclear exchange which could have led to an all-out nuclear war? The issue is debatable, because such an agreement can be viewed as an attempt to increase the threshold for the use of nuclear weapons. The risk of a nuclear attack alongwith the consequences that would follow remained.

More than a decade has passed since the end of the Cold War. The lack of ideological differences between the erstwhile antagonists has reduced the possibility of a global nuclear war. However, in the politico-military arena of international high stakes, nuclear weapons continue to be regarded as a 'currency of power'.

The inability of the international community to 'de-value' nuclear weapons has witnessed a surge in the number of nations seeking to acquire nuclear weapons. This has led to what some analysts refer to as the advent of the 'second nuclear age'. The nuclear tests by India and Pakistan in May 1998 are considered as important benchmarks of the second nuclear age but these are not the only events or trends. The discovery of Iraq's secret nuclear weapons programme before the first Gulf War, Iran's desire to acquire nuclear technology in utter disregard to world opinion, the discovery of AQ Khan's proliferation network in 2003, North Korea's nuclear tests of 2005 and the general desire of countries in the Middle East and Gulf region to acquire nuclear technology, are all indicators of the second nuclear age. The rising concerns about nuclear weapon proliferation has galvanised an equally powerful trend towards finding a solution to reduce the risk from them.

Disarmament, Arms Control and Non-Proliferation

The increasing desire of many 'states' to acquire nuclear weapons is matched by growing world-wide abhorrence among 'people' against these weapons of mass destruction. This has resulted in various initiatives for their complete elimination. 'Nuclear Disarmament' lies at one end of such initiatives, which proposes a total elimination of nuclear weapons through steps like de-valuing or de-legitimising their use. Disarmament initiatives can follow multilateral, regional or even individual approaches. The Delhi Declaration of Rajiv Gandhi for a 'Nuclear Weapon Free World' made at the UN General Assembly in 1988 or the launch of the 'Global Zero' initiative by 100 internationally renowned political, military, business and civic leaders in December 2008, for complete elimination of nuclear weapons, are a few examples of this approach. The latest initiative for global nuclear disarmament comes from none other than US President Barack Obama. On 04 April 2009, in a historic speech at Prague, he spoke eloquently of the moral responsibility of the US, the only nuclear weapon power to have used nuclear weapons, to pursue the elimination of nuclear weapons.

However, most analysts feel that global and universal nuclear disarmament is a utopian idea and difficult to reach under present circumstances. Such people focus on 'Arms Control', which seeks to stabilise military competition, thus reducing mutual suspicion and fear. Arms control usually aims at some kind of restraint in qualitative design, quantitative production, deployment, protection, control, transfer and planned, threatened or actual use of arms for politico-strategic purposes. At a macro level, nuclear disarmament and arms control, at least conceptually, seek to reduce the possibility of the use of nuclear weapons, if not the complete elimination of such a threat. The fact that their actual practice or implementation may not have reached a desired end-state, does not dilute the basic premise that by eliminating nuclear weapons or reducing their inventory, the chances of their use automatically get reduced.

Nuclear non-proliferation can also be viewed as yet another facet of the same concept to reduce the threat from nuclear weapons. Non-proliferation aims at preventing the spread of nuclear weapons technology to newer entities and thus the threat from such weapons. However, most of the nuclear non-proliferation initiatives till now have addressed 'horizontal proliferation', which prevents the emergence of new Nuclear Weapon States (NWS) than the issue of 'vertical proliferation', which seeks to reduce the existing armoury of established NWS. The new avatar of this concept is counter-proliferation, albeit with elements of coercion built into it. The Proliferation Security Initiative announced by President George W Bush at Krakow, Poland, in 2002, is an example of counter-proliferation.

Regional Risk Reduction

Nuclear weapons are considered by India as political weapons, which are to be used for deterrence and not for actual war-fighting. However, eulogising the concept of deterrence will not reduce the threat, howsoever low it may be. Some analysts feel that the nuclearisation of the sub-continent has ushered in stability. Operation Parakram and Operation Vijay are touted as examples of it. Deterrence can and has worked in democratically elected states that are responsible to their electorate and hence rational in their approach. Will it work for totalitarian regimes, dictatorial states, anarchists and terrorists? The point is that the consequences of a nuclear strike can be so devastating that relying on deterrence alone to eliminate the possibility of their use will be foolhardy. Hence, there is an overarching need to reduce the overall risk of use of nuclear weapons.

In the Indo-Pakistan context, talks on Nuclear Risk Reduction Measures (NRRM) are being conducted through an expert level dialogue as part of nuclear Confidence Building Measures (CBM). The broad framework was agreed on at Lahore in 1999 during the visit of the Indian Prime Minister.[3] While an agreement on non-targeting each other's nuclear facilities was already concluded in 1988, based on which a list of nuclear installations is exchanged every year on the first of January, the latest dialogues have finalised agreements on pre-notification of ballistic missile tests, immediate notification of accidents that can create radioactive hazards, establishment of a hotline between foreign secretaries, upgrading of communication links between Directors General of Military Operations and national measures to guard against accidents. As part of this process, India had also submitted a draft for 'reducing accidental and unauthorised use of nuclear weapons' to Pakistan in August 2005. Some other issues which NRRMs can address are the declaration of respective nuclear doctrines, a more transparent nuclear command and control structure, de-alerting or de-mating of nuclear assets and establishment of dedicated nuclear risk reduction centres in both countries. Sino-Indian NRRM talks have not been possible because China does not consider India as a NWS under the narrow definition of the nuclear Non-Proliferation Treaty (NPT). However, as the ranges of India's ballistic missiles cover larger parts of China, including its economically developed eastern coast, it will have to engage

India in such a dialogue sooner than later. Nuclear risk reduction measures, as the name suggests, seek to 'reduce' the danger of a nuclear exchange. Since such a possibility still remains, the aspect of 'nuclear defence' assumes importance.

Deterrence and Nuclear Defence

There is a succinct difference between deterrence and defence. Deterrence denotes a policy of dissuasion based on threatening, the results of which would outweigh the benefits hoped for. Defence is a policy of dissuasion based on counter-posing of forces and capabilities, so that an attack would fail or may not meet desired results. Defence comes into force when war begins; deterrence is to prevent war from breaking out.[4] So when deterrence breaks down, defence comes into play. Unfortunately, the possession of nuclear weapons can deter but cannot defend. Hence, in case of a nuclear stalemate, everything must be done to ensure that deterrence does not break, while up-shoring aspects of nuclear defence. From the argument, it emerges that nuclear warfare has two distinct facets. Its offensive element involves the threat of use of nuclear weapons for deterrence or actual use, in case of its breakdown and aspects of nuclear defence.

Nuclear defence[5] includes both active and passive measures. Active measures aim to prevent nuclear attacks by destroying the vectors carrying the nuclear warhead to their targets. Any attempt to destroy the nuclear warheads or their vectors before they are actually launched would fall under the realm of counter-force targeting. Active nuclear defensive measures include 'missile defence' and 'air defence'. The technology for the former is still in the developmental and experimental stages because it is believed that counter-missile defence is relatively easier and cheaper than missile defence. Notwithstanding the argument, the US is planning to build National and Theatre Missile Defence systems to protect itself and its allies from future missile threats. India too is making efforts to either acquire a missile defence system or build one indigenously.

Passive nuclear defensive measures could either be those that reduce target vulnerability by camouflage and concealment, deception, dispersion etc., or civil defence measures. Pre-strike civil defence includes measures undertaken to reduce the number of casualties among the unprotected population by constructing protective shelters or the evacuation of people to safer areas as well as measures to reduce economic damage from a nuclear strike. Civil defence aspects in a post-attack scenario can be referred to as 'consequence management' operations and includes casualty evacuation, medical management, relocation, rehabilitation and reconstruction. The defensive aspects of a nuclear war, as far as the armed forces are concerned, includes measures that provide the ability to a force to minimise damage from a nuclear strike, ensure survival and then, if required, to undertake conventional operations in contaminated conditions. Both active and passive defensive measures increase the credibility of 'deterrence', because it conveys the will and capability to undertake military operations and consequent management measures, even after the use of nuclear weapons, to deny victory to the aggressor. The measures being taken at various levels to reduce the risk from nuclear weapons and aspects on nuclear defence along with the institutions responsible to pursue these are explained with the help of Diagram 2.

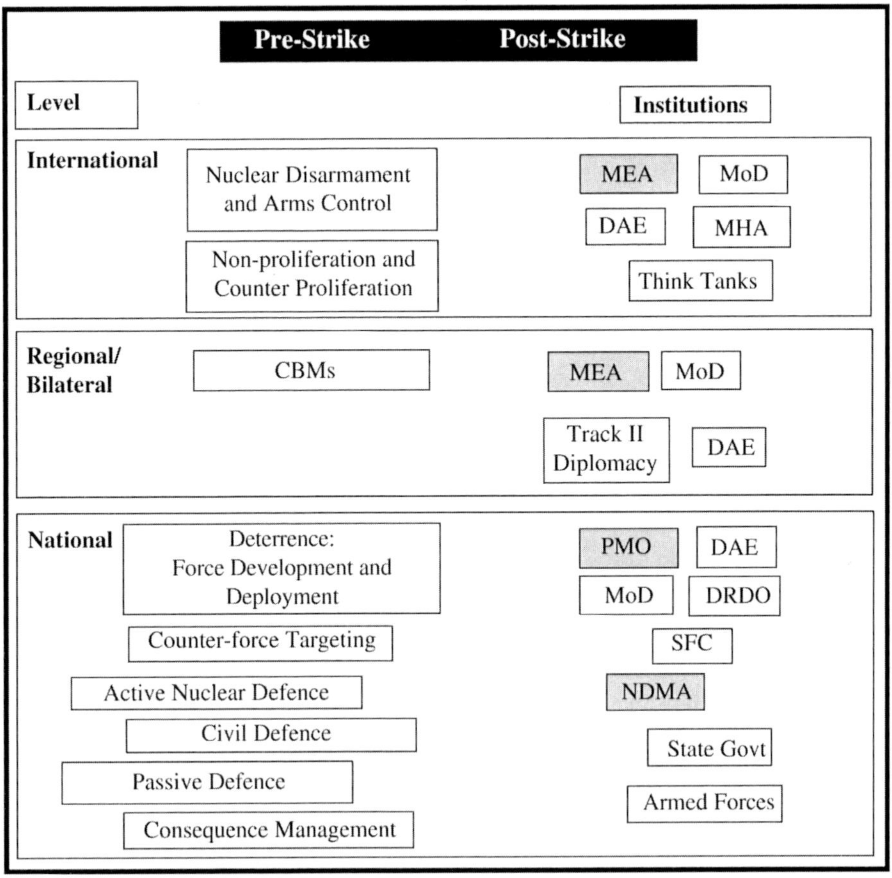

Diagram 2: Reducing Risk from Nuclear Weapons

ENDNOTES

1. George Perkovich, *India's Nuclear Bomb: The Impact on Global Proliferation* (New York: Oxford University Press, 1999), p. 313.
2. The ABM Treaty presently stands abrogated since 2002.
3. "India-Pak Nuclear CBM Talks: More Meetings to Follow," *India News Online*, http://news.indiamart.com/news-analysis/india-pak-nuclear-cb-3615.html, accessed on 28 February 2009.
4. Raman Sudha, *Nuclear Strategy: The Doctrine of Just War* (New Delhi: Manas Publications, 2006), p. 12.
5. Some nuclear pacifists consider the use of the word 'Defence' with 'Nuclear' as offensive, because they consider that there is no prospect of defence against a nuclear attack.

13

Post-Strike Military Operations

India's Nuclear Doctrine, prepared by the National Security Advisory Board (NSAB) and released by the former National Security Adviser (NSA), Brijesh Mishra, on 19 August 1999, was purportedly approved by the Cabinet Committee on Security (CCS) on 04 January 2003. The Doctrine states that "the Indian Armed Forces shall be prepared to conduct operations in a NBC environment with minimal degradation."[1] This precept is in sharp contrast to the Indian Army Doctrine, which considers that "all future operations will be conducted under a nuclear backdrop."[2] Clearly, the Indian Army Doctrine relegates nuclear threat to a 'backdrop', whereas the possibility of conducting military operations in contaminated conditions, as a consequence of use of nuclear weapons, is obviously visualised in the Nuclear Doctrine.

This divergence in perceptions can be attributed to the fact that the control over India's nuclear weapons programme has always been exercised at the highest political level and the armed forces have been excluded, not only from the development programme of this strategic capability, but probably also from its employment strategies. This 'hands-off' approach on nuclear issues, which essentially related to the 'offensive' facet of nuclear warfare, has permeated down to the 'defensive' aspect also.[3] It is probably perceived that a nuclear crisis, if at all it ever arises, will be handled at the highest level and the role of the Army in such a situation, will be limited. After all, nuclear weapons are considered 'political weapons', to be used as 'weapons of last resort'. The use of this ultimate weapon may draw the curtain on the war itself.

India's strategic community also considers that the probability of the use of nuclear weapons on counter-value targets is more than counter-force targets because such a potent weapon is unlikely to be frittered away in the TBA. So in the 'unlikely event' of a full-scale war breaking out, firstly, nuclear weapons may not be used at all and secondly, even if the threshold of their use has been breached, they are more likely to be used on cities. Since this reduces the threat to the armed forces to negligible levels, it has failed to draw the desired attention of the Army. The lack of a credible threat, ambiguity of role in such a crisis and inability to distinguish between offensive and defensive aspects of nuclear warfare has led to diminished interest in nuclear warfare in general and its defensive aspects in particular.

Most of the threat assessments carried out in the armed forces are generally based on 'enemy capability' and 'intent'. An alternate model to assess threat could be based on evaluating 'probability' and 'consequences'. For example, the probability of terrorists striking in the rear areas during war remains very high, but the consequences of such a strike will not affect the outcome of the battle in a theatre and certainly not the course of the war. After all, the Army has always considered the threat of fifth columnists, partisans and enemy's special forces operating in their rear. The probability of the use of nuclear weapons in the TBA remains low but the consequences will be catastrophic and may decide the outcome of a battle in a theatre. Hence, it would be prudent to be prepared by considering this low probability threat as realistic and credible. Preparations by half measures, to meet such an eventuality, which is based on inadequate or half-baked knowledge, can lead to a larger tragedy in all its dimensions, i.e. human, spatial and environmental. Accordingly, there is a need to look at the defensive aspects of nuclear warfare with increasing seriousness by the entire armed forces.

The armed forces have to be prepared for survival and fighting during a nuclear strike. They also have to be prepared to assist the civilian administration, in case any of our cities or towns become the targets of such a strike rather than the armed forces. The human tragedy of such a nuclear strike on a city will be so colossal that all the organs of the government, including the armed forces, will have to get involved in mitigation efforts. The success of any multi-dimensional response will depend upon the coordination achieved and preparatory work undertaken during peace time. This preparedness will include aspects like increasing awareness among likely responders, promulgating operating concepts and guidelines, formulating drills and standard operating procedures and upgrading preparedness for operating in radiologically contaminated conditions in terms of equipping and training of troops. While this section primarily deals with military operations in the case of a nuclear strike in the TBA, some of the aspects will have a correlation, including lessons for management of such a disaster to the civilian domain also.

Pre-Strike Measures

Vulnerability Assessment: Potential nuclear targets, especially the ones in the TBA, when considered from a defender's point of view, have a distinct advantage over counter-value targets. A pre-assessment of their vulnerability can assist military commanders in formulating 'courses of action', which can allow mission accomplishment at acceptable risks. This essentially entails redeployment of combat assets for achieving the desired 'ends', albeit through slightly different 'ways', while not subjecting the 'means' to any additional danger. The means to reduce vulnerabilities in case of our towns and cities would be tantamount to the removal of all hazardous and inflammable material; creating fire lanes to reduce the vulnerability to massed fires or even evacuation of population. Such redeployment or re-engineering may not be practical or even possible. However, in the case of military targets, it is recommended that all contemplated military operations must be assessed for their vulnerabilities to nuclear strikes during all phases and stages of the battle, and modifications, if required, to reduce casualties, must be made. Even if no alternatives can be visualised, either due to tactical or geographical constraints, at least the commanders will be mentally more prepared in terms of the immediate reactions and intended actions that they will have to initiate, in case their command is subjected to a nuclear strike. Vulnerability Assessment is carried out in a similar manner as damage assessment, using the Tables and Graphs discussed in Chapter 1. Most of the parameters like details of own deployment, likely meteorological conditions and protection available to troops in the likely target area would be known, the only variable being the yield of the nuclear strike. This may also be bracketed on intelligence assessments.

Pre-assessment of own vulnerabilities can assist in arriving at 'critical decisions' in a better timeframe during a crisis. Some of these 'critical decisions' could be as follows:

- Upgrading the state of preparedness, including Mission Oriented Protective Posture (MOPP) levels, as per assessment of the threat.
- Issue of warning to troops likely to be affected by the nuclear fallout, including their re-deployment, if necessary.
- Gearing up of medical echelons in rear areas for anticipated casualties.
- Plan for relief or replacement of units likely to be affected by nuclear strike.
- Measures to be initiated for limiting the spread of radioactive contamination.
- Mobilisation and positioning of specialist NBC units.
- Earmarking suitable sites for decontamination and their preparation.
- Issue of NBC protective equipment to troops earmarked for restoring the adverse situation likely to be created after the strike.
- Laying down of radiation exposure criteria for contemplated operations.

Radiation Exposure Criteria (REC): Operations in contaminated areas are based on the twin axioms of 'Hazard Avoidance' and in case that is not possible, to 'Minimise Exposure'. Exposure to radioactivity can be minimised by shielding, increasing distance from the source of radioactivity,[4] reducing time spent in the contaminated area by sharing the contamination burden and delaying entry into the contaminated area till radioactivity has reduced considerably. However, it may not be possible to undertake all these precautions during active hostilities or when time is at a premium for saving human lives. Troops may have to enter radiological contaminated areas for operational reconnaissance, search-and-rescue missions, casualty evacuation or for the conduct of actual combat missions. Since radiation can neither be seen, heard or smelt and can only be detected or measured with the help of instruments, it should be the duty of all commanders to ensure that troops entering radiologically contaminated areas are provided adequate radiation detection and measuring instruments and a limit for their exposure to radiation is laid down.

Radiation exposure limits can be laid down only if commanders at all levels have some guidelines and criteria for acceptable radiation exposure. The REC must define the negligible, moderate and emergency risk that commanders can undertake while employing troops in radiologically contaminated conditions. There is a need to lay down such a criterion for both war and peace time conditions.[5] While the war time criteria would be applicable to the armed forces and para military forces (PMF), peace time criteria should be extended to civil defence units, fire brigade personnel and DAE personnel earmarked for management of nuclear disasters. While a suggested radiation exposure guideline for war is given in Table 50, similar guidelines also need to be evolved for peacetime. Since during peacetime there will be no threat from the enemy, the radiation exposure guidelines must be commensurate with those laid down for civilian workers employed in the nuclear industry by the Atomic Energy Regulatory Board (AERB) of India.[6] Suitable enhancement can be made when tasks in contaminated areas are of a life-saving nature or which will prevent spreading of contamination to newer areas.

Radiation Exposure State (RES): The effects of radiation exposure on the human body are also cumulative, especially when the time lag between two exposures is restricted to weeks or months. This is to say that if a person has been exposed to a total dose of 30 rads during an operation, he should not be exposed to beyond 20 rads in the next operation, in order to maintain his risk exposure as negligible. Hence, there is a need to maintain (RES) of troops, so that troops having a history of previous exposure are not subjected to radiation beyond prescribed limits.

Laying and Implementing the REC: Based on actual operations being contemplated, the laying down of the REC by all commanders is an important aspect of pre-strike planning. Besides being an operational requirement, it also has a moral dimension to it. Most of our troops may not be fully aware of the invisible and insidious nature of the threat posed by exposure to radiation because depending on the degree of exposure, the adverse affects will only manifest after a period of time. Hence, laying the REC limits for all operations must be seen as

Table 50: Recommended Radiation Exposure Guidelines during War[7]

S. No.	Nature of Operation or Task	Enemy	Suggested Total Dose	Remarks
1.	Actual offensive or defensive combat with enemy troops including operational manoeuvres in the combat zone to prevent breakthrough by the enemy or to pursue a breakthrough	In the face of the enemy. (Enemy troops are also likely to be exposed to similar levels)	70 to 100 rads	The total Dose can be varied within the laid down limit depending upon the importance of the operation/sector etc.
2.	Operational manoeuvres like redeployment or reinforcement including crossing or temporary holding of contaminated ground to thwart enemy action	Not in the face of the enemy	50 to 75 rads	-do-
3.	Radiological reconnaissance by air or on ground	In the face of the enemy	30 to 50 rads	Time will be at a premium hence a larger risk can be taken
4.	Radiological reconnaissance by air or on ground	Not in the face of the enemy	20 to 30 rads	–
5.	Radiological survey	Not in the face of the enemy		Survey is a time-consuming activity and if the REC limit is kept low, the task will never be completed
6.	Casuality evacuation from NIGA affected area or from the fallout zones	Humanitarian considerations	10 to 20 rads	Total dose can be varied depending upon the urgency of the mission
7.	Search and rescue operations Humanitarian considerations	Humanitarian considerations	30 to 50 rads	-do-
8.	Decontamination of equipment/ vehicles/tanks during lull in battle	Not in the face of the enemy	30 to 50 rads	Equipment may be required at short notice
9.	Medical and non-medical personnel involved in decontamination of casualties	Not in the face of the enemy	10 to 20 rads	–
10.	Medical personnel providing life saving treatment to contaminated casualties	Not in the face of the enemy	1 to 10 rads	–
11.	Preventing the spread of contamination by removal or turning over of top soil during peace	Not in the face of the enemy	1 to 10 rads 1 to 5 rads	Operations can be delayed if not a priority task
12.	Deliberate decontamination of equipment/vehicles/tanks after cease fire	Peacetime activity	As per civil guidelines of AERB	–

a moral obligation also. Laying down of REC for a particular operation is one issue, whereas overseeing its implementation is an entirely different matter. The latter can only be carried out if troops are equipped with suitable instruments for detecting and measuring radioactivity. Such instruments must measure both dose rates and accumulated dosage. Instruments measuring accumulated dosage will be required to maintain the REC status of individual soldiers. Commanders must note that there will be a large variation in REC guidelines for peace from that laid down for war and hence the equipment authorised to the Army for war may not be sensitive enough to be of any use during peace time.[8] This issue must be borne in mind while providing aid to civil authorities in nuclear disaster situations. In fact, there may be a need to review the requirement of dosimetry in the armed forces to meet the twin requirements of war and peace, including training.

ARCHITECTURE OF NBC DEFENCE

Physical Protection: This is a function of individual and collective protection measures and essential to fight and survive in a NBC environment.

Detection and Identification: This involves the employment of units equipped with specialist NBC equipment to detect and identify the nature of threat. It helps in:

- Warning and reporting.
- Contamination avoidance.
- Upgrading of MOPP.
- Contamination Control.
- Employment of troops in contaminated conditions.

Warning and Reporting: It is a two-way process. Forward troops report suspected or confirmed attacks, which are then analysed at HQs and their hazards predicted. Troops likely to be affected are then warned.

Medical Counter Measures: These include prophylaxis, medical self aid and the administration of antidotes once symptoms of exposure have manifested and treatment of large-scale casualties.

NBC Training: A value-added service or force multiplier, which enhances the value of NBC defence.

Post-Strike Operations

NBC Defence: Post-strike operations will involve simultaneous action by troops, staff and commanders at all levels. Most of their actions will be guided towards limiting the damage that has already occurred and would hence fall under the realm of NBC Defence. Since the strike on a military target has a very high probability of being a surface or low airburst, there will be an urgent need to carry out hazard prediction of the local fallout, followed by damage estimation. While the former will prevent radioactive fallout from contaminating unexposed troops, especially in the downwind direction of the strike, the latter will provide useful inputs for the type and quantity of medical effort required.

Hazard Prediction: The process involves estimating the yield of the strike based on cloud morphology and the GZ. These are then interpolated with meteorological parameters to predict the limit of major hazard zones and the time of arrival of the fallout. The procedure for a simplistic manual prediction of the movement of radioactive fallout has been dealt with in the previous chapter. There is, however, a need to automate the procedure so that units that are likely to be affected are warned in time to undertake evasive action, or, if that is not possible, to adopt a more stringent protective posture.

Damage Assessment: The methods and techniques for damage estimation is the focus of Chapter 1. The use of similar procedures has been advocated for the reduction of own vulnerabilities against the use of nuclear weapons in the TBA. Like hazard prediction, there is a need to automate damage estimation also so that if parameters like HOB and yield are defined, the desired damage circles are automatically plotted on a GIS map containing target information. However, post the use of nuclear weapons, the damage estimation can be accurately plotted by aerial reconnaissance, including the use of unmanned aerial vehicles.

Command and Control

In a post-strike scenario there is a strong possibility that major command and control elements might become non-effective and units functioning under them get isolated. This calls for decentralisation of control to such a level that it ensures effective functioning without compromising unity and integration. Duplication of HQs is one of the measures advocated to maintain continuity of command and control in a nuclear environment. In case both the main and adhoc HQs are targeted and are lost during a nuclear strike, then the HQ of a neighbouring formation must be prepared to assume immediate charge.

Post-strike consequence management will require a full-time dedicated HQ. This HQ must be divorced from all other operational duties and made responsible for controlling the operations of combat and specialist NBC units in contaminated areas only. The normal staff of the HQ must be supplemented by NBC warfare experts from specialist NBC units and from the Faculty of NBC Protection (FNBCP), College of Military Engineering (CME), Pune, at the earliest. DRDO representatives from Defence Laboratory, Jodhpur, and from the radiological safety division of the DAE must also be brought in, as soon as the operational situation permits, to provide technical advice to the local commander. Since such a HQ would be functioning in close proximity of the contaminated areas, they will require collective NBC protection shelters (initially inflatable variety, which must be replaced by containerised ones) and other NBC protective paraphernalia.

Radiological Monitoring, Reconnaissance, Survey and Marking

Specialist NBC units are generally employed in radiological contaminated areas for radiological monitoring, reconnaissance, survey, sampling and marking in the hope or understanding that these would provide sufficient inputs that will facilitate the employment of combat echelons or Search and Rescue (S&R) teams in contaminated areas. Such a deduction is true, but only partially. There is a need to understand these tasks and the method of their execution in relation to the NBC equipment held by our formations so that troops are not employed on dangerous missions without achieving the desired payoffs. Let us take the example of a 10 kiloton strike on a forward node[9] with linear wind speeds of 24 kmph without shear. In case of an idealised fallout pattern, the 30 rads/hour contour is likely to cover approximately 73 by 4.5 kilometres, but the predictions do not indicate exactly where the fallout will occur or what dose rates will be there in specific areas. This is because fallout will be affected by local wind conditions and the layout of the terrain. Hence, confirmation of fallout zones becomes necessary before the employment of troops. This is done by radiological monitoring, reconnaissance and survey.

Monitoring: Radiological monitoring is carried out to determine the presence and intensity of residual radiation (fallout and NIGA) at a particular place and is usually done while remaining static.[10] Units that are likely to be affected by fallout and have been ordered due to operational exigencies to remain deployed can be tasked for monitoring. Basically, the task involves measuring radioactivity dose rates during fallout, which are expected to peak on the arrival of the radioactive cloud above the monitoring location and thereafter, decrease in intensity due to decay. The monitoring reports from many locations, when correlated at a higher HQ, present a coherent picture of the contaminated areas. However, monitoring presupposes the availability of radiation monitoring instruments like portable dose rate meters or pocket dosimeters with all units besides their accessibility to protected bunkers or armoured vehicles which can afford some shielding from fallout radiation. The last two parameters must be taken into account by commanders before tasking units to monitor radioactivity after a nuclear strike. Monitoring was important during the Cold War, when NATO forces expecting a heavy breakthrough by Soviet armour formations, following a number of tactical nuclear strikes, saw merit in holding ground likely to be affected by fallout. Radiological monitoring has limited utility in our context because in the case of single or limited nuclear strikes, a radiological survey by specialist NBC units (platoon or company) can also determine the areas affected by radioactivity and its intensity. There seems to be little tactical merit in putting combat units to risk by making them stay put in areas that are likely to be affected by fallout. They could re-enter these areas for combat missions and stay put for longer durations after fallout has ceased. Such an approach will also obviate the need for early decontamination of such units.

Reconnaissance: Unlike monitoring, which was done from a static location, radiological reconnaissance is detecting the presence of radiation while on the move.[11] It is conducted to 'initially detect' or 'determine' the extent of contamination. Radiological reconnaissance focuses on location rather than intensity, thus providing information on 'clear' or 'contaminated' areas, which would be of assistance to 'follow on' units in avoiding the contamination hazard. Radiological reconnaissance is not carried out as a principal mission by units and the information they provide is incidental. In the example of a nuclear strike on the node, a mechanised infantry battalion-based S&R team could also be tasked to carry out radiological reconnaissance. The information provided by the team could guide the S&R team following in soft-skinned vehicles so that they can avoid contaminated areas. Another important aspect that commanders need to realise is that 'contamination avoidance' is a bit of a misnomer, especially in the case of fallout radioactivity because there can be no clear-cut boundary between 'clean' and 'contaminated' areas. Contamination avoidance should not be equated to bypassing drills of mechanised units, where an enemy location can be avoided altogether. It also needs to be remembered that the boundary of a contaminated area will keep shrinking rapidly due to radioactive decay. Armour and mechanised units whose armoured vehicles are normally equipped with roentgen meters can be tasked for radiological reconnaissance. However, the dose rate that, in the commander's opinion, would constitute 'contamination', must be made clear to them. In case specialist NBC units are to be employed, they must be tasked for radiological survey rather than reconnaissance.

GUIDING PRINCIPLES: RADIOLOGICAL SURVEY

- Survey is done after fallout has ceased.
- Order survey if the operations situation permits and operations are planned in contaminated areas
- Survey teams to operate within laid down REC.
- Marking of contaminated areas to be done concurrently.

Survey: While radiological reconnaissance provides general information for immediate operations, radiological surveys are conducted to find the extent and intensity of contamination, so that future operations can be planned and executed based on the findings of the survey.[12] A radiological survey basically involves finding the dose rates at different locations at a particular time after the nuclear explosion. The dose rate established during the radiological survey is normalised to the dose rate that would have been prevalent at H plus 1 hour and based on this data, iso-dose rate maps of the contaminated area are prepared. Since the findings of the survey may be based on approximations, these are good for field use only. Re-survey, if carried out after a few days, will increase accuracy and also take into account the inaccuracies that have come about due to weathering etc. A radiological survey requires trained personnel and is a time-consuming activity. During the survey, trained personnel will get exposed to radiation, although within the laid down REC limits, and hence, the duration of their reutilisation will get progressively reduced. Therefore, specialist NBC units need to be utilised judiciously. In addition, radiological surveys must be carried out only if the operational situation permits and further operations are planned in contaminated areas. In case combat operations are not planned in contaminated areas, this survey can be delayed till the intensity of radiations comes down due to radioactive decay. Radiological surveys can be carried out either by air, using helicopters or on ground using armoured vehicles. Some doubts that may still nag commanders while ordering a survey are discussed below:

- When to order a survey? Technically, it must be done immediately after the fallout has ceased, so that dose rates can be normalised for H plus 1 hour, as accurately as possible. Tactically speaking, it would be unwise to conceive that counter-force nuclear strikes can be carried out by an adversary in isolation and without plans to exploit the resulting imbalance in the operational situation. Hence, tactically also, surveys must be carried out as early as possible so that the movement of combat echelons in areas likely to be exploited by the enemy can be facilitated.
- How should the REC be laid for survey? Commanders need to consider that if the laid-down REC is very high, say, in the range of 100 rads or above, then the troops who carry out this task cannot be reused. On the other hand, in case the REC is kept very low, say in the range of 20 rads, then the turn back dose rate for the survey team will be 10 rads/hour, which means that Iso-dose rate maps will have no contour showing a higher intensity of radioactivity. Such maps will be of no use after some time.
- How much resources are to be committed for the survey and for how long? To find an answer to this problem, let us visualise the idealised fallout pattern from a 10 kiloton strike. The dose rate contour representing 30 rads per hour would be spread over 73 by 4.5 kilometres. A detailed radiological survey of such a large area will require about four to six NBC reconnaissance vehicles, employed for three to four hours each. So, if the survey commences at H plus 3 hours and is completed by H plus 7, the radiation dose rate of 30 rads per hour prevalent at H plus 1, would have fallen to 6 and 3 rads per hour by H plus 3 and 7, respectively. The survey team would have been exposed to a cumulative radiation dose between 15 to 20 rads during the operation.

Marking of Contaminated Areas: One of the tasks that a radiological reconnaissance or survey team can be asked to perform is the 'marking' of contaminated areas. The doubt that generally arises is the dose rate line that needs to be marked by the team. A higher dose rate line will unnecessarily overexpose troops carrying out the task, whereas a lower dose rate will become irrelevant after some time due to radioactive decay. Ideally, it should be the 'turn back' dose rate for the team which should be marked. Turn back dose rate is generally taken as half of the REC laid down for the task. This also gives us a fair idea of the number of markers to be carried on NBC reconnaissance vehicles.

Sampling: 'Sampling' will be required when the dose rate or the decay rate in a contaminated area becomes unpredictable. This may happen in case 'salted' weapons are used by the adversary. Radioactive samples may be collected by reconnaissance or survey teams of specialist NBC units and sent to the rear for further analysis in mobile or static NBC laboratories.

Search and Rescue (S&R) Operations

In case of a nuclear strike on a defensive node, the area enclosed within a circle of two to three km radius (depending upon the strike parameters like yield, HOB, etc.) would be completely devastated by craters, blown down trees, upturned equipment, damaged bunkers and communication infrastructure and hence, it will be physically impossible to approach the area. In addition, this area will also have very little possibility of survivors, besides having very high levels of radioactivity to attempt any meaningful S&R operations. This area should be identified as an absolute destruction zone. S&R operations should be focused in a circular area that is contiguous to the absolute destruction zone. In addition, S&R operations, albeit of a minor nature, may also be required in areas affected by fallout, in case these have not been vacated.

GUIDING PRINCIPLES: S&R OPERATIONS

- Casualties having greater chances of survival must be rescued first.
- S&R teams must not be exposed to radiation beyond that recommended as part of REC. REC will dictate their time of stay and the earliest time of entry into the hazard area.
- The S&R teams must be based on the actual requirement and their number kept to a bare minimum.
- S&R effort must not spread contamination to newer areas.
- Speed in mounting operations is essential for the survival of victims and to reduce exposure of S&R teams.

S&R Zones: The search area must be divided into two S&R zones as per the seriousness of the casualties that are likely to be encountered. S&R Zone 1 will be contiguous to the immediate destruction zone and S&R Zone 2 adjoining Zone 1. Comparatively, Zone 1 will be more difficult to approach; the casualties in this zone will be suffering from more than one effect of a nuclear detonation and will have to be physically evacuated. Casualties in Zone 1 will also have lesser hopes for survival unless evacuated at the earliest. Zone 2 will be more approachable and most of the casualties would be of the 'walking wounded' type.

Organisation of S&R Teams: The damage estimation of a brigade-sized node being subjected to a 10 kiloton nuclear strike had put the maximum possible casualties at 1,296. These casualties are expected to be evenly distributed in S&R Zone 1 and Zone 2. While Zone 2 casualties can be picked up in soft-skinned vehicles, casualties in Zone 1, due to higher radiation levels are recommended to be evacuated by teams equipped with armoured personnel carriers or infantry combat vehicles. To search and evacuate even 80 percent of anticipated casualties from Zone 1, there will be a requirement of at least two mechanised infantry battalions. Similarly, to pick up casualties from Zone 2 in soft-skinned vehicles, there will be a requirement of about 40 to 50 Stallion vehicles or an equal number of high mobility vehicles. These figures give us a rough idea of the S&R effort required in terms of manpower and vehicles. Teams earmarked for Zone 1 must be supplemented with armoured recovery vehicles and dozers, as they will have to traverse severely damaged terrain features. Needless to add, the S&R teams will be equipped with full spectrum NBC protection and radiation detection equipment, including NBC suits, boots and gloves, gas masks, canisters including spare canisters, personnel dosimeters with readers and dose rate meters or roentgen meters.

Relief of S&R Teams: It will not be possible, even in the best of circumstances, for one S&R team to pick up all the survivors, especially from Zone 1. Besides the physical difficulty of approaching the area devastated by a nuclear strike, the S&R teams will have to operate within the laid down REC. To give a rough idea about the problem, let us assume that the S&R is being attempted three hours after the nuclear strike and the REC laid down by the commander for the operation is 40 rads. The intensity of radioactivity in Zone 1 at H plus 3 is expected to come down to between 10 to 30 rads per hour, thus giving the team about two hours to complete their mission. Since one team may not be able to pick up all the survivors, there will be a need to earmark and equip suitable reserves.

Large-scale casualty collection and evacuation, post a nuclear strike, can be simplified through formulating the concept of casualty collection points as part of formation SOPs. After all, there will be a large number of 'walking wounded' type of personnel, some just suffering the trauma from the effects of a huge explosion without any physical injury. Two or three casualty collection points can be established at sites that are located upwind of the immediate destruction zone. These could be located at a suitable distance from the GZ, depending upon the fallout and NIGA considerations. The walking wounded casualties will need to walk up to these points. These sites could be identified by firing of coloured flares or smoke and the victims informed to collect there with help of loud hailers or dropping of leaflets.

Organising the Medical Effort

Provisioning of emergency treatment and rearward evacuation of large number of casualties in a short period of time will be a highly critical activity during post-strike operations. This, to a large extent, will depend upon an efficient system of sorting and classification of casualties, to ensure optimum utilisation of the available medical effort. The success of medical support to a great degree will also depend upon the adequacy of pre-war logistics planning and preparation. The organisation of medical support in the field for conventional warfare is well established and time-tested. There may not be a need for any drastic changes in the organisation of various echelons of medical support. However, this medical support is based on 'casualty planning data' laid down long ago and does not take into consideration the likely use of WMD on the battlefield. Accordingly, there would be a need to augment various medical echelons in terms of manpower and equipment and also create suitable reserves at all levels.

Nature of Casualties: In the case of a 10 kiloton nuclear strike on any compact defensive position, about 1,200 to 1,400-odd casualties can be expected. A nuclear strike like this may occur as a closing finale to a short intense war. Medical echelons already saddled with normal battle casualties would have to undertake this additional burden of nuclear casualties. A rough analysis of Tables 46 to 49 indicates that about one-third of the casualties will be suffering penetrating or blunt injuries from blast effects and first degree burns (primarily flash burns). The remaining two-third would be suffering from blast related injuries as well as thermal burns (flash or flame burns) and a small number of these would also be suffering from exposure to initially nuclear radiation. The implication of this analysis is as follows:

- Most of the second degree burn cases (about 800) will require special care in static hospitals. Lack of sufficient sterile wards to treat burn cases in all the military hospitals of a theatre, may necessitate that the casualty evacuation is spread both vertically and horizontally over a larger number of hospitals.
- Clinically, the first degree burn cases can be retained in forward casualties holding and treatment echelons. However, their current capabilities are limited as they are only geared to take on casualties of a conventional conflict. The capacities of forward medical echelons will have to be suitably regimented. Alternately, casualties could be evacuated to these units or to static hospitals in the rear.
- Since there will be a requirement to attend to a large number of casualties in a short time frame, there will be a need to establish Minimal Treatment

Centres (MTC) at all medical echelons. A MTC houses those patients who cannot return to duty but also do not require regular hospitalisation or intensive care. The basic purpose of the MTC will be to carry out triage and provide medicines only. Intimate care for lightly wounded cases is either not required or left to the individual. Such a concept will help reach out to a large number of people with superficial injuries, who are suffering from the trauma and shock of a major catastrophe. Casualties expected in the MTCs are the walking wounded casualties or the ones being evacuated by S&R teams from Zone 2.

Mobile Medical Team (MMT): Life-saving first aid, if provided within the first few hours, can enhance the chances of survival manifold. Hence, besides Advance Dressing Station (ADSs) and Forward Surgical Centre (FSCs), there would be a requirement of small self-contained first aid squads to provide life saving first aid and treatment. These MMTs could be grouped as part of S&R teams This is essential because the victims of a nuclear strike, even if trained in administering first aid, may not be able to do so. One to two MMTs must be grouped with S&R teams earmarked both for Zone 1 and Zone 2.

Rearward Evacuation: Extreme care will be required during rearward evacuation to prevent the spread of contamination. It will, therefore, necessitate decontamination of casualties before evacuation. Evacuation planning must be based on an efficient and flexible plan, with the basic aim to enabling forward medical echelons to retain their capability to receive more casualties. Generally, evacuation plans are based on the assumption that the chain of ground or surface evacuation will remain available. This may not be true in a post-strike scenario. However, availability of dedicated air evacuation resources would enable bypassing of intermediate medical echelons and would keep them free for the care of long-term cases. In case large-scale air evacuation from the incident site is planned, selection of suitable helipads will become crucial for the control of contamination.

RADIOLOGICAL HAZARDS DURING FALLOUT

- **Whole Body Gamma Exposure:** Radioactive dust from fallout on the casualty will not only affect him but also those evacuating and treating him. This can be reduced considerably by shaking off the dust or change of clothing.
- **Beta Contact Hazard**: This may pose sufficient risk in terms of radiation burns unless removed early. Removal will require washing and scrubbing.
- **Internal Contamination**: This may be caused due to inhalation or ingestion and will require chelation therapy for removal.

Casualty Decontamination Centre (CDC): Patients being evacuated from S&R zones may have their outer body surfaces contaminated with fallout residue in the form of dust, dirt and debris, which may be loosely attached to the clothing and skin of the patient. There will be need to decontaminate such patients so that they do not pose a radiological hazard. Since a large number of casualties will require decontamination, medical echelons will be required to be augmented in terms of manpower so that trained medical personnel can be spared for providing expert medical care. CDCs will be necessary for ADS and FSCs, and will have to be created by the formations out of available resources to augment the medical echelons. CDCs will also be required at military hospitals earmarked to handle NBC casualties.

Prophylaxis: While operating in a radiological contaminated environment, it is possible that minute radioactive particles could be inhaled or ingested by unprotected soldiers. This may lead to internal contamination. While there is no prophylaxis against external exposure to radiation, to prevent internal contamination, potassium iodide tablets are recommended. These prevent the accumulation of radioactive iodine in the thyroid glands by saturating the gland with normal iodine and thus preventing cancer of the throat. Hence, troops who are to be employed in contaminated affected zones, including medical personnel who also would be coming in close contact with radiological contamination, are recommended to be given potassium iodide tablets.

Recommendations: On the face of it, there seems to be a perceptible shortfall in the existing medical capabilities to handle a situation that may arise following a nuclear strike in the TBA. However, a nuclear threat remains nebulous and even if it prevails, its manifestation cannot be predicted with certainty in both time and space. Hence, across-the-board type upgradation of medical infrastructure is neither necessary nor required. The upgradation must be carried out on a selective basis.

- **Military Hospitals:** The risk profiling of various regions and types of operations provides sufficient indicators as to which areas need priority. Primarily, military hospitals located in Rajasthan must have CDCs and special wards to treat burn casualties. The spillover of casualties should be taken over by military hospitals located across the country, including civil hospitals. An in-house evaluation of the existing capacity to handle a nuclear strike in the TBA is necessary and must form the basis of a detailed evacuation plan.
- **Medical Brick:** Treatment of radiation exposure (both internal and external) and burn cases will require special medicines and drugs. These can be stocked centrally as a brick, which must be turned over regularly. The composition of the brick, level of stocks and placement must be decided by the general staff in consultation with medical authorities.
- **NBC Equipment:** Medical personnel working as part of MMTs, MTCs and CDCs will perforce have to operate in Individual Protective Equipment (IPE). Such equipment must be catered for and personnel

trained to operate with it. However, in order to permit medical echelons to carry out specialised treatment in a contaminated environment without the encumbrances of the IPE, it would be desirable to provide collective NBC protection to establishments like divisional and corps field ambulances. Collective protection shelters, like medical bricks, can be stoked centrally and must be used on an as-required basis.

- **Mobility**: Operations in a NBC environment require a high degree of mobility to ensure dispersion and ability to concentrate when required. Supporting medical echelons, especially those of strike formations, should also be fully mobile with own organic transport and communication systems.
- **Coordination with Civilian Agencies**: In an NBC scenario, despite augmentation from integral resources, medical resources are likely to remain inadequate in the aftermath of a nuclear strike. It would be essential, therefore, to coordinate with civil medical agencies. This should be done during peace time to enable both the counterparts to know the capabilities, limitations and mode of functioning of the other.

GUIDING PRINCIPLES: COMBAT OPERATIONS

- Enter contaminated areas only if you must.
- Operate within REC.
- Enemy threat to decide time of entry, and REC, the duration of stay.
- Decontaminate at the earliest.
- If possible, operate on sides of contaminated areas rather than inside it.
- Prophylaxis treatment against radiation hazard is a must.
- Armoured vehicles to operate with hatches closed and NBC filtration switched on.

Combat Operations in Contaminated Environment

Combat operations in contaminated areas will be peculiar because, besides fighting the enemy, there will be a need to protect troops from over exposure to radiation. Hence, commanders must plan for mission accomplishment with minimum risk of exposure. Mechanised troops, especially with heavy tanks, are ideally suited for combat in radiological contaminated areas due to the protection factor afforded by armour against gamma radiations. This protection factor implies that troops can be employed for longer duration within the laid down REC for that particular operation. Mechanised troops, before entering contaminated areas, must close down hatches and switch on their NBC air filtration units. They must operate within laid down REC with the help of roentgen meters fitted on their vehicles. Infantry units, when tasked to operate in contaminated areas, must be equipped with full-scale NBC protection.

Combat operations in contaminated areas will be based on how the adversary plans to exploit the situation due to the temporary unbalancing of the defender. A cursory look at the post-strike situation given in Map 8 highlights the two main dilemmas that will confront the enemy. First, the enemy is likely to exploit the areas contaminated by nuclear fallout only if its troops are sufficiently protected against the hazard. Second, he may have to delay his entry into contaminated areas, especially near the GZ, until the radioactivity levels come down. This is because his exit from the contaminated areas will be dependent upon the resistance he will experience from the opposite side. The enemy may avoid contaminated areas and choose to exploit a new flank. While it may choose from the two options available, the operations of the defender can be broadly classified into three major types.

- **Unopposed Crossing of Contaminated Areas:** These could be part of reinforcement, occupation of counter-penetration positions or movement for counter-attack. In such cases, the shortest route must be chosen and the mission accomplished at the earliest.
- **Temporary Defence of Terrain Features in Contaminated Areas:** This task can be performed by mechanised or normal infantry units suitably equipped with NBC equipment. Since the REC limits laid down by the commander will dictate the duration of stay in the contaminated area, the staff must plan for the timely relief of such units. Units while forced to occupy ground in contaminated areas must take measures to reduce surface radioactivity by overturning the topsoil.
- **Operational Manoeuvres including Actual Fighting:** This task must be carried out by armoured units and formations because of the protection enjoyed by them against gamma radiation.

Contamination Control

Once the local fallout has settled over the ground, it is likely to remain there unless disturbed by wind or rain or the frequent passage of men and material through contaminated zones. Hence, one of the major responsibilities of commanders conducting operations in a post-strike environment will be to prevent radioactivity from spreading to newer areas. Limiting the spread of contamination will not only help in reducing the decontamination burden but will also reduce unwarranted exposure of troops to radiation. Since contamination control involves restricting the movement of personnel and equipment into contaminated areas, it is easier said than done. Units have to be sent into contaminated areas for S&R, casualty evacuation, recovery of important equipment and conduct of tactical manoeuvres, including actual combat with enemy troops, if necessitated due to operational reasons. Some of these, like S&R operations are time critical and cannot be delayed beyond a particular time for radioactivity to decay. Commanders and staff officers will have to frequently review the requirement of conducting

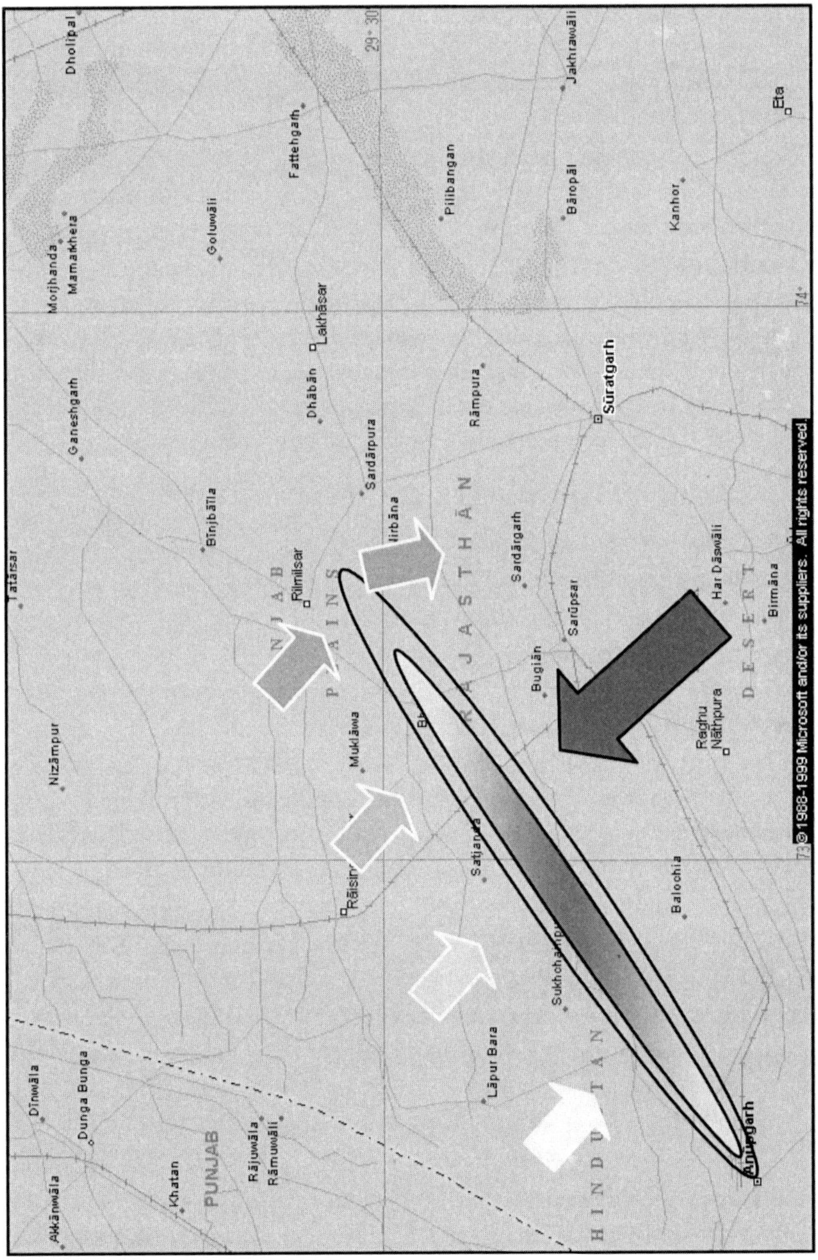

Map 8: Enemy Options after a Counter-force Nuclear Strike

operations in contaminated zones and make constant efforts to keep them to a bare minimum. Some additional measures that can be undertaken to limit the spread of contamination are as follows:

- **Controlled Entry and Exit:** The entry into and exit from contaminated areas will have to be restricted and when required, must be conducted from specified locations.
- **Route Restrictions:** Most of the units exiting from contaminated areas will be first moving to decontamination areas. Routes for movement to decontamination sites must be earmarked and monitored periodically.
- **Radiation Monitoring Detachments:** Somewhere near the formation's rear boundary, there will be a requirement to establish radiation monitoring stations for checking contamination levels on vehicles moving rearwards. These monitoring detachments can be co-located with existing traffic control posts. These detachments must be equipped with radiation detection gates rather than hand-held detection equipment.

GUIDING PRINCIPLES: DECONTAMINATION

- Decontaminate as soon as possible.
- Decontaminate only what is necessary.
- Decontaminate as far forward as possible.
- Decontaminate by priority.

Decontamination

Contaminated material poses problems of varied nature. Not only can it spread contamination to newer areas, it can also be lethal to unprotected troops. Operating with contaminated equipment means stringent MOPP levels for personnel and hatched down conditions for armoured vehicles. All these reduce fighting efficiency and increase fatigue among soldiers. Hence, decontamination is essential to restore fighting efficiency of contaminated units. This must be done at the earliest and as near to the incident site as is technically feasible.

Decontamination Types: The type of decontamination that may be resorted to by units and troops is dependent on the operational situation and level of contamination. Although academic, the types of decontamination are being mentioned to bring out the diversity of resources required as part of NBC equipping for the armed forces.

- **Emergency Decontamination:** Emergency decontamination forms part of personal decontamination and is done as a life saving measure by immediately neutralising or removing contamination from the exposed portion of the skin. It should be started as soon as the fallout has ceased or immediately after exiting from contaminated areas. Emergency decontamination kit must form part of a soldier's IPE.

- **Partial Decontamination:** Partial decontamination removes or neutralises all visible or detectable contamination from individual clothing and equipment and from those surfaces or equipment that operators or crew must touch to perform their mission, e.g., the operator's controls, weapons firing controls, and the exit and entry paths. Such selective decontamination inhibits the spread of contamination and also sustains the combat potential of the contaminated force. Partial decontamination kits must be authorised on all 'A' vehicles and 'crew served weapon' systems.
- **Complete Decontamination:** Complete decontamination is anything that reduces all or most of the contamination hazard to a level that permits removal of the protective mask and gloves. The aim is to restore combat effectiveness by eliminating the need for soldiers to fight and operate while wearing all their MOPP gear. To attain this goal, decontamination efforts must reduce residual contamination to negligible risk levels.

Decontamination Burden: A nuclear strike in the TBA will entail partial or complete decontamination of hundreds of vehicles of various types on an almost daily basis. On the first day, S&R operations by two mechanised infantry battalions will mean that almost 100 armoured vehicles will need to be decontaminated. This does not include the surviving armoured vehicles present in the target area or the NBC reconnaissance vehicles of the specialist NBC units carrying out radiological survey. From day two onwards, the decontamination effort will depend upon the employment of combat units in contaminated areas, besides the conduct of S&R and salvage operations. Such large-scale decontamination effort in a short period of time will require automation during pre-wash, application of decontaminant and post-wash activities, which are an essential part of the decontamination procedure. Since the resources of the affected formation will generally be inadequate to meet such a large requirement, the resources of neighbouring formations will also need to be pooled.

Decontamination Sites: While complete decontamination for restoration of fighting efficiency will be time-consuming and resource-intensive and must be carried out during a lull in the battle, partial decontamination can be carried out by the establishment of a hasty decontamination site within the TBA, to partially restore fighting efficiency. The site must be large enough so that sufficient dispersal of vehicles, equipment and personnel can be managed. Since water is an essential consumable in any decontamination operation, the site must be close to a water source. The area should provide natural drainage so that waste water can be canalised into a limited area after decontamination. Care should be taken that the contaminated waste water does not contaminate the water source. Decontamination sites, especially in high threat areas, can be earmarked and prepared in advance if required.

Disposal of Waste: The decontamination site is likely to be heavily contaminated and may pose a hazard to follow-on troops. The decontamination site is recommended to be marked with appropriate flags depicting radiological contamination. Time permitting, the hasty decontamination sites must be sprayed using universal decontaminants. Deliberate decontamination operations after the war will attract more stringent procedures for waste disposal.

Miscellaneous Aspects

Disposal of the Deceased: In an NBC environment, to prevent contamination from spreading, corpses contaminated by chemical or biological hazards are recommended to be incinerated, whereas those suffering from radioactive contamination are required to be buried. Hence, most of the fatalities among soldiers and civilians, irrespective of their religious denominations, must be buried. The major decision dilemmas facing military commanders in such a situation should not be 'how to do it', but 'when to do it'. Early disposal of the deceased is a moral obligation but involves sending personnel to high radiation zones near the GZ, where most of the bodies would be located. Inordinate delay will make the task more repulsive and unpleasant, besides increasing the chances of spreading secondary contamination as well as disease. Whenever a taskforce is formed to dispose of the deceased, it should be well protected and suitably grouped with trained personnel and heavy earth-moving equipment. In all cases, the dead are not recommended to be buried outside the contaminated areas.

Refugee Control: The national census of 2001 gives an average population density in the State of Rajasthan as 423 persons per square kilometre. Considering that the fallout is spread over 300 square kilometres, it implies that a maximum of about 126,900 persons will be required to be temporarily relocated. This should be the task of the state government and the Army will have little role to play in it. However, the problem that will confront the local commanders will be from a larger number of people who would be fleeing in panic. Such an uncontrolled exodus can contaminate fresh areas; hamper monitoring of people affected by contamination for treatment, besides interfering with the Army's post-strike consequent management operations. While there may be a need for relocation of genuinely displaced persons, there will be an operational need to stop directionless and panic-stricken crowds from roaming about aimlessly. Local commanders will have to work in close coordination with the civil administration and provide them necessary guidance and advice. In order to prevent this uncontrolled exodus, the civil administration can consider banning mechanical transport for a few days in the vicinity of the strike area as well as take measures to reassure the people.

Management of Contaminated Areas: Specialist NBC units of the Army, while carrying out a radiological survey, would have marked the contaminated areas. These temporary markings can be related to a dose rate between 10 to 30 rads/hour, prevalent at the time of the survey. This activity level will take about 5 to 6 years to come down to permissible radiation exposure limits laid by the AERB for yearly exposure of workers employed in the nuclear industry in India. Obviously, the contaminated area will have to be vacated of permanent settlements as stay beyond a year would be hazardous, as per AERB guidelines. The initial markings of the area will need to be converted into permanent fences with suitable sign posts to prevent people and cattle from straying in. In addition, soil from radiation hot spots may have to be treated, removed, overturned or even buried under fresh soil to reduce the surface activity levels. These tasks will have to be performed by personnel of the state agriculture department, NDRF battalions of the NDMA or even NGOs under the expert advice of DAE personnel. The Army's role in such tasks will be non-existent or minimal at best. The assistance it may provide should be limited to handing over the radiological survey reports carried out during the initial stages or during resurvey.

NBC Equipment

The capability of our armed forces to conduct operations in a contaminated environment with minimal degradation, as envisaged in the nuclear doctrine is, to a large extent, dependent upon the availability of NBC equipment, besides development of drills and procedures for various missions that the army may be required to undertake in contaminated areas. Some of the guiding precepts for drills and procedures have been enunciated but there is a need to look at the requirement of NBC equipment.

Types of Equipment: A wide range of NBC equipment is available globally and also manufactured indigenously. The NBC equipment of the strike and defensive formations of the Indian Army must primarily assist them to 'survive and fight' in a contaminated environment and should not be focused for 'consequence management'. NBC equipment of specialist NBC units needs to be more diverse. Most of these aspects have been amplified when covering the nature of post-strike operations.

Personnel Protective Equipment: It is often wrongly believed that NBC suits and masks provide protection against nuclear radiation. Fallout radiation, which are primarily gamma rays, cannot be stopped with NBC suits. These suits prevent internal contamination by preventing the inhalation of radiological dust. Hence, troops entering contaminated areas will need to be suitable equipped with IPE. The IPE must also contain emergency decontamination kits as well as drugs and medicines, both for prophylactic treatment and administration of antidotes.

Collective Protection: Collective NBC protection is required to provide a contamination free environment for command and control elements; medical echelons; personnel working in decontamination sites; and for the rest and relief of combat units. NBC shelters should be a mix of inflatable types, which can be quickly erected or containerised, which provide better protection. Integrated field shelters, which are usually constructed underground and provide protection from blast, thermal and nuclear radiation, have little utility in our context because the threat can never be accurately assessed in either time and space.

Radiation Detection and Measuring Instruments: These equipment measure 'dose rate' and 'accumulated dose' and assist troops to work within the laid down REC. While the detection equipment of combat units must be sensitive in ranges of expected REC, the equipment of specialist NBC units needs to be more diverse to detect very faint to intense radiation levels. Besides hand-held detection equipment, there is also a requirement to consider unmanned radiation monitoring gates for contamination control and post-decontamination monitoring. This calls for a wider range of detection equipment to be inducted for specialist NBC units.

Decontamination Equipment: Since operations in contaminated areas will be mostly led by mechanised troops, the decontamination burden of armoured and soft-skinned vehicles will be colossal. In order to save time, an 'assembly line' type of decontamination system would be needed for hasty decontamination. Deliberate decontamination including removal of internal contamination from vehicles will, however, remain a manpower-intensive activity, for which a vehicle-based mobile decontamination station is more suited.

Brick System of Equipping: NBC equipment is expensive and most of it has a short shelf-life. Hence, across-the-board equipping for all soldiers of the Indian Army will be a prohibitively expensive proposition. In any case, the Army is not expecting to fight in a heavily contaminated battle field resulting from large-scale use of nuclear weapons, something which was envisaged by the Soviet Union and Western nations during the height of the Cold War. The possibility of counter-force strikes, though greater than counter-value strikes, will not only be limited in numbers but also restricted to specific areas. Any further escalation may graduate to counter-value strikes. Hence, a brick system of equipping is recommended. A basic NBC brick, comprising of essential NBC equipment, can be used for combat or combat support units of the infantry, artillery or engineers. Armoured formations can have an enhanced scaling of NBC items like decontamination equipment in their bricks. Medical bricks must be authorised to select medical establishments. However, specialist NBC units must have their NBC equipment authorised on their war establishment tables. NBC bricks should be stocked as per 'risk profiling' of various sectors. The level of stocking in a theatre will depend upon the nature and scale of operations that are planned to be undertaken in the sector.

ENDNOTES

1. "Draft Report of the National Security Advisory Board on Indian Nuclear Doctrine," 17 August 1999, http://www.indianembassy.org/policy/CTBT/nuclear_doctrine_aug_17_1999.html, accessed on 20 November 2008

2. Indian Army Doctrine, http://ids.nic.in/doctrine.htm, accessed on 20 December 2008.
3. The Indian Army Doctrine, while describing the 'Types of War', mentions only the offensive use of nuclear weapons under 'Nuclear Warfare'. There is no mention of NBC defence.
4. This is possible in the case of point source only. In case of fallout radiation, troops may have to enter contaminated areas for operational tasks.
5. Radiation Exposure Guidelines are known as Operational Exposure Guidelines (OEG) in NATO parlance. These lay down exposures of up to 50 rads, between 50 to 70 rads and between 70 to 150 rads during war as negligible, moderate and emergency risks respectively. OEG Criteria both for war and peace is a subject of debate and under revision.
6. Radiation exposure limits laid down by AERB for workers employed in the nuclear industry is 30 milli-siverts (mSv) per year.
7. The radiation exposure guidelines have been suggested by the author for various tasks based on own knowledge and experience. They have no medical sanctity.
8. The nuclear detection equipment of the armed forces will be customised to measure higher dose rates because REC limits will be higher during war. Most of the detection equipment has a margin of error, which is usually about 10 percent. Use of such instruments will be of little use during peace time when REC limits will be low.
9. A node is a strong defensive position that is usually occupied in the desert.
10. Army Field Manual FM 3-3, *Chemical and Biological Contamination Avoidance* (Washington, D.C.: Department of the Army, 1992), pp. 3-7.
11. Ibid, pp. 3-31.
12. Ibid, pp. 3-16.

14

Post-Strike Response in a Metropolis

Introduction

Hiroshima and Nagasaki, the only two incidents of a nuclear strike over populated areas, occurred at a time when no effective mechanism in terms of 'preparedness' or 'response' was in place for facing the disaster that was to follow. Local municipal authorities, civil defence personnel, health officials, or even the specialised intervention by a team of US military and scientists after the nuclear strike, had no knowledge of the long-term effects of radiation on human beings. Fortunately, both the nuclear strikes were air bursts and hence produced no local fallout or else fatalities as a result of an 'uninformed and hasty response' would have increased the casualties dramatically. Since then, the world has witnessed two major nuclear accidents. The Three Mile Island (TMI) accident near Pennsylvania in 1979 and the Chernobyl disaster in 1987, both leaked substantial amounts of radioactivity into the environment. However, even a serious nuclear accident like a 'reactor core meltdown' does not result in a detonation, because the release of energy is not instantaneous. Apart from the TMI and Chernobyl episodes, minor accidents involving radioactive release include the criticality accident at Tokaimura, Japan, in 1999. The experience gained from such incidents has led to the development of a more technical and scientific response mechanism to handle situations involving the release of radioactivity into the environment.

The US has conducted almost 1054 nuclear tests till date. While most of them have been conducted to develop or perfect designs of nuclear weapons, some have been conducted to study the 'effects', including those from fallout radiation. Since the use of nuclear weapons during the Cold War was a distinct threat facing the US and its NATO allies, a large number of 'drills and procedures' were evolved to conduct military operations in a radiologically contaminated environment. These resulted in the publication of a large number of field manuals (FM) on the subject. However, what needs to be noted is that most of these were theoretical models and had never been tested in an actual environment, for obvious reasons. Some of these FMs also form the basis of NBC training in the Indian Army.

In the Indian context, no models, case studies or research works are available that lay down even broad guidelines for tackling a large-scale disaster that will follow a nuclear strike over a densely populated area. Owing to the disproportionate number of casualties due to a nuclear strike on a counter-value target, as compared to a purely military one, this section will rely on synthesising the mitigation techniques of conventional disaster management with the drills and procedures for post-strike military operations and also include some lessons learnt from accidents involving radioactive material. However, while adapting the military method of post-strike consequence management on a larger canvas of a metro like Delhi, all the concepts and templates cannot be applied without necessary modification. There is a need to consider some fundamental differences that exist between the two situations:

- In case of a counter-force strike, troops will be better prepared both mentally and psychologically as compared to the civilian population, owing to their better training, and probably, an advance warning of an impending nuclear strike. Being a disciplined body, they are likely to respond as directed even after a strike. In contrast, the civilian population is likely to panic, which may result in all-round chaos. In such a situation, rumours are likely to spread thick and fast. Hence, one of major tasks of the government and disaster management institutions will be to establish early contact with the affected citizens to restore their confidence.
- A defensive military deployment like a brigade node, even after being hit with a 10 kiloton nuclear weapon, will be approachable from any direction due to the vast open stretches of land surrounding it. This will not be possible in a large metropolis, where most of the routes will be blocked by a fleeing population. Hence, the mounting of consequent management operations is likely to be more exacting.
- There will be a large number of displaced personnel in a metropolis. Even though they may not be injured to the extent that they require hospitalisation, they will have to be provided shelter. The sheltering of temporarily displaced personnel will not be a problem in a military situation but will be a major problem in a city. Overcrowded temporary shelters with inadequate facilities may have their own problems like the maintenance of public order, sanitation, outbreak of diseases, etc.
- Unlike a soldier, a civilian is not trained to administer first aid. The requirement of administering immediate first aid and the requirement of specialised facilities for the treatment of a very large number of injured will be a major problem.

- Disaster relief efforts of the government during natural calamities are often supplemented by NGOs, including social and religious organisations. In the aftermath of a nuclear strike, such organisations will neither be equipped nor trained to handle relief efforts in contaminated conditions. Hence, per force, the relief effort will have to be undertaken by trained and suitably equipped personnel.

Institutional Framework for Disaster Management

In India, an institutional framework for dealing with natural disasters has been in existence for quite some time. This framework is headed by the Cabinet Committee for Management of Natural Disasters (CCMND), National Crisis Management Committee (NCMC) and the Crisis Management Group (CMG). However, after the passage of the National Disaster Management Act and the establishment of NDMA in 2005, the institutional framework for disaster management has been further streamlined and strengthened. The existing framework caters for the implementation of disaster prevention and mitigation, including plans for long-term recovery and rehabilitation. It also caters for providing the required political direction and higher leadership as well as a mechanism for coordination between various ministries and departments of the Government of India to deal with a large-scale disaster. The charter of NDMA includes preparation and response to man-made disasters, apart from the naturally occurring ones and accordingly it is in the process of formulating separate Standard Operating Procedures (SOPs) and guidelines for chemical, biological, radiological and nuclear disasters.[1] Since a broad framework for the management of large-scale disasters including those having a nuclear dimension already exists, prima facie, there is no need for a new organisational set-up to deal with the aftermath of a nuclear strike. Notwithstanding the fact that some apex organisational institutions may not survive a nuclear strike on the national capital or their effectiveness may be severely eroded, there is a need to look at the broad framework that will come into play after a nuclear strike.

- **Cabinet Committee on Security** (CCS): The highest decision making body at the centre is the Union Cabinet headed by the Prime Minister. Although there is a separate CCMND, but in the unfortunate event of the nation being targeted with nuclear weapons, it will be the CCS that will provide the overall political leadership and guidance. Punitive retaliation, which is an intrinsic part of India's nuclear doctrine, will also be decided by the CCS, but this aspect is not being factored in. In addition, it is assumed that the Prime Minister or his designated successors will survive to facilitate the higher decision-making process.
- **National Disaster Management Authority** (NDMA): The NDMA constituted in 2005 has the Prime Minister as its chairman. It has nine members including the Vice Chairman. At the functional level, the

NDMA has various sub committees to address various aspects of a disaster like relief, rehabilitation, etc. Usually, the NDMA constitutes an advisory committee of experts in the field of disaster management. There are also groups that specialise in various types of disasters, including CBRN disasters. The NDMA will have the responsibility of laying down policies, plans and guidelines for management of disasters.

- **National Executive Committee (NEC):** A NEC of secretaries to the central ministries and departments assists the NDMA. The NEC is required to prepare a National Disaster Management Plan in consonance with national policy laid down by the NDMA and in consultation with state governments and expert bodies and organisations in the field of disaster management.
- **National Crisis Management Committee (NCMC):** The NCMC had been in existence much before the constitution of the NDMA by the government. The Cabinet Secretary is the Chairman of the NCMC and it has secretaries from MHA, MEA, MoD, Ministries of Railways, Power, Petroleum and Natural Gas, Civil Aviation and Departments of Animal Husbandry, Drinking Water and Supply, Food and Public Distribution, Health, Road Transport and Highways and Rural Development, besides the Planning Commission. The Services are represented by the Chief of Integrated Staff Committee (CISC).
- **Crisis Management Group (CMG):** The CMG normally functions under a special secretary from the MHA to deal with matters related to major natural calamities. The CMG is basically subordinate to the NCMC and translates its decisions into action by closely interacting with the various ministries and departments in the Government of India. The CMC has joint secretaries as members from practically all ministries and departments represented in the NCMC.
- **Organisational Structure at State and District Level:** The National Disaster Management Act of 2005 provides for the establishment of State Disaster Management Authorities (SDMA). However, most of the states are still in the process of setting up state authorities for disaster management. The SDMAs, once operational, will have the respective Chief Ministers as chairpersons, with ministers from various departments as members. It is envisaged that the SDMAs will have four functional groups that will be assigned tasks like 'Hazard Mitigation', 'Preparedness and Capacity Building', 'Relief and Response', and 'Administration and Finance'. The state governments are also required to establish district-level Disaster Management Authorities (DDMA) with the District Magistrate as the chairperson and elected representatives of the local authority as co-chairpersons. The other members of the DDMA will include the Superintendent of Police, Chief Medical Officer and two district-level officers.

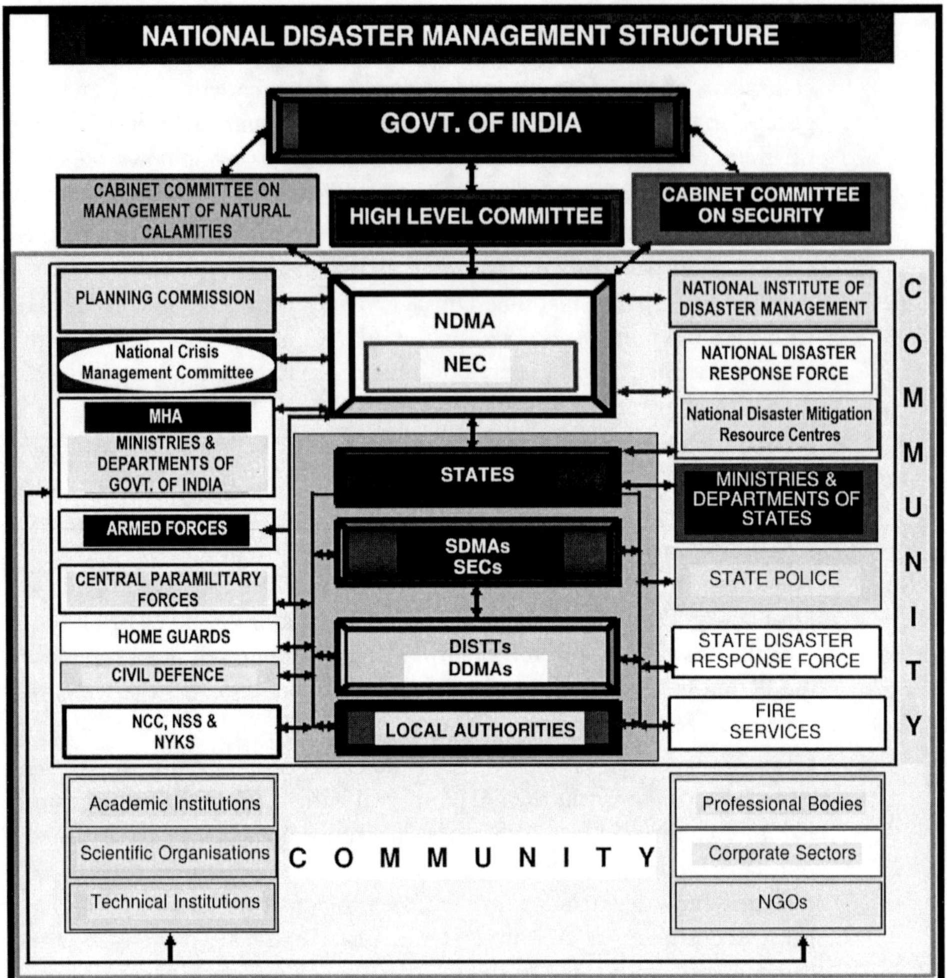

Notes: 1. This diagram reflects interactive linkages for synergised management of disasters and not a hierarchical structure.
2. Backward and forward linkages, especially at the functional level, are with a view to optimise efficiency.
3. Participation of the Community is a crucial factor.

Figure 7: Broad Disaster Management Structure at National Level[2]

Nuclear Disaster Management

In India, the DAE has been identified as the nodal agency for the management of man-made radiological emergencies in the public domain. Accordingly, since 1987, the DAE maintains a separate Crisis Management Group. In case of a nuclear emergency, the CMG of DAE will be required to co-ordinate between the local authority in the affected area and the NCMC. The CMG comprises of senior officials drawn from various units of the DAE like the Nuclear Power Corporation of India Ltd (NPCIL), Bhabha Atomic Research Centre (BARC), Heavy Water Board (HWB) and the Directorate of Purchase and Stores (DP&S) besides senior officials from the regulatory authority, the Atomic Energy Regulatory Board (AERB).[3] Several resource agencies from the BARC also back up the CMG. They can provide advice and assistance in the areas of radiation measurement and protection and medical assistance to radiation affected personnel.

The DAE visualises four types of nuclear emergencies in the facilities being operated by them. These are 'Emergency Standby', 'Plant Emergency', 'Site Emergency' and 'Offsite Emergency'. Among these, only an offsite emergency may release radioactivity into the public domain. To tackle such hypothetical scenarios, detailed response plans have been drawn up for each site by concerned district administrations and the NPCIL. The response plans extend to about 16 kilometres from the nuclear plant and this area is referred to as the 'Emergency Planning Zone'.[4] In addition, the DAE also maintains two Emergency Control Rooms (ECRs) in Mumbai, at two different locations, which are manned and operated round-the-clock and on all days of the year. These ECRs maintain continuous contact with all the critical facilities of the department with a variety of communication links.

In order to prepare the different state disaster management agencies to face the challenges of nuclear and radiological emergencies, the NDMA on 24 February 2009 came out with a comprehensive plan which included, among other things, setting up of an Emergency Response Centre (ERC) in all major metros.[5] In the first phase, all cities having a population of above 20 lakhs are to be covered by the ERCs and in phase two, the remaining metropolitan cities having populations of above 10 lakh will be covered. The establishment of ERCs in all major cities will mean that there will be a basic framework available in most cities to deal with nuclear emergencies.

Response Organisations

NDRF: The NDMA has raised eight battalions of paramilitary forces for specialised emergency response during disasters and designated them as the National Disaster Response Force (NDRF). The eight battalions can provide 144 S&R teams of 45 personnel each. Four of the NDRF battalions are specially mandated to handle CBRN disasters. These battalions are located at Pune, Delhi (Noida), Chennai and Guwahati. The general superintendence, direction and control of the force is vested and exercised by the NDMA and the command and supervision of the force is vested with the Director General NDRF. So, besides the NDRF battalion located at Delhi, there will be a need to mobilise the other three battalions by air to strengthen the response element. In fact, the air mobility of NDRF battalions in times of a crisis must be part of the standard operating procedures.

DAE: Each nuclear power plant in the country can mobilise a few teams each from its emergency response element. These DAE teams with their radiation monitoring instruments will be an asset. Besides the response element for disaster management, there will be a need to monitor and survey the affected areas after fallout has settled. Teams from the BARC or other establishments of the DAE must be incorporated in this effort.

Armed Forces: The Indian Army is in the process of creating a capability to conduct operations in a CBRN environment. Besides the issue of protective NBC equipment to select formations, the process entails raising of specialist units for carrying out tasks like NBC reconnaissance, monitoring, survey, marking and decontamination. The army possesses a handsome capability in terms of mobile medical echelons, which can come in handy for rapid deployment in a disaster situation. Specialist NBC teams and the medical echelons of the army, if uncommitted in actual operations, can be mobilised to strengthen the response elements.

State Government Resources: The response element of the concerned state government, in terms of medical teams, fire brigade personnel, home guards and local police, will be the first to be employed in any disaster, including one having a nuclear dimension. Their continued support will be essential for the success of consequent management operations being organised under the aegis of the NDMA.

Ministry of Health and Family Welfare (MoHFW): The bulk of the medical teams, in the case of a nuclear disaster, will be provided by the MoHFW. The NDMA will have to lay down suitable guidelines for the mobilisation of medical resources in consultation with MoHFW.

Foreign Assistance: The scale of the disaster following a nuclear exchange will be so huge that it may be impossible for one nation alone to meet the challenge by itself. Like in natural disasters, foreign assistance will be offered and the government may be forced to accept it. Foreign assistance could be from individual countries or offered under the auspices of the UN. It could range from urban S&R teams to medical hospitals, consignments of drugs and medicines, tents etc.

Command and Control

All response elements in the disaster zone will operate as per a National Response Plan under the overall supervision of the NDMA. These response elements will be organised into mission-oriented composite task forces. To obviate the problems of coordination and control, the NDMA will have to set various guidelines for interoperability among the diverse response elements, by laying down a core set of concepts, operating principles and common terminologies and techniques for carrying out the task. The armed forces will prefer to maintain their chain of command, especially if they are a major contributor and nominated as the lead agency for consequent management operations in the aftermath of a nuclear strike. In case their participation is limited to a few specialist teams, they must receive tactical and technical direction from the nominated task force commander. The close supervision of task forces must follow the Incident Command System by establishing an Incident Command Post (ICP). This system is recommended because the authority of the ICP will span multiple jurisdictions and will allow various agencies with diverse legal, geographical, financial and functional authorities to work together. During the initial stages, the state resources are likely to be committed first and the national resources are expected to build upon them. The SDMA may well establish their operations centre on which the ICP must be superimposed by the NDMA.

Incident Command Post (ICP): The management of the disaster following a nuclear strike will require a multi-disciplinary response from all organs of the government. Such a situation also necessitates that the consequent management operations in contaminated areas are guided by professionally competent people in a scientific and technically sound manner. The existing institutional mechanism for the management of natural disasters is adequate to elicit the desired response and cooperation of various ministries and departments but it cannot be entrusted with the management and supervision of post-strike operations. To exercise close control over post-strike operations, there will be a need to establish the ICP. It will have two broad responsibilities. First, to function as a link between the NCMC and CMG so that other ministries and departments could be tasked; and second, to guide day-to-day operations of the response teams in contaminated areas through a task force commander. The concept is explained in Diagram 3.

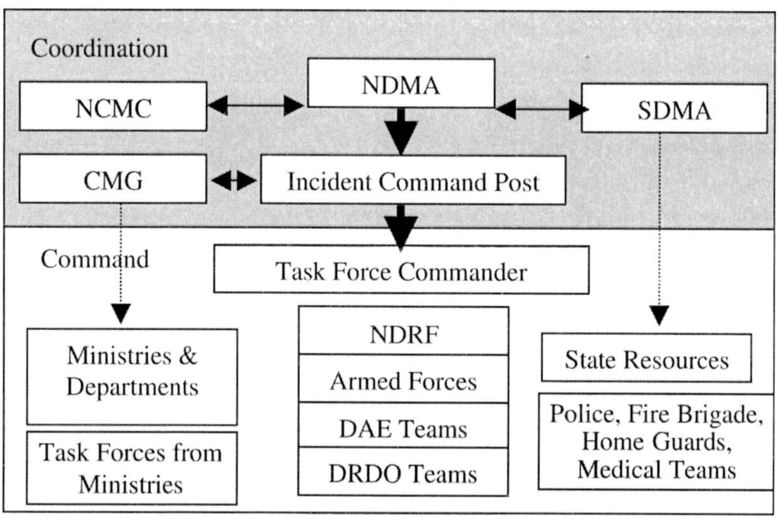

Diagram 3: Recommended Command and Control Structure

Tasks and Responsibilities: The tasks of the ICP will be to guide and coordinate a post-strike response through the task force commander. Its tasks will include the following:

- Assess the damage information being received.
- Coordinate with CMG about the involvement of various ministries and departments.
- Coordinate with SDMA for the employment of local resources.
- Prepare situation reports.
- Update the CCS and the NCMC on the current situation.
- Brief media on the latest situation.
- Advice the task force commander on the employment of various response elements.
- Guide the task force commander on technical matters like survey, monitoring, contamination control, decontamination, etc.

Command and Control: The ICP must function under the vice chairman of the NDMA.

Composition of ICP: The composition of the ICP must be laid down as part of the SOP on the management of post-strike responses. The ICP should be composed of persons from the NDMA (nuclear division), DAE (radiological safety and nuclear medicine department), DRDO (scientists working in the field of radiations—Defence Lab, Jodhpur and INMAS, Delhi) Faculty of NBC Protection, College of Military Engineering, Pune, DDG NBCW, Army HQ, MHA and DG NDRF.

Location of ICP: The ICP members should physically assemble at the disaster site immediately after the incident. Since most of the members would have to be 'flown in', ideally, the ICP should be established near an airport. Here, it would also be able to receive and guide various response elements. It can be housed in two or three aircraft hangars to provide it the required working space. These must be made available by the Ministry of Civil Aviation or the Airport Authority of India, along with elementary communication, which must be augmented by the Department of Telecommunications as soon as possible.

Method of Functioning: Situation awareness is important to understand the operational parameters in a contaminated environment. This awareness generation for the ICP must be based on Geographical Information System (GIS) maps for the city, if available. In the absence of GIS maps, normal maps with overlays of hospital data, emergency services, transportation networks, hazard-affected areas and weather can be used. The ICP must function in a corroborative environment. Since its tasks are enormous, it will have to form various sub-groups to monitor them. Some of these could be as follows:

- Mitigation sub-group.
- Medical services and public health sub-group.
- Emergency services sub-group to look after tele-communications, water supply and power.
- Information sub-group.
- Infrastructure sub-group to deal with transport, road, rail and air communication and public works.
- Human services sub-group to look after the requirement of housing, tents and relocation of people.
- Law and order, public safety and security sub-group.
- Fire fighting and hazardous material handling sub-group.
- Long-term recovery and rehabilitation sub-group.

Task Force Commander: The response elements assembled for nuclear disaster management could by commanded by the Director General NDRF, with an Army officer as his deputy. The task force commander will be responsible for the deployment of field teams based on priorities laid down by the ICP. Initially, S&R and medical teams may get priority, based on the assessment of the situation. Deployment in later stages will be based on survey reports. Some of the major responsibilities of the task force commander would be as follows:

- Exercise intimate command and control over various task forces.
- Allot appropriate missions and obtain feedback.
- Allocation of resources to the task forces.
- Lay down REC for various missions.
- Monitor movement of radioactive cloud.
- Organise the survey of fallout affected areas by employment of aerial resources or ground teams.

Type of Operations

The post-strike operations of the armed forces were focused to negate the possibility of the enemy exploiting an adverse situation created by a nuclear strike. In a counter-value strike, the over-riding criteria must be to limit the catastrophe and save as many lives as possible. Broadly, the operations that are recommended to be undertaken in such a situation are as follows:

- Information Operations.
- Medical Management Operations.
- S&R Operations.
- Radioactive Monitoring and Survey.
- Relocation of People.
- Disposal of the Deceased.

Information Operations

The general public in India is unaware of basic civil defence measures that need to be adopted during hostilities like precautions during an air raid or fire fighting drills. Hence, it would be highly unreasonable to assume that they would even be remotely aware of preventive or post-strike measures that need to be taken during a nuclear attack. This is because the awareness level of Indians on nuclear aspects is abysmally low. A post-election national opinion poll in 1999 had found that over half the Indian population had not heard of the May 1998 nuclear tests.[6]

A nuclear education and awareness campaign, especially in a period of heightened tension before the outbreak of hostilities or after their commencement, will be avoided by any government as this can create unnecessary panic. Such action was not initiated during the nuclear crisis of sorts during the Kargil war as also during Operation Parakram. Hence, it would be realistic to conclude that, in case of a nuclear attack, most people would be unaware of basic precautions or survival measures. However, the political leadership and the civilian bureaucracy who would be part of the NCMC or CMG should be educated, because they too, may be oblivious to what needs to be done in such a crisis.

Like in all disasters, a lot of people will be seeking information and guidance. These will include survivors of the strike, people unaffected but in close proximity of the strike, media, relatives and friends of people whose cities has been targeted, NGOs and various departments of the government. Besides providing general information, there will also be a need to pass on instructions to many complex and heterogeneous groups, which broadly fall under three categories:

Category 1: The primary focus of consequent management operations should be on the injured survivors of a nuclear strike. These people will need to be told about immediate first aid measures which they can administer to themselves or to their co-survivors, elementary survival measures like how to carry out personal decontamination, what to consume, how to prevent fallout from entering homes etc. In addition, they need to be guided to designated areas within walking distances, where they may receive medical attention. Most such information can be broadcast on AM or FM radios or telecast to these survivors but unfortunately after a nuclear strike, there is a high probability that most of the user-end instruments like TV sets, radios and even mobile telephones would have been rendered unserviceable due to the EMP effect.[7] Providing information to people will be an essential element of post-strike disaster response, because most of the people would not have been educated on these aspects during peace time and any attempt to enhance their awareness level in the midst of a conflict would amount to creating panic, which any government would avoid. Hence, to pass the required instructions to the affected public, the NDMA may consider distributing disposable AM/FM tuners as the first important post-strike measure. These disposable receiver sets, along with a radio station, can be stocked centrally in an EMP-shielded environment. An FM radio station can be established next to the ICP and tuners-cum-receivers distributed aerially over the disaster zone.

Category 2: The EMP footprint of an airburst nuclear detonation will extend beyond the slant ranges affected by heat, blast or thermal radiation. Hence, most people who are immediately outside the disaster zone would also be devoid of any information. This is as good as the entire population of Delhi. These people, if not given timely information, may panic and cause a serious impediment to the mounting of rescue operations in the actual disaster zone. They have to be informed about the areas already affected or likely to be affected by fallout, areas which need to be vacated, areas which are safe from radiation, clear routes for evacuation, and so on. They may also have to be informed about the dangers from radiation which are not visible to the naked eye. In case there is no imminent danger from fallout, the people need to be assured that since they have survived a nuclear strike, they are not in any immediate danger. The means of passing information and instructions are the same as has been recommended for Category 1 personnel.

Category 3: The panic that will grip the survivors of a nuclear strike on a city will be nothing in comparison to the hysteria such a strike may generate in other cities, which may fear a similar strike on them. There will be a need to reassure the population of other cities as well as to educate them about the actual dangers as brought out for Categories 1 and 2. The task of educating the public cannot be left to the media, Indian or foreign, which may unwittingly churn out totally unprofessional advice, leading to more panic. The passing of timely and factually correct information is possible only if elementary audio and video capsules on subjects like the effects of nuclear weapons, nuclear radiation, civil defence measures, first aid for burn and splinter casualties, personal protective measures, decontamination drills duly modified for home use etc have been prepared in advance by the NDMA, and on occurrence of the disaster, are distributed to the media. In fact, finalising the list of subjects itself and the preparation of short and crisp audio and video tapes in consultation with experts on NBC warfare, psychologists and eminent educationalists, would be a major exercise in itself. This should be the first step of civil defence that the NDMA must undertake to upgrade preparedness of the nation to meet such an eventuality.

Medical Management Operations

Nature of Casualties: Part II of the study has estimated that a 50 kiloton nuclear strike over New Delhi will result in the immediate death of about one to one and a half lakh people. In addition, close to five lakh people will be injured, whose medical management will assume priority. A cursory look at Tables 39, 40 and 41 indicates that the range at which the effects of blast, heat and radiation will produce fatalities is largely dependent on the yield. For lower yields, the casualty producing effects of radiation will be more pronounced at longer ranges than the effects of heat or blast, whereas, in the case of higher yields, thermal radiation will be the major contributor for fatalities. Since a nuclear strike on populated areas will invariably be of a higher yield, more casualties could be expected from thermal radiation. In case of a 50 kiloton strike, about three lakh people are likely to suffer minor injuries from the blast, accompanied by first degree burns, but with no exposure from prompt nuclear radiation. Another two and a half to three lakh people are likely to suffer from second degree burns, with penetrating or blunt injuries from the secondary effects of blast. Only about 50,000 people will suffer from severe blast injuries, accompanied with third to second degree burns and exposure to radiation.

Nature of Medical Problem: The estimate of casualties and the nature of their injuries are not the only factors that will guide the medical effort. The type of medical problems facing the survivors after a few days will present a different picture. The nature of problems that the medical authorities of the city will face is amplified in Table 51.

Table 51: Medical Problems during a Nuclear Attack

Medical Issue	H hour	D day	D plus 1 to 7	D plus 7 onwards
Flash burns	Yes	-	-	-
Blast injuries	Yes	-	-	-
Flame burns	Yes	Yes	-	-
Initial nuclear radiation	Yes	-	-	-
Fallout radiation	Yes	Yes	Yes	-
Lack of first aid	NA	Yes	Yes	
Lack of specialised medical care	-	-	Yes	Yes
Communicable diseases	-	-	Yes	Yes
Cancer/genetic problems	-	-	-	Much later

Medical Resources: To grasp the enormity of the crisis that the local administration will face in the aftermath of a nuclear strike, there is a need to evaluate the existing medical resources available in our cities and the likely problems they will face. This is being done by taking the example of New Delhi.

- **Doctors and Paramedics:** A survey carried out by the Associated Chambers of Commerce and Industry of India (ASSOCHAM) in August 2008 on the availability of doctors in New Delhi, states that "leading government hospitals such as AIIMS, Safdarjung, Ram Manohar Lohia, Guru Teg Bahadur, Lok Nayak Jaiprakash Narayan, St. Stephen's and various dispensaries and leading health charitable trusts such as Ganga Ram hospital etc. have on their payrolls doctors totalling about 10,000."[8] Since the doctors are residing in various parts of the capital, a large number among them will survive the nuclear attack, but how many will be willing to work in areas affected by contamination and how many of them will be able to reach the incident site is anybody's guess. Even if an optimistic figure of 20 percent is taken, then the ratio between the anticipated 5 lakh casualties and the doctors would be around 1:250. If a doctor was to spend 10 minutes[9] with each patient and worked continuously for 24 hours, he would be able to see only 144 casualties in a day. Mathematically, it would take about 48 hours before most of the casualties are attended to by any qualified doctor or physician.

- **Hospitals and Clinics:** The existing medical resources in the case of Delhi or for that matter any metropolis are well spread out and most of them would survive a single nuclear strike either unscathed or with minor damage. In the case of a 50 kiloton strike on Vijay Chowk, the Ram Manohar Lohia and Sucheta Kripalani (Lady Hardinge) hospitals may be destroyed. The Lok Nayak Jaiprakash Narayan, Maulana Azad and Govind Ballabh Pant hospitals will suffer minor damage but will be able to function. If, in the broad definition of 'medical resources', we also include private hospitals, nursing homes, polyclinics, private medical practitioners and their clinics, most of them would also survive a nuclear strike. The same does not hold true in the case of small towns, where most of the private nursing homes, medical clinics and the government hospital are all generally located within a radius of 2 km from the centre of the town, which is also the likely GZ. None of these facilities are likely to be available after the strike. Hence, unlike in major metros, post-strike medical management in the case of smaller towns will have to be based entirely on 'outside assistance'. Medical management in a metro will be a mix of internal resources and outside assistance. In the instance case, the total bed capacity of all medical institutions in New Delhi is given in Table 52. This capacity of 30,484 is in no way near the figure of anticipated casualties. In any case, the medical support plan for a nuclear disaster cannot be based on private medical resources, which must be considered as an additional asset. Another problem facing the Delhi administration will be that in normal times, most of the bed capacities are normally full due to heavy patient load. Discharging of seriously ill cases, even if desired in such a crisis, will be a major dilemma that will haunt the medical community.

Table 52: Bed Capacities of Medical Institutions in Delhi[10]

Type of Medical Institution	Number of Institutions	Number of Beds
Government Hospitals	70	19,287
Primary Health Centres	8	79
Maternity Homes	31	321
Private Nursing Homes	460	10,797
Total	**569**	**30,484**

- **Special Facilities:** A large proportion of the casualties will be suffering from burn injuries. Optimal therapy for severe burns requires sedation, oxygen administration and large intravenous infusion of fluids, electrolyte and plasma expanders.[11] For example, a patient weighing 70 kilograms, having burn injuries over 30 percent of his body surface will require fluid replacement in excess of 6000 ml. In addition, antibiotics, tetanus prophylaxis and local wound care will also be necessary. Severe burn cases are normally treated in special wards to prevent infection. In the case of Delhi, while the Safdarjung Hospital has a capacity of 156 beds for treating burn cases, which is the largest in Asia, it does not have standard air circulation and temperature monitoring systems. The state of the other three government hospitals, i.e., RML, LNJP and Guru Teg Bahadur, which are equipped to handle burn cases, is no better.
- **Ambulances:** The Centralised Accident & Trauma Services (CATS) of Delhi, which started functioning in 1991, has only 30 ambulances deployed in about 30 stations.[12] While there are a large number of private ambulances available, medical management plans cannot be based on them.
- **Drugs and Medicines:** Drugs and medicines required to treat casualties of a nuclear attack will include ordinary bandages, splints, antibiotics, sterile dressings, pain killers, burn creams and lotions. Any city will run out of these stocks in case they have to treat the large number of patients that would be expected during a nuclear attack.

Medical Management: The NDMA has already issued 'Medical Preparedness and Mass Casualty Management' guidelines in 2007, primarily focusing on natural disasters. However, an extraordinary crisis that will follow a nuclear strike will require extraordinary solutions and out-of-the-box thinking. The basic medical plan for consequent management in a metro can take a leaf or two from the way the armed forces plan to deal with a nuclear strike on the TBA. Such a model would involve the establishment of an organisation for providing an orderly process of medical management, triage of the injured as per urgency of the problem, deciding on the priority of treatment and evacuation of casualties to safer areas. Civil defence planners must, however, take into consideration the disproportionate number of casualties in the two scenarios. Some of the measures that could be undertaken are as follows:

- **Mobile Medical Team (MMT):** In Western countries, due to higher literacy levels, the general population is aware of emergency first aid procedures. This will be a major handicap in our case as we will have to rely entirely on trained and qualified doctors and paramedics to administer emergency first aid. The NDMA can consider employing MMTs as part of the initial S&R teams, the concept recommended for the conduct of post-strike military operations. The MMTs will have to be earmarked both by the MoHFW and the Delhi Government. Their employment, including marrying up with S&R teams of the NDRF battalions, should be the responsibility of the ICP. Over here, it is pointless to quantify the number of MMTs that may be required, because any number will always fall short of the desired, especially during the first few days of the disaster. Ironically, their requirement during this period will be most crucial.

- **Adhoc Medical Facilities**: The treatment of five lakh non-fatal casualties will be a major challenge for the Government of Delhi and the NDMA. A major portion of these casualties (about 3 lakh) would be suffering from first degree burns and minor cuts and bruises. If not treated in time, some of these cases could turn serious. Since the existing bed capacity of hospitals in Delhi is limited, there will be an urgent need to open up new medical facilities. These facilities will have to be commissioned in areas which are easily accessible to large crowds of people. During the Katrina crisis, the Federal Emergency Management Agency (FEMA) of the US had established rehabilitation centres in existing sports stadiums. The NCT has seven[13] sports stadiums, two of which are covered. While three of these can be expected to be destroyed during a nuclear attack, the balance can be converted into adhoc hospitals. These can accommodate about 20,000 patients each. In case of open-air stadiums, tented facilities can be built upon them. Apart from these stadiums, there will be a need to identify open and unoccupied stretches of land, like on the Ridge and in the Delhi cantonment, which can also be used. The NDMA has plans to field three mobile hospitals in times of major disasters. These mobile hospitals must be container-based, which can be placed in open spaces of the city, like stadiums, with helicopters.
- **Evacuation of Casualties**: The mismatch between the anticipated casualties and survivable medical facilities indicates that Delhi, or for that matter, any metro will not be able to absorb all the casualties of a nuclear attack. These will have to be distributed to neighbouring states of Haryana, Punjab, Rajasthan, Uttar Pradesh and Uttarakhand. The planned destinations must be worked out in two tiers, which can be activated depending upon the scale of the disaster. Medicines and drugs for the management of casualties in the destination towns and cities must be stored in the form of medical bricks, with plans to requisition additional doctors and specialists. This large-scale movement of casualties to tier 1 and tier 2 cities can be affected by special ambulance trains. The Delhi government's disaster management plan must include the requirement of trains and entraining stations corresponding to each destination. This will depend upon the bed capacities available in destination towns and cities. The plan must be based on several entraining stations as suggested in Table 53. The entraining stations of Delhi

cantonment and Shakur Basti are ideal due to open spaces around them and relatively less crowded approaches. Disaster management plans must earmark at least two to three casualty evacuation stations and the DDA must ensure that the areas around these stations remain de-congested and free from encroachment. The casualty evacuation could also include air resources by hiring of civil aircraft. In a post-strike situation, the aviation industry would be the worst hit and most of the airlines would be only too happy to offer their otherwise idle aircraft. Air evacuation can ensure that the serious casualties are distributed throughout the country.

Table 53: Stations for Ambulance Trains

Station	Destination	Railways
Delhi Cantonment	Jaipur	Northern Railway
Shakur Basti	Rohtak, Ferozepur	Northern Railway
Sabzi Mandi	Karnal, Ambala	Northern Railway
Hazrat Nizammudin	Faridabad, Mathura, Agra	Central Railway
Shahdara	Dehradun, Saharanpur, Aligarh	Northern Railway

- **Reorganisation of Existing Hospitals:** Existing hospitals will have to be geared for immediate sorting out of casualties. The triage must decide the priority for admissions in existing hospitals. To deal with casualties that are likely to be denied admission, the concept of adding a MTC to existing government hospitals is recommended. The hospitals will also have to establish a CDC in a post-attack crisis, for which necessary work must commence during peace time. The necessary technical guidelines for the construction of CDCs can be issued by the NDMA in consultation with the DAE to the concerned state governments.
- **Medical Logistics:** The medical plan must also cater for the movement of drugs and medicines to earmarked hospitals. The medical management sub-group of the ICP will have to fly in the drugs based on the requirement of the city till the normal method or re-supply is restored.

Prophylaxis: During a nuclear detonation, radioactive iodine is released into the atmosphere which can be inhaled or ingested by the unprotected population. This iodine can get accumulated in the thyroid gland and later on may lead to cancer. To prevent internal contamination, potassium iodide tablets are recommended by health officials because normal iodine saturates the thyroid gland thereby rejecting radioactive iodine. The recommended dose is 130 mg tablets for a week. The timely distribution of potassium iodide tablets to the general populace is likely to be affected by local fallout and distribution before its actual arrival is a proposition of a very tall order. However, plans must be made to distribute these to the local populace, in case sufficient warning of a nuclear attack is available. These tablets must also be distributed to relief workers of NDRF,

Army and DAE units which will be employed in radiologically contaminated areas besides medical personnel, who would be coming in close contact with radioactive contamination. It may be noted that there is no prophylaxis against external exposure to radiation.

S&R Operations

In the case of a 50 kiloton strike over New Delhi, S&R operations will be spread over five kilometres from the GZ, covering an area of approximately 78 square kilometres. Out of this, approximately nine square kilometres at a distance from one and a half kilometres from the GZ would be completely devastated. Due to intense radioactivity levels, no S&R operations must be planned in this absolute destruction zone. However, taking a cue from military methodology, S&R operations can be planned by designating the balance area in two S&R zones. These zones will cover 22 and 47 square kilometres, respectively. The efforts of the 18 S&R teams of the NDRF battalion located in Noida can be supplemented with teams of the Army, DAE or other uncommitted NDRF battalions.

- **S&R Zone 1:** In this zone, areas that are approximately 1.2 kilometres from the GZ would be affected by NIGA radiation dose rate of about 2 rads per hour. This is when the nuclear strike over Delhi is considered as an air burst. In case of a surface burst or low air burst, the fallout considerations would apply. Unlike the scenario of post-strike operations on counter-force targets, where Army S&R teams could be based on Infantry Combat Vehicles, such equipment, even if made available to the S&R teams of the NDRF, would be of no use due to the lack of open spaces for their movement. There would be a need to group road clearing teams equipped with heavy earthmoving equipment with S&R teams operating in this zone.
- **S&R Zone 2:** The operation of S&R teams in this zone will be handicapped by crowds. Since these teams would also be encountering large and comparatively less serious casualties, there may be a need to group MMTs with them. The MMTs must be broadly aware of the medical management plans, especially the areas where 'walking wounded' type of patients need to be directed.

Urban Rescue: A post-disaster urban setting will be characterised by a requirement to reach well above the ground as well as underground, increased risk of fire due to the presence of combustible material, large electrical cabling and gas pipelines juxtaposed against shortages of water, confined spaces that will hamper the deployment of specialist equipment and unexpected risks due to the presence of hazardous material. Hence, S&R operations in an urban setting will require the deployment of specialists in urban rescue. NDRF battalions must have elements trained for such high-risk rescue operations.

Heavy Demolition Teams: There will be a need to assess buildings, especially high-rise buildings that have been partially damaged and are likely to collapse. Special demolition teams will be required from the PWD, duly assisted by Army engineers, to pull down structures that may endanger human lives or obstruct traffic.

Disposal of the Deceased

Among the many health problems that will face any metro in the aftermath of a nuclear strike will be the disposal of the deceased. In case of a 50 kiloton nuclear strike, the immediate fatalities estimated are between one to one-and-a-half lakh people. While some of the dead near the GZ will be instantly vaporised or incinerated in the resultant firestorm or secondary fires, there will still be a large number of corpses that the municipal authorities will have to dispose of immediately. In addition to immediate fatalities, a large number of injured people could be expected to die in the next few days. The figures of the persons dying daily will peak after two weeks due to the latent period after radiation exposure and before the onset of the Acute Radiation Syndrome. In fact, the daily deaths in the city will exceed the normal average for the next six to eight months before returning back to somewhere near normal.

The prompt disposal of the deceased will be essential due to the dangers that they will pose to public health. Unattended corpses can lead to the breakdown of an epidemic through their increased interaction with vectors like flies and rodents. The main problem of disposing of the deceased would be that most of them deceased would be near the GZ, where residual radiation will be most intense, thus making the task hazardous, especially for unprotected responders. After a few weeks, most of the dead bodies will accumulate near the existing hospitals or makeshift medical camps established by the State Government or the NDMA. Hence, the requirement of prompt disposal of the deceased from these areas will become more acute and demanding on municipal authorities.

Nuclear disaster management plans for most cities, including Delhi, must be under preparation. The plans of the Delhi government for the disposal of the deceased are not fully known, but if some old reports are to be believed, these border on the ludicrous and lead one to believe that the authorities are not aware of the type of disaster that would follow in the wake of a nuclear attack. One such suggestion proposed for the identification of corpses is tagging them as H for Hindu, M for Muslim and S for Sikh and so on. Such proposals can be laughed off because they would have been made keeping religious sentiments in mind, rather than the technical aspects of disposing contaminated corpses. The city administration in such a situation should not worry about finding different tags, but on earthmoving equipment, trained and motivated drivers and the necessary space for burying the dead. The requirement of space will not be a one-time requirement but will arise with regular frequency for the next few weeks, if not months. Metaphorically speaking, the crisis can also be seen as a 'great leveller'. In an instant, it will evaporate all caste, religious and socio-economic divisions of society. Every one will be on one side of the divide, i.e., being a victim of the crisis, and would be treated equally.

Radioactivity Monitoring and Survey

In the event of a nuclear strike over Delhi, either a surface or low air burst resulting in nuclear fallout, a detailed radioactive survey will be required. Since the affected areas would be inaccessible to ground-based elements, the initial survey could be planned by using UAVs or helicopters.[14] Later on, specific areas could be selected for long-term monitoring. Such monitoring must be based on unmanned sensors programmed to feed inputs on a required basis to a central facility. The regular monitoring of radioactivity levels in residential areas will be necessary because based on these inputs, the NDMA or the state government can declare the area safe for re-occupation. The NDMA must consider authorising suitable equipment to NDRF units earmarked for CBRN disasters. In addition, the NDMA and DAE may consider a radiological survey of all metros during peace time so that background radiation levels of various cities are known. These reports will assist in carrying out radiological surveys and monitoring of fallout affected areas as part of post-strike crisis management as well as dealing with cases of accidents or incidents involving radioactive material.

Radiological Exposure Criteria (REC)

The overriding consideration while laying down REC criteria and guidelines for war was whether the operations were being conducted in the face of the enemy or not. During peace time, a higher risk should be accepted if the operations involve saving human lives. Some suggested REC guidelines that can be followed for envisaged consequent management operations are given in Table 54.

Table 54: REC Guidelines for Peace

Operation	Exposure in rads		Remarks
	During 24 Hours	During One Week	
S&R	20	30	Saving human life
Operations of MMT	20	30	Saving human life
Disposal of Dead	10	20	–
Radiological Survey	5	10	–
Radiological Monitoring	1	3	–
Decontamination	10	20	Preventing spread of contamination
Terrain decontamination	5	10	Preventing spread of contamination

Theoretically, there would be a time when the dose rate in the fallout affected area has reduced to such an 'insignificant level' that the area can be termed as "safe for re-occupation". This insignificant 'dose rate' level needs to be identified by the NDMA in consultation with the scientific community. The ICRP guideline for safe radiation exposure for civilians during peace time is one mSv per year. This is an extremely low dose rate to be followed during the crisis that the nation will be facing in the aftermath of a nuclear strike. A safe dose rate level for re-occupation of an area by the civilian population will have to be established based on Indian health standards for the speedy rehabilitation of people.

Re-location of People

Even if Delhi has the misfortune of being hit with nuclear weapons, one should hope for it to be an airburst and not a surface or low airburst. In case of the latter, the people residing in a fallout affected area of approximately 200 square kilometres will have to be relocated. With an average population density of 11,436 persons per square kilometre, the number of affected people translates into a mind-boggling figure of 10 to 15 lakh. Since it will be practically impossible to shelter such a large number of displaced persons in Delhi, they will have to be relocated in rural areas adjoining the city and temporarily housed in tents. This will be a major administrative and logistic nightmare for the city administration.

The relocation will also have a socio-economic dimension attached to it. Will the government be able to acquire land in rural areas without coercion? Will such a large-scale relocation create tension between the owners of the land and the re-settled people? Some affected people would be middle class city dwellers who would lose their only houses for the next 2 to 3 years. Will such people be physically, mentally and psychologically ready to face such relocation? What about their jobs, children's education, etc. There can be no clear-cut solutions and readymade answers for such socio-economic problems that will be created after a nuclear attack on a city. However, the authorities must be aware of these while formulating relocation plans so that these can be implemented with least resistance during a crisis.

Traffic Management

There are close to 54 lakh vehicles, including two wheelers, registered in Delhi. Even if a quarter of Delhi's population decides to leave Delhi in the wake of a nuclear attack, all roads leading to the outskirts or neighbouring states will be choked with traffic. To put the problem in perspective, one lakh cars in a bumper-to-bumper mode will occupy nearly 25 kilometres of road space. However, most of the chaos will not be because of the volume of cars but because people will be driving on both sides of the divider in order to escape faster. The non-functional traffic lights inside the city will add further confusion to the chaotic situation. Only an ordinary resident of Delhi can understand the magnitude of the problem because he is witness to such chaos whenever there is a 'protest rally' or traffic is stopped or diverted due to VIP movement. Ironically, such a chaos will be created by personnel who would be unaffected by the nuclear strike. Unless controlled, such a situation has portents to become a disaster in itself. It will also be detrimental to medical management and S&R operations. Unless the roads are clear, no fire fighting can be carried out, no S&R missions attempted, debris cleared or dangerous structures demolished. The only silver lining to the grim situation being painted is that most of the vehicles may not function due to the effects of an EMP, at least in a 10 kilometre radius around the GZ.

The traffic congestion resulting from an uncontrolled exodus of people can be managed if people are forced to discard private transport in favour of public transport for travel within the city for at least one week. People wanting to leave the city must be allowed to do so systematically by laying down priorities for different localities and information provided on clear routes. Since the exodus will not be restricted to roads only, the management of crowds at airports, railway stations and bus stands will assume equal importance.

Law and Order

The crisis is likely to bring out the best and worst of Delhi in its extreme. There will be a large number of people who will respond to their inner conscience and will willingly come out to help the needy. On the other hand, there will be a large segment of the populace that may take the law into their own hands and take this opportunity to make a quick buck by targeting shops, stores, houses, banks, etc. There will be yet another category which will try and profit from hoarding essential commodities and black-marketing. In a city where road rage can kill at the least provocation, anxiety caused by the crisis may lead to increased instances of violence among people. This increased violence in its worst form may take a communal colour or a socio-economic tinge. The Delhi government will have to think of various ordinances and decrees that it may be required to proclaim in case such a situation comes to pass. Special powers to deal with hooligans and mafia must be vested with local police and NDRF units, who would be at the forefront of handling such a crisis. The normal procedure followed while rendering aid to civil authorities, of a civil magistrate handing over the situation to the armed forces, will not work.

Restoration of Infrastructure

Water Supply: Among the elementary needs of man, water occupies a life-saving status. Most city dwellers may not survive beyond a day if the water supply is disrupted. Hence, restoration of water supply to the city at the earliest should be a major priority for the city's administration. It also needs to be noted that the demand for water in a post-strike situation will go up manifold. Water will be required for fire fighting, hospitals will require additional supplies to treat patients, heat and dehydration will mean more water for ordinary people, who will also need water to decontaminate themselves. On the other hand, the timely restoration of normal water supply will be a major problem as some of the damaged pipelines and pumping stations will be located in contaminated areas. The municipal authorities will have to rethink bypassing heavily contaminated areas and restoring supplies by rerouting of water pipelines etc. Another major problem facing the administration will be the provision of contamination-free water. The water works and reservoirs may get contaminated by increased dust, smoke, dead carcasses and possibly fallout. The water supply will require increased surveillance and regular testing to prevent the outbreak of diseases and epidemics.

Power: Some sceptics may claim that the citizens of Delhi can stay without electricity for days because frequent power outages have made them used to it. While this may be true in the case of individuals, the running of essential services like hospitals, telecommunications, water treatment plants, airports and railway stations will all need an uninterrupted flow of electricity. The loss of a few electricity pylons or substations to blast or thermal effects may not cause grave damage to the national or regional power grid. However, the EMP effects may affect a larger area, which may result in a major power outage. If planned properly, restoration should be possible within a few hours or days, as most of the facilities affected by EMP would be outside the contaminated area. In case limited power supply is available, restoration of supplies to hospitals, water pumping or purification units, transportation and communication networks, industry etc., must be given priority over connections to individual households.

Telecommunications: Tele-connectivity is an inseparable part of daily life. The backbone of the telecommunication infrastructure will have to be restored at the earliest, even if user-end instruments are unavailable as a result of EMP effects. Towards this end, the Telecommunication Regulatory Authority of India may have to force telecom operators to invest in mobile towers that can be installed in disaster affected areas immediately. Such towers can also provide additional call routing options, thus decongesting the network.

TV and Radio: Most of the user-end instruments including the Direct to Home (DTH) dishes and cable network may break down due to the EMP effects of a nuclear attack. However, telecast or radio broadcasts per se are unlikely to be affected, which must continue.

Rail, Road and Air Connectivity: There is unlikely to be any inbound traffic to any city that has been hit by nuclear weapons. Air and rail connectivity will be required to assemble men and material for relief operations or for evacuation of casualties. Unless targeted, air facilities are unlikely to be disrupted. Immediate repair of railway tracks in heavily damaged and contaminated areas may be a problem but rerouting should be possible within the existing network. The Ministry of Railways and the NDMA must make contingency plans for such an eventuality in consultation with the Delhi government.

Reconstruction and Rehabilitation

Rehabilitation and reconstruction is an essential part of any disaster management plan. In a nuclear disaster, the reconstruction and rehabilitation plans will depend upon the extent and intensity of residual radioactivity. Even in case of an airburst, there will be some areas around the GZ that will not be habitable for a few years, from the public health point of view. In case of a surface or low airburst, the uninhabitable areas will increase manifold, thus enhancing the scope of rehabilitation and reconstruction. The broad options that can be contemplated by the city administration are to either seal the contaminated area for a few years or attempt deliberate decontamination operations. The latter will require select buildings to be demolished, roads and topsoil to be scraped and all the accumulated debris to be buried. The process will be tedious and its economic viability must be balanced against the likely loss of real estate in the centre of the city. On this issue, the government must be guided by the advice of experts who, in turn, must base their opinion on radiological monitoring and survey reports.

ENDNOTES

1. Some of these can be accessed at the website of National Disaster Management Agency, at http://www.ndma.gov.in.
2. "National Disaster Management Structure," http://www.ndma.gov.in, accessed on 28 February 2009.
3. "An overview of Nuclear Emergency Response Plans in the DAE," http://www.dae.gov.in/cmgweb.htm, accessed on 28 February 2009.
4. The DAE follows a zoning system around its nuclear power plants. In an 'Exclusion Zone' of 1.6 kilometres, no habitation is allowed to come up. In 'Sterilization Zone' up to 5 kilometres from the reactor, the activities are controlled so as to check undue increase in population.
5. "Government Lays down Guidelines for Nuclear Emergencies," *The Times of India,* 25 February 2009.
6. Yogendra Yadav, Oliver Heath and Anindya Saha, "Issues and Verdict," *Frontline*, 13-26 November, 1999.
7. A 50 kiloton airburst will affect most electronic devices within a radius of 30 kilometres from the GZ.
8. "Delhi Short of Over 12,500 Additional Doctors: ASSOCHAM," 25 August 2008, http://www.assocham.org/prels/shownews.php?id=1653, accessed on 20 November 2008.
9. 10 minutes has been randomly selected, although it would be grossly inadequate to treat or even diagnose casualties suffering from all three effects of a nuclear detonation, which would include second or third degree burns, haemorrhage and acute radiation sickness.
10. Government of Delhi, "Economic Survey of Delhi, 2001-02," http://delhiplanning.nic.in/economic20%survey, accessed on 24 February 2009.
11. Victor W Sidel, "The Physician's Role in Post-attack Period," in Christine Cassel, Michael McCally and Henry Abraham (eds.), *Nuclear Weapons and Nuclear War: A Sourcebook for Health Professionals* (New York: Praeger Publishers, 1984), p. 162.

12. Government of Delhi, 2001-2002, n. 10.
13. The seven major stadiums in Delhi are the Feroz Shah Kotla, Dr BR Ambedkar, Jawaharlal Nehru, Indira Gandhi, Shivaji, Talkatora and the National Stadium. The last three are expected to be destroyed.
14. Bhabha Atomic Research Centre (BARC) has developed an Aerial Gamma Spectrometry System (AGSS) and CARINS that can be mounted on a helicopter and an UAV, respectively, for radiological survey.

15

Approach to Preparedness and Capacity Building

Introduction

The effectiveness of any response mechanism during disaster management is directly dependent upon the quality of preparatory work undertaken to meet the eventuality. The same paradigm holds true while dealing with the aftermath of a nuclear strike, especially in a densely populated urban setting. The actions required to be undertaken by institutional bodies and response organisations must be thought through in their entirety, so that a credible, workable and technically feasible post-strike response plan is developed. The plans for dealing with the aftermath of a nuclear strike should be area-, or rather, city-specific, to cater for the peculiarities in its size, layout, availability of medical infrastructure, connectivity etc. These are recommended to be developed by the NDMA in consultation with the respective state governments and local municipal authorities at least for the states who have emerged as more vulnerable during the risk profiling carried out earlier.

A nuclear strike over a densely populated area will result in a number of fatal and non-fatal casualties. However, if adequate measures are instituted, the fatalities could be reduced, especially in scenarios involving single or limited nuclear strikes. Preparatory work for consequence management after a counter-value nuclear attack would generally fall under the realm of civil defence. The important aspect here is the preparation of the population to face a nuclear strike and hence, community participation is important towards capacity building.

Nuclear Civil Defence

Civil defence in a nuclear environment can be broadly classified as active and passive. Active civil defence is designed to destroy incoming weapons whereas passive civil defence reduces the danger from weapons that reach their intended targets. The focus of this section is passive civil defence measures which can be undertaken prior to the outbreak of hostilities. The usual components of such a defence are dispersal of industrial assets, evacuation of population and construction of protection shelters. In addition, "a passive defence programme will include development of warning and notification systems; communication for damage control and damage assessment; measures for ensuring continuity of the government; stockpiling of food, medical supplies, temporary shelters and other necessities for immediate post-attack period; and training of emergency personnel and the general populace."[1]

Since the possibility of the use of nuclear weapons remains low, the preparatory work for dealing with the aftermath of a nuclear strike must not invite a heavy financial burden on the exchequer. It must not be based on grandiose plans for providing security to all, as for example, the nuclear civil defence plans of some countries like Sweden and Switzerland, both non-nuclear weapon states and neutral countries. Since there is a major difference in the number of people who need to be protected and the economic resources that these countries can commit, in comparison to India, no practical lessons can be drawn. There is, hence, a requirement to analyse the Cold War experiences of the US and the erstwhile Soviet Union, both of which had a large population, in meeting the challenges of civil defence.

The United States: Passive civil defence measures in the US were taken, by and large, in 'fits and starts' – more often than not in fits, which occurred whenever there was an alarm over the Soviet Union having developed a new system or taken a technological lead. The entry of the Soviet Union into the nuclear club in 1949, followed by the invasion of South Korea a year later, saw the US Congress pass the Federal Civil Defence Act and the Defence Production Act. The latter ensured the dispersion of US defence industries. The speed on civil defence programmes soared once again when the Soviets launched the Sputnik in 1957 and during the Cuban missile crisis of 1962. Most of the funding for civil defence in the US was consumed by two programmes, namely 'evacuation and relocation plans' and 'construction of shelters'. There is a need to evaluate their applicability in the Indian context.

Soviet Union: The Soviet civil defence plans, on the face of it, were not any different from that of the US and followed the accepted model of dispersion, camouflage and concealment, construction of underground shelters and plans for the evacuation of the population from threatened urban centres. The focus of Soviet civil defence during the initial years was to disperse its defence industrial base and provide underground shelters for their work force. But even with these measures "the Soviet Union did not seek to protect more than a fraction of its total population."[2] The USSR also managed to construct a few hardened granaries and underground defence plants but all these were insufficient to meet the recovery requirements of a large-scale nuclear war. However, the growth of the Soviet defence programme during the initial years produced considerable alarm in certain quarters of the US administration, where it was interpreted as part of a Soviet plan to forgo active defence, in which the US had a technological advantage, in favour of passive defence, where the USSR had a programmatic lead.[3]

Deterrence and Nuclear Civil Defence: The protagonists of instituting civil defence measures against a nuclear attack in the US also found it as an important tool for 'escalation control'. According to them, "the US could not be willing to escalate to a strategic exchange if it were evident to the Soviet Union, the US people, and the world in general, that it had made no attempt to protect its population from a Soviet attack. With such preparations, the Soviet Union would take seriously our (US) declared intentions; without such provisions, it will be clear to all that the US is unwilling to risk escalation from tactical to strategic warfare, and therefore probably unwilling to risk a full-scale conventional confrontation."[4] (It was assumed that a conventional conflict in Europe would escalate to a nuclear one due to the use of tactical nuclear weapons). So without civil defence measures in place, it was assumed that the politicians would be unable to risk the use of nuclear weapons. Whether such an analogy is applicable in the Indian context is debatable. However, civil defence preparations can be seen as one of the means to increase the credibility of national and political will to live through a nuclear threat and hence, the willingness to retaliate with nuclear weapons. It thus strengthens deterrence. As far as the Indian Army is concerned, its argument that there is enough space for conventional operations in spite of the enunciated nuclear 'red lines' drawn by Pakistan and that they will exploit this space during a conflict will get buttressed, if they build up a capability to undertake operations in the aftermath of nuclear strikes in the TBA.

By the middle of the 1970s, it was clear to both the US and USSR that there can be no major breakthrough in civil defence technology that can afford increased protection or reliability at decreasing cost for large-scale defensive measures. On the other hand, developments in offensive technology saw the advent of Intercontinental Ballistic Missiles (ICBM) which reduced warning time and the introduction of Multiple Independently-targetable Re-entry Vehicles (MIRV) technology, which afforded greater flexibility in the selection and engagement of targets. The dictum that any increments of passive defence could be overwhelmed by less expensive increments in offensive technology had gained general acceptance.[5] The subsequent period witnessed decreasing interest of both the super powers in large-scale passive defence measures.

Evaluation of Civil Defence Measures

Underground Shelters: The underground nuclear shelters, constructed in the US and the Soviet Union during the Cold War, were of two types. Some afforded protection against nuclear fallout only and others against blast effects as well. In Indian cities, where there in no space to construct public utilities like toilets, car parks and where there are hundreds of destitutes who do not have a simple roof over their heads, the thought of constructing underground nuclear shelters seems to be too far-fetched an idea. Nevertheless, there is a need to examine their utility from the practical and technical points of view.

- **Blast Shelters:** These shelters, as their name suggests, can provide protection against blast effects. Such shelters were mostly constructed in basements of buildings and were able to withstand static overpressure to the tune of 10 psi. Theoretically, blast shelters can only be effective if the people are huddled inside them before an attack. This will require a satellite-based surveillance system to detect real time launch of nuclear missiles, dedicated communication arrangements with local municipal authorities of all major cities, besides adequate warning resources and time. Any false alarms will do no good to the credibility of the government and hence, such shelters may never come into use.
- **Fallout Shelters:** Most of the nuclear civil defence plans of Western nations have focused on fallout shelters rather than blast shelters. This is because nuclear fallout can travel much further and will affect a larger segment of the population. People are expected to stay in these shelters till radiation levels come down to relatively safe levels. Since fallout shelters will come into play after the movement of fallout has been predicted following a nuclear strike, their utility from the point of view of time and space is also doubtful. In South Asia, we are not expecting the large-scale use of nuclear weapons of the Cold War variety that will force people to stay in fallout shelters for weeks and months, just because there is no contamination-free area left in the near vicinity.

Underground shelters have not found favour even within the US and the erstwhile Soviet Union because people from different social backgrounds are forced into confined spaces, leading to multiple problems related to public safety, crime and psychological stress due to conflicts over limited space, food or water. Even the usage of utilities like underground parking lots, shops, underground subways, or even underground stations and the track network of Delhi Metro in times of a nuclear emergency is doubtful, although it has been suggested by some eminent personalities.

Delhi Metro: As part of New Delhi's nuclear civil defence plans for the public, it is reported "that the Delhi government has issued instructions to the Delhi Metro Rail Corporation that underground tunnels being constructed in the city be damage-proof against a possible nuclear attack".[6] The Delhi Metro line is a combination of underground and overhead sections. The underground section will be able to provide protection against blast effects. It may also prevent airborne contamination from entering if its air conditioning system includes NBC filters and curtaining of the underground section from the overhead one. However, the utilisation of the underground section of the Delhi Metro as a blast shelter during a nuclear threat on the city is not recommended. Its utility before or even after an attack is limited because more people may die from a stampede and suffocation, thus leading to a larger tragedy. In case a major portion of the Metro network survives a nuclear strike, it must be used for consequent management operations like the evacuation of people and transportation of mitigation teams.

Evacuation: One of the alternatives to 'sheltering' considered by the Federal Emergency Management Agency (FEMA) of the US during the initial stages of the Cold War was 'massive evacuation' of urban centres and 'relocation' of the populace in rural areas. The civil defence plans of FEMA were based on a total of 6,559 megaton nuclear attacks on the US, which if launched without warning would kill about 133 million people immediately or in the first few weeks after the attack.[7] Such an attack would leave the population of urban centres defenceless unless massive funding was approved for the construction of blast-proof underground shelters. FEMA also assumed that "the Soviet Union would not launch a pre-emptive strike on the US without first protecting its own population, as much as would be possible, from the effects of a US counter-attack, and would thus first execute its own civil defence plans and begin evacuating all major cities and population centres around industrial plants."[8] This would provide three to five days of warning time to the US, during which it was proposed to carry out large-scale evacuation. It is not hard to imagine that such a plan would have run into problems like large-scale traffic snarls, law and order problem in vacated areas, all-round chaos, all happening under conditions of great stress and strain for the general public. Besides the immediate problems, the later ones will include the problem of housing and feeding a large population in an alien environment. "Recognising these problems, many local and state governments in the US refused to prepare evacuation plans."[9]

Warning: Another important aspect of nuclear civil defence is advance warning of an impending attack, which can range from a few minutes to a few days. In case of very little warning time, the least that can be done is to warn the general population so that they can undertake personal evasive action. This can be done with the help of radio or TV broadcasts or sirens as is done in case of air raids. In case adequate warning is available, the evacuation of cities can be considered as was conceptualised by FEMA. The analogy of 'adequate warning time' could be applied in the Indian context also, in case Pakistan, especially as part of its first strike policy, decides to address counter-value targets only. Even if the Pakistani population is not warned and evacuated, there will be some shifting and relocation of important assets, people, organisations or their HQs. Such movement can be picked up by satellite or human intelligence. Let us assume that the government is in receipt of definite indicators of an impending nuclear strike. Will it ask people to evacuate Delhi or major cities knowing fully well that this may lead to panic? Since there is no way of knowing the targeting intent of the adversary, especially in terms of specific locations, evacuation plans may also not work in India. However, certain feasibility studies for evacuating important cities can be carried out by the NDMA. Such scenarios may come into play if India decides to escalate to counter-value strikes in response to the adversary's counter-force nuclear strikes.

The efficacy of shelters, evacuation plans and warning methodology has been questioned by Professor R Rajaraman and others in their study *Nuclear Civil Defence in South Asia: Is it Feasible?* The concept of shelters had been rejected by them because it was feared that homeless people may occupy them. The idea of stocking of fallout shelters with non-perishable food and water in cities where millions live on daily wages was considered preposterous at best. Evacuation was impractical, because most citizens will have to rely on government transport, which is grossly inadequate in most cities. The study had concluded that "none of the major nuclear civil defence measures considered and partly put into operation in Europe, the US and the Soviet Union, such as city-wide evacuation or provision of nuclear blast-proof on fallout shelters are feasible in South Asia. Warning and communication systems such as sirens would have to be greatly improved beyond what is being contemplated."[10] Some of the practical nuclear civil defence measures suggested by the study are as follows:

- Each city should have a reliable, recognisable warning system that can alert the population.
- People should promptly seek shelter in a nearby building upon receiving the warning.
- Each city should have emergency radio stations scattered around the city to instruct people who have taken shelter.
- Radio broadcast stations must be designed to survive a nuclear attack and to serve as radiation monitoring centres.
- Emergency medical supplies must be stockpiled at schools throughout the city.

While some of the recommendations mentioned above have already been considered as part of the response mechanism, there is a need to look beyond 'shelters' and 'evacuation' as part of national capacity building to meet the challenges of a nuclear attack.

Capacity Building

Stocking of Drugs and Medicines: There will be a need to stock drugs and medicines as per the nature and number of casualties that are anticipated. These stocks could be distributed in all major private and government hospitals to obviate the problem of turnover. In fact, all major metros can stock one 'medical brick' each to treat a specific number of nuclear casualties and medicines can be flown into the city which has the misfortune of being under a nuclear attack. The composition and stocking levels can be decided by the NDMA in consultation with the Ministry of Health and Family Welfare (MoHFW).

Stocking of Food: Stocking of food including the construction of underground granaries was undertaken during the Cold War, due to an exaggerated threat of an all-out nuclear war. Strategic planners on both sides believed that long-term contamination of agricultural areas may affect the harvest, thus leading to food shortages. Some extreme scenarios like the 'nuclear winter' even postulated a shift in cropping patterns. However, in a scenario of limited or single nuclear strikes, severe food shortages are unlikely but there can be a temporary disruption of supplies, especially of fresh vegetables, for which all metros are dependent on neighbouring areas. The temporary shortages can be exploited by unscrupulous elements by hoarding and black-marketing. This can be avoided if the concerned state governments maintain some buffer stocks and replenish their public distribution system. Legal action against hoarders must also be taken to tide over the temporary food shortages.

Specialist Units: Presently, the NDRF has four battalions earmarked to handle CBRN disasters. These are located at Delhi (Noida), Chennai, Pune and Guwahati. The specialist units of the Army can be taken as a bonus but consequence management cannot be planned on these as their availability in times of war is not certain. The resources, if mobilised, can take care of one major disaster. The establishment of ERCs in all major cities which is being contemplated by the NDMA will serve as a central resource pool and can be mobilised for consequence management in contaminated areas.

Training: Training of all response elements in handling post-strike disaster management is an important element of national capacity building. Apart from the training of individual units and organisations in a 'stand alone mode' on their own roles and tasks, there will be a need for these units to take part in a collaborative manner with other response elements like specialist NBC units of the Army, civil defence personnel including home guards and NCC, fire brigade personnel and the local police. Annual mock exercises must be planned to iron out coordination aspects. The actual feel of managing a real disaster cannot be created in any mock exercise. Hence, such exercises leave a large amount to the imagination of the participant. This imagination can be brought close to reality by way of table-top exercises, discussions or screening of films on nuclear strikes. The efficient employment of response elements in radiologically contaminated environments will be possible if personnel are confident of the reliability of their detection instruments and the soundness of the drills and procedures. 'Caution' and not 'fear' of radioactivity must guide the responders in the conduct of their mission. Hence, there will be a need to create simulated conditions with live radioactive sources. Responders must be trained in the detection, survey and handling of live sources to inhibit their fear of radioactivity. There may also be a need for 'psychological training' while preparing troops to operate in radiologically contaminated areas as well as for handling large-scale casualties. While the training of response elements is important, the success of any disaster management will also depend upon coordination in the higher organisational setup. Mock exercises must practise drills for the establishment of Integrated Command Post (ICP) and the mobilisation of various task forces to fine-tune coordination between NDMA and the Crisis Management Group (CMG) or the National Crisis Management Committee (NCMC).

Awareness Building

Role of Civil Defence: Civil defence in India, till the outbreak of the Sino-Indian war of 1962, remained confined to 'paper plans' for protecting major cities and towns. However, the 1962 Sino-Indian and the 1965 Indo-Pakistan wars provided it the necessary impetus, which culminated in the enactment of the Civil Defence Act of 1968. Currently, civil defence provides protection to individuals, properties and establishments against any hostile acts. It is functional in only 121 out of the 225 categorised civil defence towns. Over the years, the relevance and efficacy of civil defence has steadily deteriorated. To remain relevant, civil defence may have to look for new roles like fighting against terrorism, assistance in natural calamities or human induced disasters. Some of the state governments are already utilising the services of civil defence volunteers for post-disaster response and relief as also for pre-disaster activities related to mitigation and preparedness. In a nuclear environment, civil defence volunteers can assist in awareness building during the preparatory phase and in the post-strike phase, they could be employed in uncontaminated areas for crowd control, and relocation and rehabilitation type of tasks. To achieve this, the civil defence infrastructure of select cities needs to be strengthened by bringing the home guards under it. In addition, some of the youth organisations like National Cadet Corps (NCC), National Service Scheme (NSS) and Nehru Yuva Kendra Sangathan (NYKS) can also be involved, particularly in the field of community capacity building and generating public awareness.

Awareness building programmes can only succeed if there is participation of the local community in these programmes. Hence, there is a need to build awareness in the local population about the threat of nuclear weapons without causing undue alarm. Nuclear warfare or the 'effects of nuclear weapons' are new subjects for the Indian public and there can be some misinformed perceptions. There is a need to remove these and here civil defence can play an important role. In the national awareness building exercise, the NDMA should take the lead in developing information, education and communication material. Disaster Management is now a subject in all school curriculums. Topics related to nuclear defence can also be included into the curriculum. Besides targeting the common public, awareness programmes must also address the higher decision-making authorities who are in charge of formulating policies.

Preparedness and Response

To meet the challenges of a nuclear threat requires, as some analysts put it, 'defence in depth' or a 'layered response'. It also requires the involvement and active participation of all national and state disaster management agencies, both during the preparatory and response stages. Diagram 4 summarises the processes involved in meeting the challenges of a nuclear strike.

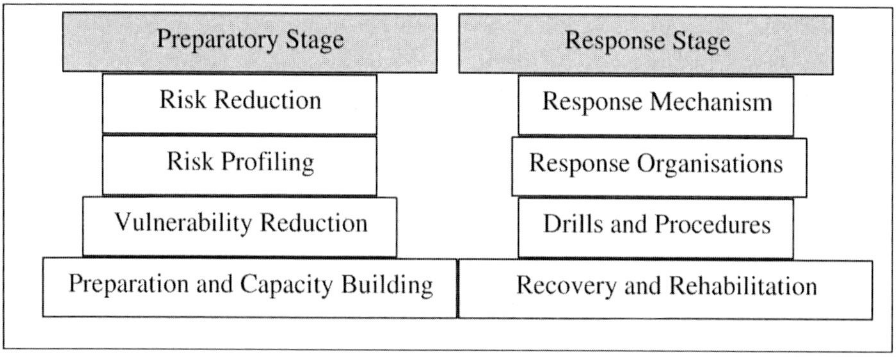

Diagram 4: Defensive Response to a Nuclear Challenge

Capacity Building for Other Nuclear Disasters

The Indian nuclear industry is likely to witness a major growth in the next few years. While there is no co-relationship between 'nuclear disasters' and this 'growth', the possibility of nuclear accidents may get enhanced. Besides nuclear accidents, there is also the increased possibility of terrorists using radioactive material. Hence, our capacity building to handle a nuclear strike must also take into consideration the possibility of nuclear disasters, accidental or man-made. Some of the incidents for which we must be prepared are listed in decreasing order of seriousness:

- Reactor core meltdown in a nuclear power plant.
- Criticality accidents in nuclear facilities.
- Accidents involving fissile material, including transportation accidents.
- Use of Radiological Dispersal Devices (RDD), so-called 'Dirty Bombs' by terrorists.
- Radiological threats emanating from accidents in neighbouring countries.
- Use of Radiological Emitting Devices (RED) by terrorists.

Nuclear Accidents: The physical response for mitigation efforts after a nuclear accident will be similar to that a nuclear detonation, although accidents like core meltdown will produce a much higher intensity of radioactivity. Other accidents being minor in nature, the response required will be much smaller in scale. Since the probability of a nuclear accident is more than that of a nuclear attack, our response can be more focused. During such an event, there is always a possibility of forewarning. Nuclear power plants in all nations, including ours, employ radiological detection equipment around their periphery. The radiological sensors are programmed to detect any abnormal increase in radioactivity levels from the background levels and set off automatic alarms in a central monitoring facility. The NPCIL has made elaborate disaster management plans for such contingencies in all nuclear power plants being operated by them, in close cooperation with the local administration. These plans are not only subject to a detailed review by the regulatory authority, i.e. the AERB, but also put to test on a yearly basis.

Terrorist Threats: Some scenarios also speculate on the possibility of our nuclear power plants being subjected to terror attacks. The prevention of such attacks lies in the domain of physical security measures, because to cause a deliberate accident in a captive nuclear power plant before the arrival of armed response, is extremely difficult and will require detailed knowledge and expertise. The possibility of accidental leakage of radioactivity in such scenarios is minimised due to design features like containment domes in all nuclear power plants. However, the threat from the deliberate spreading of radioactive contamination by terror groups in the form of RDDs (dirty bomb) has attracted the attention of most governments in recent years. Unlike a nuclear bomb, a dirty bomb is not a WMD because it is not accompanied by a fission or fusion process which releases vast amounts of energy. A RDD is designed to spread radioactive contamination using chemical explosives with a view to cause casualties among the target population through exposure to radiation or to deny an area to the military or others for short periods of time. The best way to prevent such an attack is to deny the availability of radioactive sources to undesirable elements. This will mean having a strict control over those industries or establishments that use radioactive sources. In addition, unauthorised import or entry of radioactive material inside the country can be prevented by installing radiological detection equipment in major ports of entry. Such equipment can also be installed in various entry points of a threatened city in case there is definite information about terrorists using radioactive material. In case the background radioactivity of a city has already been mapped, it may be even possible, at least theoretically, to detect the threat through a radiological survey using aerial means. The threat from RDDs is certainly more than a nuclear attack but our preparations for the latter should also take care of such threats.

ENDNOTES

1. William H Kincade, "Repeating History: The Civil Defence Debate Renewed," in Christine Cassel, Michael McCally and Henry Abraham (eds.), *Nuclear Weapons and Nuclear War: A Sourcebook for Health Professionals* (New York: Praeger Publishers, 1984), p. 387.

2. R Rajaraman, Zia Mian and AH Nayyar, "Nuclear Civil Defence in South Asia: Is it Feasible?" *Economic and Political Weekly*, Vol. XXXIX, Nos. 46 & 47, 2004.
3. Kincade, n. 1, p. 393.
4. Jennifer Leaning, "Civil Defence in the Nuclear Age: What Purpose does it Serve and What Survival does it Promise?" in Christine Cassel, Michael McCally and Henry Abraham (eds.), *Nuclear Weapons and Nuclear War: A Sourcebook for Health Professionals* (New York: Praeger Publishers, 1984), p. 408.
5. Kincade, n. 1, p. 390.
6. AK Das, "N-Attack? Ducking for Cover is better than being a Sitting Duck," *The Times of India*, 25 November 1999.
7. Christine Cassel and Andrew Jameton, "Medical Responsibility and Thermonuclear War," in Christine Cassel, Michael McCally and Henry Abraham (eds.), *Nuclear Weapons and Nuclear War: A Sourcebook for Health Professionals* (New York: Praeger Publishers, 1984), p. 12.
8. Leaning, n. 4, p. 411.
9. Rajaraman, Mian and Nayyar, n. 2.
10. Ibid.

16

Conclusion

The possibility of the use of nuclear weapons in any future conflict involving India and its traditional adversaries remains low. In fact, even the possibility of a full-scale conflict breaking out remains remote because waging war as a continuation of state policy, to resolve political differences, is fast becoming an unpopular option. The intertwining of world economies due to globalisation has ensured that the 'economic fallout' of a regional conflict will be truly global. A conflict between nuclear armed neighbours will be unacceptable to most nations, especially to important stakeholders in the region. The efforts of the international community to prevent a major conflict in South Asia could range from coercive diplomatic efforts to offering of sops for rapprochement and reconciliation. However, can the pressures of international diplomacy or the possibility of a self-inflicted politico-military disaster, which will surely result in an economic catastrophe, prevent a future conflict from breaking out? Even if the chances of a conflict involving nuclear weapons remain low, our 'risk assessment' paradigm must consider the 'low possibility' of such an eventuality with the attendant 'high consequences', in order to appreciate the threat in its correct perspective.

It is popularly said that the world is transiting through an era of 'strategic uncertainty'. Although the phrase had been coined in the US in the aftermath of the 9/11 attacks, it has greater relevance in the South Asian context. India is living in a far more troubled and violent neighbourhood. The future of most of the states in South Asia including that of our acknowledged adversaries cannot be predicted with absolute certainty.

Our northern adversary is on the threshold of becoming an economic superpower, the benefits of which will transcend into the politico-military sphere as well. One can already discern the broad contours of a major superpower in the making from the grandiose plans made by China for the modernisation of its military including the development of strategic capabilities. Internally, its archaic political system is not compatible with the new-found economic freedom its citizens are enjoying. On the external front also, China has yet to display the maturity, vision and responsibility of a great power. Most of its closest allies and friends are viewed as 'rogue nations' by the Western world and it remains the only country that has proliferated nuclear and missile technology just to tie down a potential competitor in a regional bind. Most analysts in India consider China as a long-term threat but the shape and contours of this threat including its likely manifestation in the type, quantum or location remains nebulous at best.

Over the recent past, our western adversary has had the ignominious distinction of earning the most colourful epithets, ranging from being an 'international migraine' to a 'failing state' running a 'nuclear arms bazaar', besides being viewed as an 'epicentre of global terrorism' and hence the 'most dangerous place on earth'. The 'most sanctioned state' still manages to attract international sympathy, combined with economic and military aid, in the hope of resuscitating it from a likely internal collapse, because if that happens, it will be tragic not only for the region but for the entire civilised world. Currently, while military rule in Pakistan has become highly unpopular, the political process has not matured to provide the nation with stable governance. The army continues to call the shots from the background. It has also forced the local administration to broker a 'peace deal' with fundamentalist elements on the Af-Pak border rather than fight them. It is widely feared that chasing the chimera of 'peace' may provide the jihadis with an opportunity to fill the current political vacuum. Such 'peace' will be, as one Pakistani has put it, "the peace of the graveyard".

The only future that one can predict with certainty is the uncertainty of the future course of events, along with myriad threats and challenges that they may pose. In an environment of 'strategic uncertainty', it will be unwise to bank on our existing capabilities to hold good till eternity. Our preparedness to meet future challenges has to evolve constantly, no matter how nebulous the threat. Currently, our nuclear doctrine is based on the principle of NFU and massive punitive retaliation. This essentially translates into massive counter-value targeting. One cannot say with certainty that this paradigm will hold good for all time to come, on for all circumstances. Although any escalation of a nuclear conflict among nation states will eventually end up with massive counter-value targeting, what if the nuclear threat arises from local warlords, non-state players, satraps operating from semi-liberated areas or rogue and renegade elements of a failing state machinery? It would be unwise to rely on the absoluteness of the doctrine of NFU and 'massive retaliation' in such a case and make no efforts to develop capabilities for counter-force targeting. In case we develop such a capability and we don't require it at a later stage because the world has transformed into a peaceful place, we can always discard it. It is important to understand that one can only discard what one possesses and any talk of discarding a capability without actually possessing it will always smack of trying to achieve a hollow moral high ground. Since counter-force targeting will rely on the 'economy of force' and will avoid 'collateral damage', issues like circular error of probability of the delivery vectors, height of burst of the nuclear weapon, safety of own troops, development of damage criterion for modern structures, strategic assets and military equipment etc., will assume importance. Hence there is an overarching need to involve the military, the end users of this capability, in the development of such parameters.

India is self-reliant in nuclear technology and can take pride in the fact that most of it is an indigenous effort. It is well known that our nuclear weapons programme is an offshoot of the civilian programme. The latter was undertaken to harness the energy of the atom for peaceful purposes; primarily to meet the growing energy needs of the nation. Today, the country possesses the complete range of technologies associated with all stages of the Nuclear Fuel Cycle, right from the mining of uranium ore, to its enrichment, to reprocessing and safe disposal of nuclear waste. It is also a world leader in fast-breeder reactor technology and probably the only nation attempting to commercially use mixed oxide fuel using $Uranium^{233}$ for its next generation of fast-breeder reactors. However, being a nation with advanced nuclear technology automatically does not translate into being a Nuclear Weapon State (NWS), in spite of having demonstrated the ability to conduct a range of nuclear tests.

The responsibility that comes along with the tag of being a NWS demands much more. A NWS must have a range of nuclear capabilities not only for offensive use but also to defend itself against nuclear attack. As far as the development of offensive capabilities was concerned, India's nuclear weapons programme was driven by the scientific community, in which the military leadership had very little role to play. The military has been included after the capability was developed and successfully demonstrated. So, as far as the offensive use of nuclear weapons is concerned, the military will use what has already been developed without any say in what it would desire. Now that India has declared itself as a NWS, the military must not shy away from demanding what type of weapon systems it would need. This can be done by analysing the potential targets and their desired level of destruction without the adverse nuclear effects of such yields impacting into our territory. This can be done by following the same procedure, albeit in more scientific detail, used in this study to carry out the vulnerability analysis of Indian cities and border areas.

The joint approach that was missing in the development of India's offensive nuclear capability should not reflect in the development of defensive capabilities. The military and civil agencies that would be tasked to operate in the aftermath of a nuclear strike must work closely with the scientific community to develop this capability. Most of the defensive aspects of nuclear war are based on concepts and drills which have to be 'visualised' by the user. These, however, must be based on scientific parameters. In addition, aspects related to risk assessment, damage estimation parameters, hazard prediction, integration of meteorological aspects, automation of warning and reporting must be jointly developed by the scientific community, the armed forces and the NDMA. In case we decide to follow NATO standards and procedures that are available in open source literature, these will at least need to be validated by our scientific community.

In South Asia, nuclear weapons are here to stay. This is a reality from which the political, military and scientific community cannot shy away. We may adore these weapons or abhor them but we cannot ignore them. Hence, everything possible needs to be done to prevent their use. While these efforts can range from disarmament to deterrence, there is also a need to look at what needs to be done in the 'aftermath of a nuclear strike' – with the hope that such a crisis will never arise.

APPENDICES

BLAST EFFECTS

Distance and Overpressure Relationship Graphs

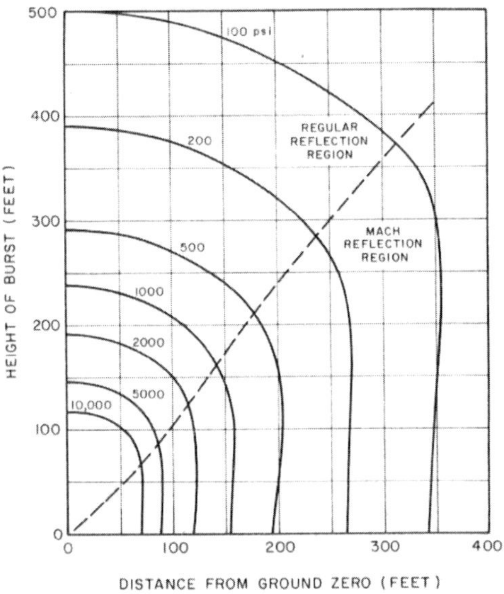

Figure 8: High Pressure Range

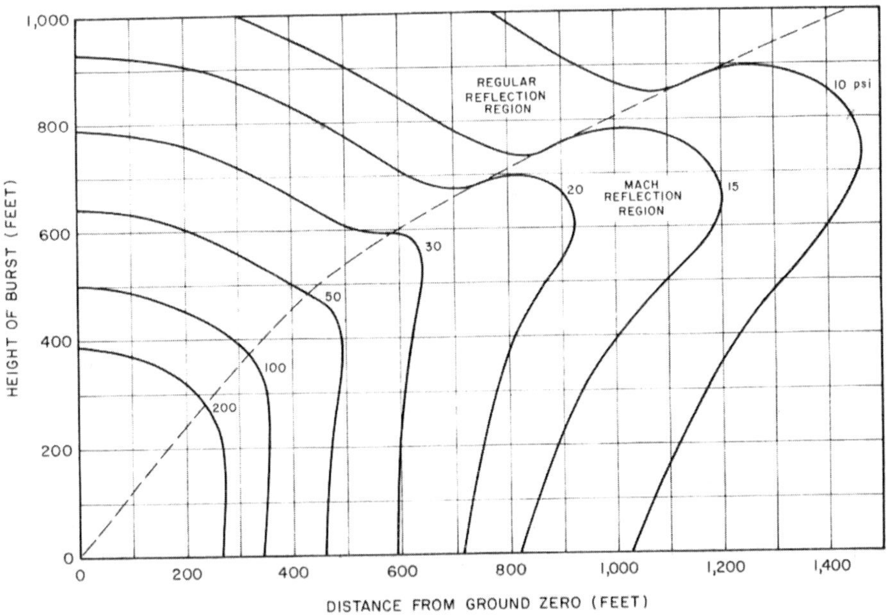

Figure 9: Intermediate Pressure Range

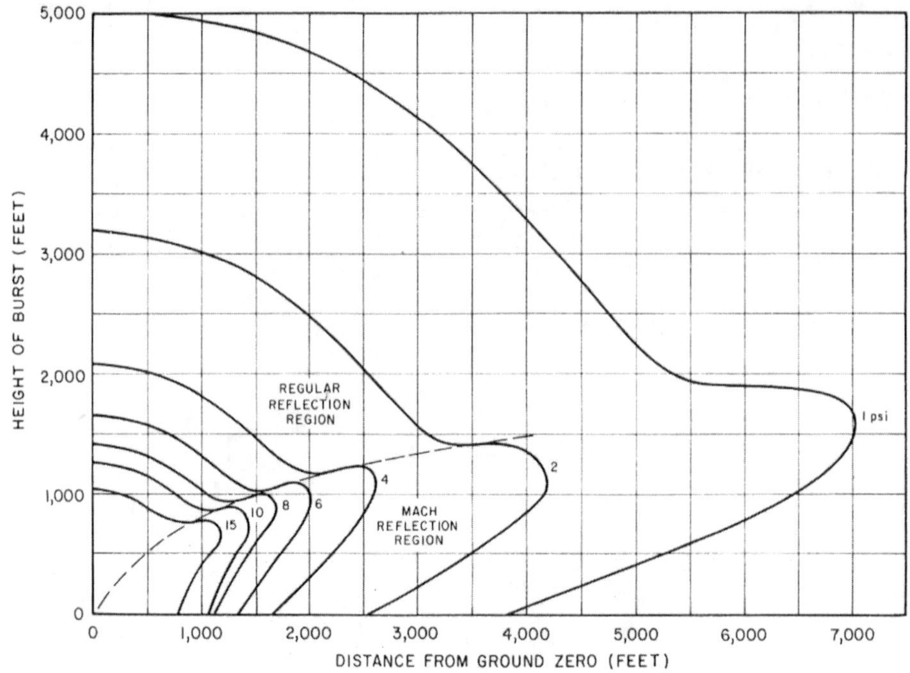

Figure 10: Low Pressure Range

Scaling Laws for Blast Effects

- As per the scaling laws, the slant distance or the Height of Burst (HOB) at which two nuclear explosions will produce similar overpressure is proportional to the cube root of their yields. This is explained with the help of the following formula.

$$\frac{R_2}{R_1} = \frac{H_2}{H_1} = \left(\frac{W_2}{W_1}\right)^{1/3}$$

Where R_2 and H_2 are the range and height till where a specific overpressure is felt from a weapon yield of W_2 kiloton, R_1 and H_1 are range and height till where similar effects are noticed from a weapon yield of W_1 kiloton.

- The distances for desired yield (R_2 and H_2) can be calculated by extracting the HOB, slant range and peak static overpressure for 1 kiloton yield from the graphs.
- For a hypothetical 10 kiloton nuclear burst at a height of 300 feet, the distance which will be affected by 10 psi overpressure is calculated as follows:

$$\frac{300}{H_1} = \left(\frac{10}{1}\right)^{1/3}$$

The scaled Height of Burst (H1) for 1 kiloton $\frac{300 \text{ ft}}{10^{1/3}}$ 140 ft

From the graph at Figure A.2, 1 kiloton burst at 140 ft will produce a static overpressure of 10 psi at 1,090 ft.

The 10 psi slant range for 10 kiloton is calculated using the scaling laws once again by multiplying 1,090 ft with the cube root of the yield

$$\frac{R_1}{R_2} = \left(\frac{1}{10}\right)^{1/3}$$

$R_2 = 1{,}090 \times 10^{1/3} = 1548$ ft $= 472$ metres.

Steps Used to Complete Table 7

- From Graphs 2 and 3, calculate the HOB that maximises slant range for 30 and 5 psi for counter-force and counter-value targets, respectively. This is located in the Mach Reflection region and equals 600 feet and 1,200 feet, respectively.
- Using the 'Scaling Laws', calculate the ideal HOB for lower yields which will be ideal for counter-force targeting (5, 10 & 20 Kiloton) and higher yields which will be ideal for counter-value targets (20, 50, 100 and 1000 kiloton).
- Use graphs to calculate the maximum distance from the GZ till where relevant overpressure ranges will extend for an ideal HOB of 600 and 1,200 feet. For example, for one psi, it comes to about 5,600 feet for counter-force and 6,700 feet for counter-value targets. For 30 psi, it comes to about 630 feet for counter-force, and at the GZ for counter-value targets.
- Use Scaling Laws to convert distance from GZ for yields of interest.
- Convert the distance from GZ and HOB from feet to metres.

THERMAL RADIATIONS

Thermal Flux and Distance Relationship

The amount of thermal radiation from an airburst from yield W, at a distance R, can be calculated with the help of the following formula.[1]

$$Q = \frac{7.94 \times fW \times t}{R^2}$$

where Q is the thermal energy in cal/cm^2, W is the yield in kiloton, f is the thermal partition factor, R is the distance in km and T is the transmission factor of the air. The thermal partition factor for airbursts in the HOB of interest is generally 35/100. The transmission factor, T for up to 15 km of visibility can be taken as 7/10.

The radius of an area that will be affected by a thermal flux of 30 cal/cm^2, from a nuclear explosion of 10 kiloton yield, can be calculated as follows:

$$30 = \frac{7.94 \times .35 \times 10 \times .7}{R^2}$$

$$30 = \frac{19.45}{R^2}$$

$$R = \left(\frac{19.45}{30}\right)^{1/2}$$

$$R = 805 \text{ metres.}$$

Steps Used to Complete Table 13. The formulae given above have been applied across the spectrum of desired yields to get R, i.e., the distance from GZ that will give 30, 20, 15, 10 and 5 Calories/cm^2 of thermal flux.

1. Samuel Gladstone and Philip J Dolan (eds.), *The Effects of Nuclear Weapons* (Washington, D.C.: US GPO, 1977), p. 317 (The distance given in the formula in miles has been suitably modified for km).

Scaling Laws for Thermal Effects

The amount of thermal radiations that two nuclear detonations will produce, is directly proportional to their yields and the distance from the GZ, where two nuclear detonations will produce similar thermal flux is proportional to the square root of their yields.

$$\frac{Q_1}{Q_2} = \frac{W_1}{W_2} \text{ and } \frac{R_1}{R_2} = \left(\frac{W_1}{W_2}\right)^{1/2}$$

INITIAL NUCLEAR RADIATION

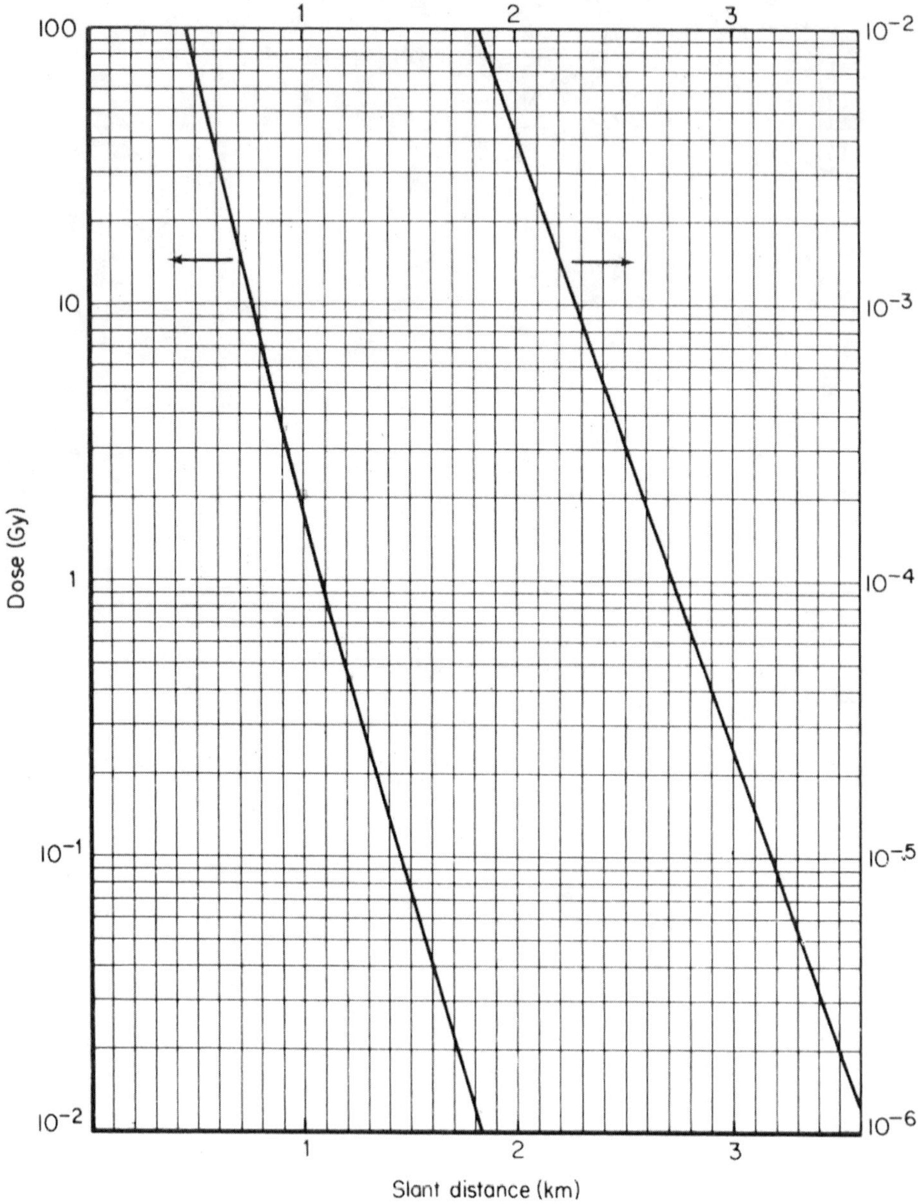

Figure 11: Neutron Dose per Kiloton as a Function of Slant Range

Source: Stockholm International Peace Research Institute (SIPRI), *Nuclear Radiations in Warfare* (London: Taylor & Francis Ltd, 1981), p. 62.

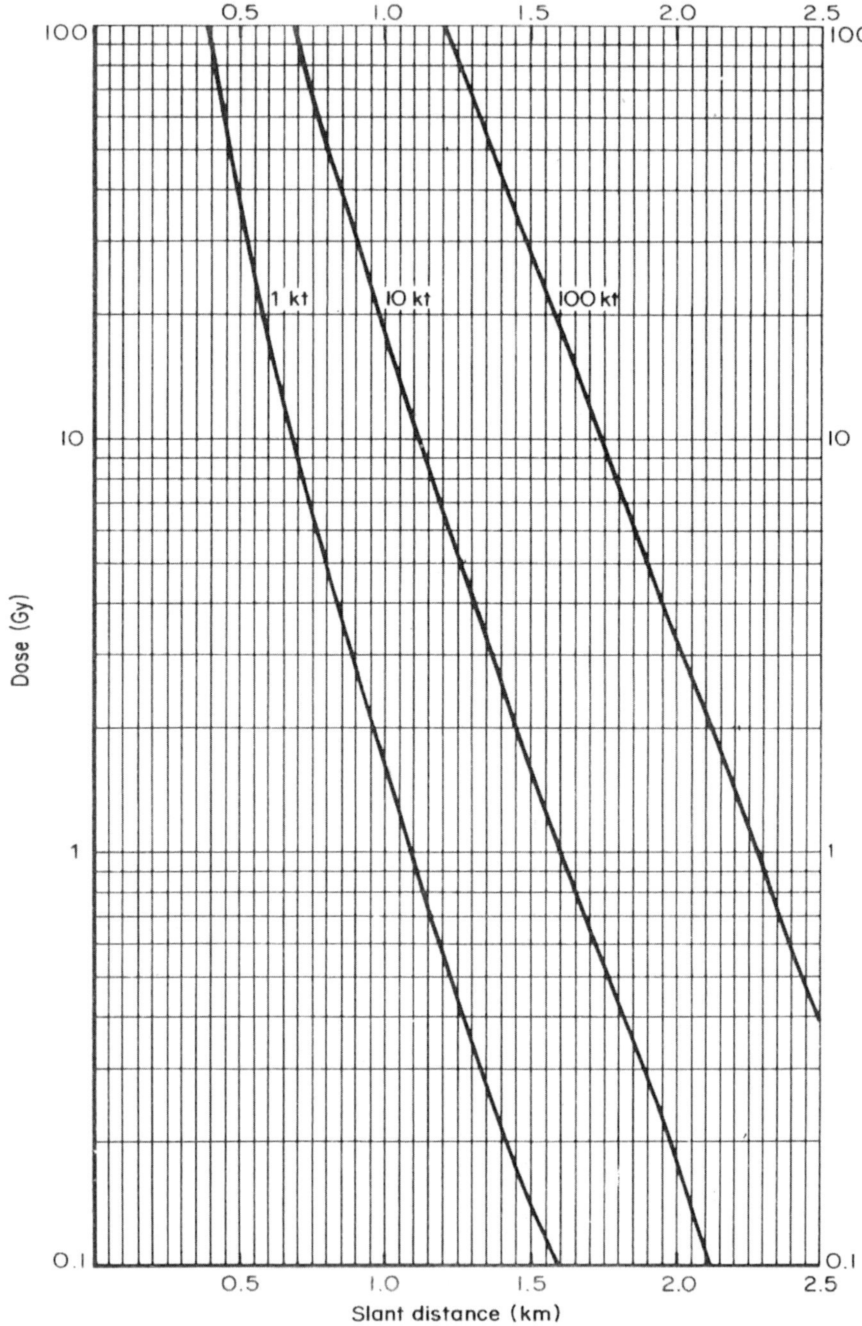

Figure 12: Gamma Ray Dose Rates as a Function of Slant Range for Fission Weapon

Source: Stockholm International Peace Research Institute (SIPRI), *Nuclear Radiations in Warfare* (London: Taylor & Francis Ltd, 1981), p. 66.

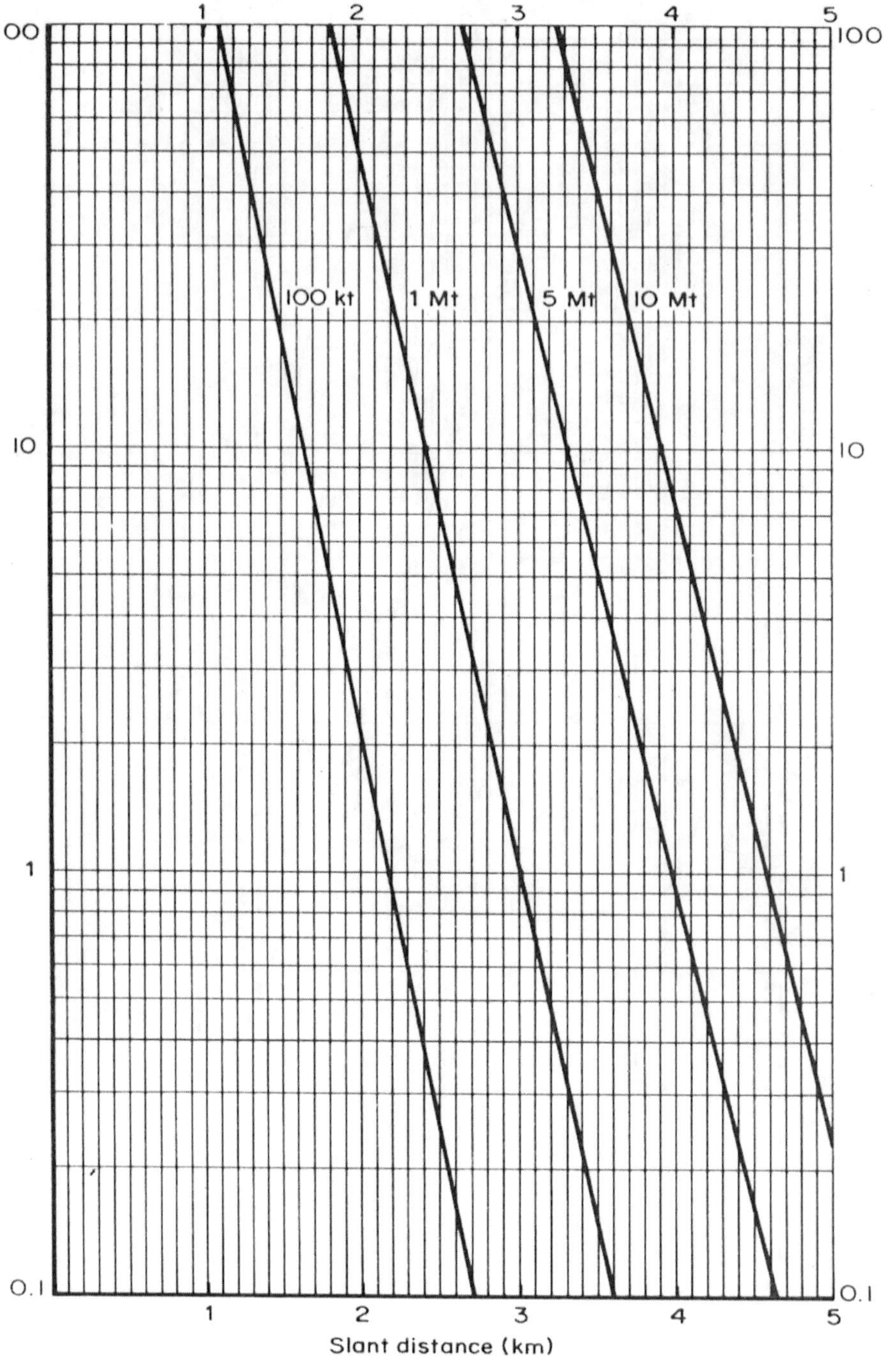

Figure 13: Gamma Ray Dose Rates as a Function of Slant Range for Thermonuclear Weapons

Source: Stockholm International Peace Research Institute (SIPRI), *Nuclear Radiations in Warfare* (London: Taylor & Francis Ltd, 1981), p. 67.

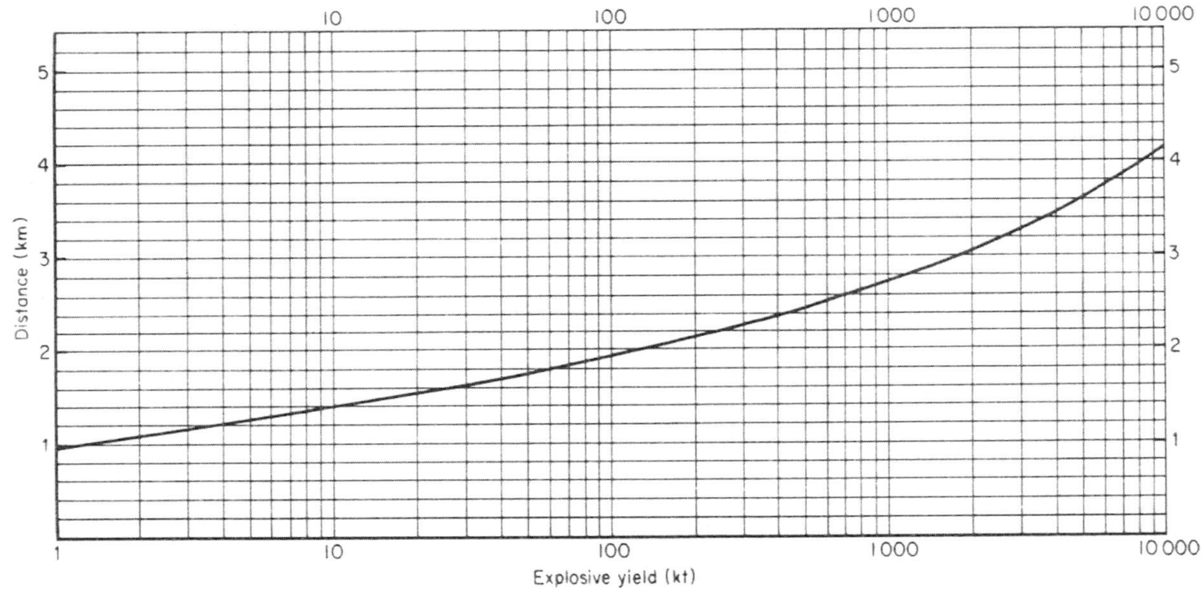

Figure 14: Distances for Lethal Radiation Doses (Neutrons and Gamma)

Source: Stockholm International Peace Research Institute (SIPRI), *Nuclear Radiations in Warfare* (London: Taylor & Francis Ltd, 1981), p. 69.

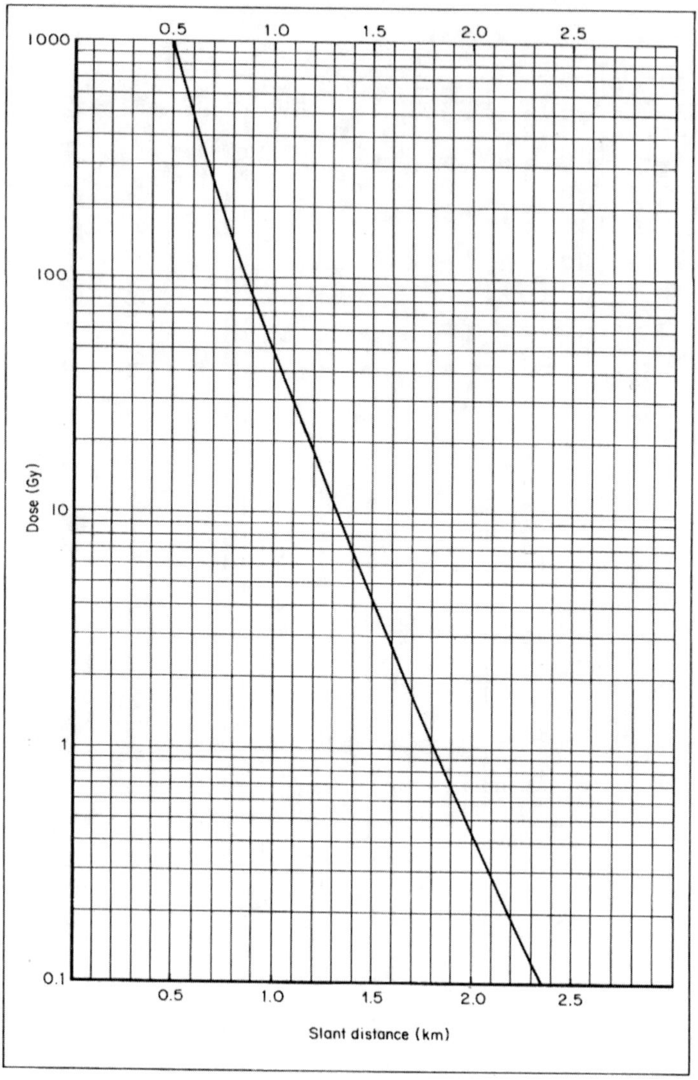

Figure 15: Neutron Dose from a 1 kt Neutron Bomb

Source: Stockholm International Peace Research Institute (SIPRI), *Nuclear Radiations in Warfare* (London: Taylor & Francis Ltd, 1981), p. 71.

LOCAL FALLOUT

Local Fallout. Tables 22 to 24 showing downwind distance, GZ radii and maximum fallout width for idealised fallout have been calculated using the following formulae:

Maximum Downwind Distances, GZ radii and Maximum Width of Fallout for Surface Burst of W kt Yield and Wind Speed of 15 mph (24 kmph)[1]

Reference Dose Rate (Rads/hour)	Downwind Distance (miles)	Maximum Width	GZ Width
3,000	$0.95 \times W^{0.45}$	$0.0076 \times W^{0.86}$	$0.026 \times W^{0.58}$
1,000	$1.8 \times W^{0.45}$	$0.036 \times W^{0.76}$	$0.060 \times W^{0.57}$
300	$4.5 \times W^{0.45}$	$0.13 \times W^{0.66}$	$0.20 \times W^{0.48}$
100	$8.9 \times W^{0.45}$	$0.38 \times W^{0.60}$	$0.39 \times W^{0.42}$
30	$16 \times W^{0.45}$	$0.76 \times W^{0.56}$	$0.53 \times W^{0.41}$
10	$24 \times W^{0.45}$	$1.4 \times W^{0.53}$	$0.68 \times W^{0.41}$
3	$30 \times W^{0.45}$	$2.2 \times W^{0.50}$	$0.89 \times W^{0.41}$
1	$40 \times W^{0.45}$	$3.3 \times W^{0.48}$	$1.5 \times W^{0.41}$

Scaling for Effective Wind – The scaling factor for downwind distances given in Table 25 has been calculated using the following scaling formula for effective wind.[2]

- In order to calculate the downwind distances for effective wind speeds of v miles per hour, the downwind distances calculated for 15 mph (24 kmph) are multiplied by a factor of F where:

$$F = 1 + \frac{V-15}{60 \text{ or } 30}$$

- For wind speeds greater than 15 mph (24 kmph) the division is by 60 and for wind speeds less than 15 mph the division is by 30.

Arrival of Fallout – The time of arrival of fallout at any location is dependent upon the wind speed and the distance of that location from the GZ. The time of arrival given in Table 26 has been calculated by dividing the distance with wind speed. Since the fallout will commence from the extremities of the radioactive cloud and not from the centre of the GZ, the radii of mushroom cloud is normally subtracted from the distance the cloud is required to travel. For example, for a 10 kiloton low air burst, the fallout arrival time at 100 km is calculated as follows:

Distance = 100 – 4.67 = 95.33 km

Wind Speed = 24 kmph

$$\text{Time of Arrival} = \frac{95.33}{24} = 3.97 \text{ hrs}$$

Calculation of Dose Rates – If, in any actual situation, the dose rate at H plus 1, or any other time is known, the dose rate at other times can be obtained simply by proportion. For example, if it is known that in a given area the dose rate at H plus 4 hours was 120 rads per hour, the dose rate at 36 hours can be calculated as follows:

From the Table given below we see that the relative dose rates at 4 and 36 hours are 15 and 1.6 respectively. Therefore, the dose rate at 36 hours is 120 × 1.6/15 =12.8 rads per hour.

Dose Rate from Fallout at Various Times After the Explosion[3]

Time (Hours)	Relative Dose Rate (rads/hour)
1	100
2	40
4	15
6	10
12	5
24	2.4
36	1.6
48	1.1
72	0.62
100	0.36
200	0.17
500	0.05
1000	0.023

ENDNOTES

1. Samuel Gladstone and Philip J Dolan (eds.), *The Effects of Nuclear Weapons* (Washington, D.C.: US GPO, 1977), p. 430.
2. Ibid.
3. Stockholm International Peace Research Institute (SIPRI), *Nuclear Radiation in Warfare* (London: Taylor & Francis Ltd, 1981), p. 81.

YIELD ESTIMATION

Cloud Parameters at H Plus 5 Minutes – To use the nomogram given below, one must know the location of the GZ and the position of the observer who has obtained the cloud width. The cloud width angle in the nomogram (right column) is joined with the help of a hairline to the distance of the observer from the GZ (centre column) to obtain the yield (left column). The flash-to-bang time (given in the centre column), if noted by the observer, can also be used to estimate the yield, but this method is considered less accurate.

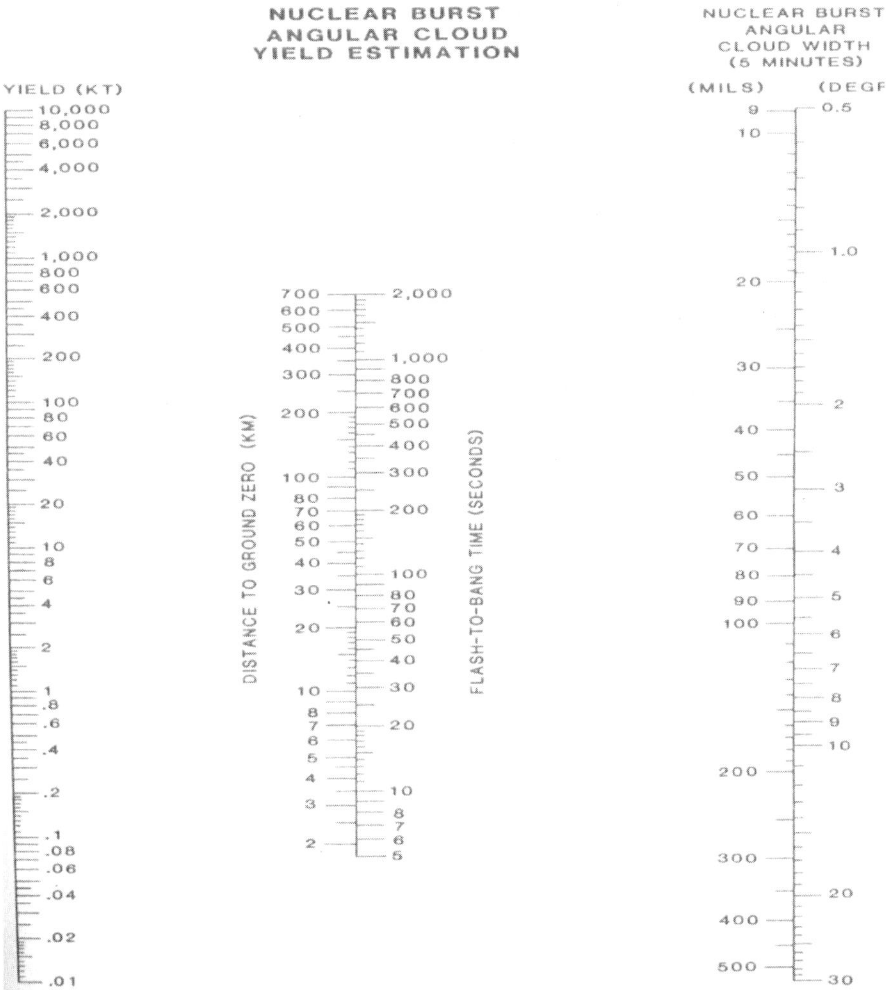

Figure 16: Nomogram for Determining Yield Estimation (Nuclear Burst Angular Cloud Width at H+5 Minutes)

Cloud Parameters at H Plus 10 Minutes. Yield estimation procedure for this nomogram is the same as given earlier.

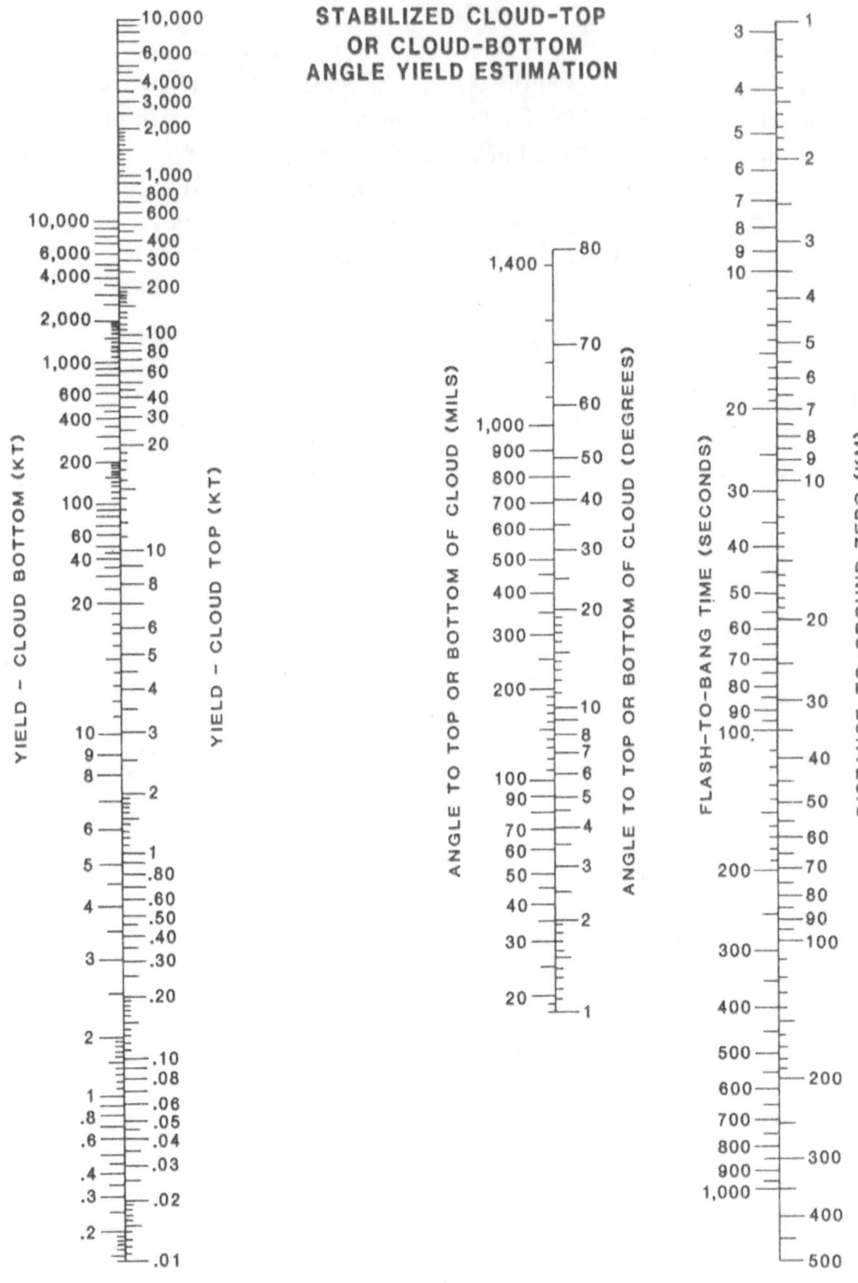

Figure 17: Nomogram for Yield Estimation (Distances between GZ and observer versus stabilised cloud-top angle or stabilised cloud-bottom angle)

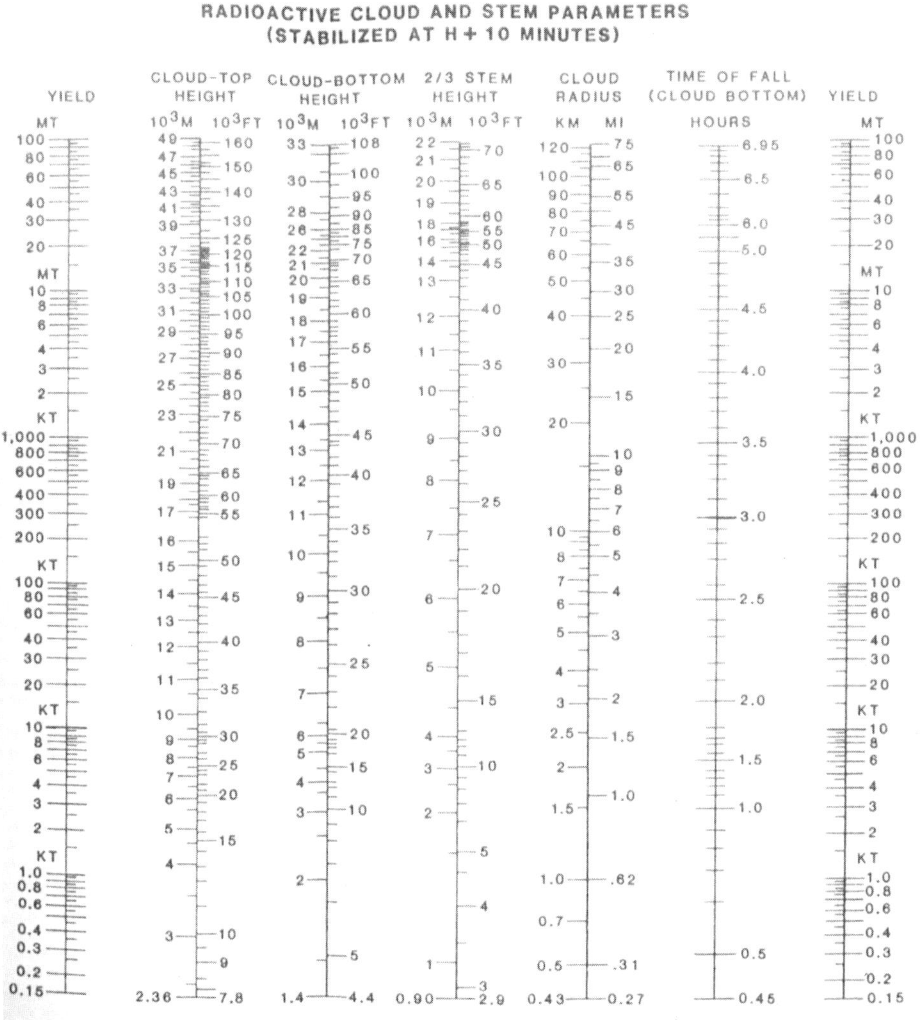

Figure 18: Stabilised Cloud Parameters at H plus 10 Minutes

Index